Andrew Young

Andrew Young

A Biography

Carl Gardner

Drake Publishers Inc
New York • London

To my mother, Gladys G. Taylor,
Who also became a politician
And did good things.

Published in 1978 by
Drake Publishers, Inc.
801 Second Avenue
New York, N.Y. 10017

Library of Congress Cataloging in Publication Data

Gardner, Carl, 1931-
   Andrew Young.

   1. Young, Andrew J., 1932-   2. United
Church of Christ—Biography. 3. Clergy—United
States—Biography. 4. United States. Congress.
House—Biography. 5. Legislators—United States
—Biography. 6. Ambassadors—United States—
Biography.
E840.8.Y64G37   341.23'3'0924   [B]   77-88945
ISBN 0-8473-1700-5

      Design by Harold Franklin

Printed in the United States of America

CONTENTS

ACRONYMS

SCLC	Southern Christian Leadership Conference
CORE	Congress of Racial Equality
SNCC	Student Nonviolent Coordinating Committee
NAACP	National Association for the Advancement of Colored People
SWAPO	South-West Africa People's Organization
SALT	Strategic Arms Limitation Treaty
OPEC	Organization of Petroleum Exporting Countries
HEW	Health, Education, and Welfare
CIA	Central Intelligence Agency
POW	Prisoner of War
KKK	Ku Klux Klan
FBI	Federal Bureau of Investigation
CCCO	Coordinating Council of Community Organizations
UDI	Rhodesia's Unilateral Declaration of Independence
CRC	Atlanta Community Relations Committee
ANC	African National Congress

PROLOGUE

Everybody was there, the priests and the rabbis and the deacons, mingling with the staunch church ladies from Philadelphia and New York and Detroit, the kids up from the hot spots in the South, fresh from dealing with Ross Barnett in Mississippi, the brave youths who had daily faced Leander Perez in Plaquemines Parish, Louisiana, and were already measuring Jim Clark for a fit in Selma, Alabama. A Freedom Train of 700 demonstrators, mostly teen-agers, had rolled in from South Carolina, Georgia, and Florida, and mixed in with the elderly Episcopalians, Catholics, Congregationalists.

Except for James Farmer of CORE, who was stuck in a Louisiana jail with 231 other demonstrators, everyone was in Washington that August 28, 1963 (with the Birmingham campaign still not quite behind us), a bright day with a high of 83, tripping over the tentpegs on the ground of the Washington Monument, then flooding out onto Constitution Avenue in ranks six, seven, eight, twenty demonstrators wide, singing, rejoicing, marching down the avenue for not quite a mile, then swinging left, under and through the trees, flooding around the Reflecting Pool and over on the parklands south of the pool that five years later would be the site of Resurrection City, lapping up to and overflowing the plaza and the broad steps of the Lincoln Memorial.

Everybody smiled and felt good about themselves and the occasion, while President Kennedy and the rest of official Washington looked on doubtfully from afar, and we, 20 percent white and 80 percent black and other persuasions, took turns occupying every inch of the edge of the Reflecting Pool and letting the water soothe our bared, overheated feet.

"The world will little remember what we say here," observed the man whose stone likeness loomed behind us. But it would remember that we came there, and why—200,000 souls when 90,000 at most had been expected. It would remember that we came, gathered, and left with not one incident of violence but just a wasp bite or two, a few cases of heat exhaustion, hysteria.

And it even turned out that, just as the sentiments that Lincoln uttered at Gettysburg one hundred years earlier were recalled after all, so a few of the many words that we hurled out into that heavy, early summer's breeze hung there for years and maybe centuries to come. No use to repeat all of Doc's speech, but you know the one, about his dream, our dream, and how it ended with the words of an old spiritual and how the crowd roared and hearts swelled in this re-affirmation of the worth of mankind, before the whole occasion faded into history and we could no longer harbor any doubts about why we had come or about the ends toward which we would continue to push, strain, struggle. . . .

> *Free at last, free at last!*
> *Thank God Almighty,*
> *We are free at last!*

Chapter One

THE VIEW

FROM KING'S MOUNTAIN

ANDREW YOUNG'S LIFE can be viewed as one long series of campaigns in a war that has raged since prehistoric times and quite possibly will end with the exit of mankind—the fight for human rights. It is also a war in which, in the long run, all victories appear only temporary and must be endlessly rewon. And it is a war which requires the selection of allies.

Andrew Jackson Young, Jr., was born on March 12, 1932, in New Orleans, Louisiana. His mother, a teacher, was Daisy Fuller Young. His father, Andrew J. Young, Sr., was a dentist.

Louisiana in general and New Orleans in particular has had a long history of the intermingling of peoples. They have lived under the flags of three nations: France, Spain, and the United States. The Cajuns or the Acadians, descendants of refugees from Nova Scotia, live in the bayous. New Orleans is characterized by the presence of enormous numbers of Creoles ("descendants of the French settlers" is one of several definitions); the arithmetically differentiated mulattoes, quadroons, and octoroons; the Griffes, who were whiter than octoroons, yet still were not quite white; and the Redbones, mixtures of black and Indian. (There were more black and Indian slave-holders in ante-bellum Louisiana than in any other state.)

Young's ancestry seems to cover almost this whole spectrum. His mother and father believe that there is Indian blood in both their lines. One ancestor, a mulatto slave, was the mistress of a Polish shipping tycoon named Czarnowski; and a group of cousins was so light skinned that they were able to pass over the color line in the thirties, assimilating into the white world completely.

11

Young has referred to his paternal grandfather as a "bayou entrepreneur." Grandfather Young ran a drugstore, a pool hall, and a saloon, in the small town of Franklin, Louisiana, and even sponsored boat excursions. He also served as the treasurer of several black self-help societies. It was within this tradition of enterprise that his son attended dental school and his grandson was able to obtain a better than average start in life.

Young grew up as a member of a well-to-do black family in a neighborhood that was otherwise filled with far less prosperous white people. He and his only sibling, a younger brother named Walter, were the "Joneses." They were the children who were most likely to have the more substantial toys, the roller skates and the football, the basketball hoop set up in their yard. Sometimes the white parents paid their children, the only available playmates, not to play with the Young boys. And sometimes there were disagreements. Andrew and his brother were given the message that has been impressed on so many black children: "When somebody calls you 'nigger,' if you don't hit him, after you come home I'll hit *you*." His father even went so far as to hire a professional boxer, a lightweight named Eddie Brown, to teach his sons the manly art of self-defense. Yet Young concedes that what he actually became an expert at was bluffing, not fighting.

By the time he was old enough to go to school, Andrew Young had already learned to read and write; he began school in the third grade. In the fifth grade, with the rest of his class he was taken by his civics teacher to observe Thurgood Marshall argue a case. Marshall, then a famous civil rights lawyer, later became the first black justice to sit on the United States Supreme Court, and it was he who swore in Andrew Young as the first black United States ambassador to the United Nations.

Andrew Young attended a private high school called the Gilbert Academy, and was graduated in 1947. He next took some courses at Dillard University in New Orleans, and then traveled north to attend Howard University in Washington, D.C. He was fifteen!

Howard's student body was almost entirely black. Its departments were stocked with excellent educators who in less segregated times might have been teaching in the Ivy League. The school was moments away from the large governmental resources of the' capital city, particularly the inexhaustible Library of Congress. Long before the spread of collegiate black studies departments, Howard's library had a huge collection of material on every aspect of the black experience. The school was truly cosmopolitan, attracting a large number of students from the West Indies and Africa, as well as from India and other parts of Asia. It wasn't big on sports, in which Young had always been interested, but excelled nationally in soccer because of the students from the Caribbean and Africa.

For those who believed that the social aspect of college ranked with the academic, there was also an array of fraternities, sororities, parties, and other activities. In fact, many believed the school to be too socially oriented and stratified. Young noticed a considerable bias of northern blacks toward those from the South. The school was dominated by students from Pennsylvania, New York, New Jersey, and Washington, D.C. To them students from the South, even if their parents had money, were fair game for the "down-home nigger" jokes. The Greek letter groups were even suspected of being segregated by skin color, which disgusted Young. Despite his eventual dismay with some of the trappings of the university, he joined the oldest of the predominantly black fraternities, Alpha Phi Alpha, whose membership included W.E.B. Dubois, Paul Robeson, Senator Edward Brooke, Justice Thurgood Marshall, and the Reverend Martin Luther King. Jr.

He took pre-med courses and sailed through his undergraduate work. But he was more interested in sports and in the social life— Howard also featured an almost bewildering array of attractive coeds—and he was on the swimming and track teams.

The president of Howard was a minister named Mordecai W. Johnson. Perhaps because he ran the school with an iron hand, everybody referred to him as Mordecai. During Young's junior year Johnson visited India, two years after Gandhi's death, and he returned with great visions of how the Mahatma's principles of nonviolent civil resistance could be applied to the push for black civil rights. He referred to Gandhi as "the little man in the diapers."

Johnson was an exciting speaker, and he introduced Gandhi into his texts so regularly that years later, Young could fondly pass on to another generation of Howard students the standing joke that Johnson's first mention of Gandhi always meant that ten minutes were left before the end of the sermon. Johnson carried his message elsewhere, including Philadelphia, where another student, Martin Luther King, Jr., was so stirred that he promptly went out and bought an armload of books on the Mahatma.

In the summer of that year, Young was working as a lifeguard in New Orleans when a man about his age dived into the pool, went

straight to the bottom, and stayed there. After Young pulled him out
and revived him, he saw that the man was an old schoolmate. One day
after some horseplay in the back of the third-grade room, the two of
them were suspended from class. Following his expected whipping,
Young returned to class the next day, but that was the last he saw of
his confederate.

The man had almost drowned because he was high on heroin.
After he finally came around, he and Young renewed their old ac-
quaintanceship. The addict continued visiting the pool and talking to
Young. He hoped they could collaborate on a book to be called *Junk*.
Young was musing on the wildly divergent courses that their lives had
taken, on the tissue-thin separation of the forces that could guide one
into a life of usefulness and another toward disaster, especially in the
black world.

Another contrast in alternatives followed. During Young's last
year at Howard, his parents invited a young minister to stay in their
home in New Orleans. While on school vacations, Young would come
in from parties near dawn and notice that while he was preparing to
sleep till noon, the minister was already arising. Young would go to
sleep and the minister would go out to help people. Despite himself,
Young was impressed. He intended to become a dentist like his
father, but all along he had really been drifting—a habit that he never
entirely lost. Years later many would suspect him of having decided
on courses of action with definite goals in mind, such as becoming
chairman of a powerful congressional committee. But that wasn't his
style. He always let things happen. He just naturally *evolved*. Earlier
he had nudged the classical authors enough to pass the humanities
courses. Now he read them anew—Homer, Plato, Marcus Aurelius—
and he began thinking seriously about Gandhi.

In 1951 Young graduated from Howard. While traveling through
the South, he customarily stayed with church groups or with friends
since as a black he was barred from most public lodgings. On his way
back home he spent the night at Lincoln Academy in King's Mountain, North Carolina. A church conference was in progress, and he
had a white roommate who was leaving soon to work as a missionary
in Rhodesia. Again this set Young to thinking. This young white
man, with the privileges, comforts, and guarantees of a comfortable
future available to him at home, was turning his back on all that to
pursue a probably difficult, possibly dangerous existence in Africa, in
order to help black people.

The next day there was a race up King's Mountain, and Young, fresh from track training, beat everybody to the top. He had about fifteen minutes in which to enjoy the solitude and the view—fifteen minutes in that clear air and the scent of pines and the silence of the woods. As he looked out over the valley, observing this beautiful work of Nature and of God, with his body relaxing from its exertions into a calm of warmth and well-being, suddenly all the pieces fell into place. He could no longer doubt that not only had some Supreme Being created such beauty, but that it was all for some purpose, and within that purpose, he had an important role to play. This was his Satori, his blinding flash of religious realization. Now if he did not know all of what he would do, at least he knew the answer to the question that had been nagging him for so long—what he would *be*. A man of God!

Instead of attending dental school Young went farther north, to Connecticut, where he attended the Hartford Theological Seminary. During the quiet years he spent there, the work of Thurgood Marshall and others back in Washington led to the landmark Supreme Court decisions of 1954 and 1955 in the case of *Brown v. Board of Education of Topeka,* which first struck down segregated school systems and then decreed that desegregation proceed "with all deliberate speed."

Later in 1955, the year in which Young received his Bachelor of Divinity degree, a seamstress and former secretary, Rosa Parks, in the latest of a series of such actions by black ladies in Montgomery, Alabama, boarded a bus and took a seat at the front. The driver ordered her out of the section reserved for white riders and to go to the back of the bus. She refused. He called the police and they took Rosa Parks to jail.

In Montgomery at that time were two other young ministers not long out of divinity school. The Reverend Ralph D. Abernathy was pastor of the First Baptist Church; the minister at the Dexter Avenue Baptist Church was the Reverend Martin Luther King, Jr.

The Rosa Parks incident aroused King, Abernathy, and many others in the black community. King, who believed in the principles of nonviolent civil disobedience taught by Gandhi, urged their use here and gravitated into leadership of the protest. All through 1956 the black people of Montgomery organized their own transportation system. They boycotted the Montgomery bus lines, and after months of agitation, through a Supreme Court decision, forced concessions from the city that led to the desegregation of the buses.

Till then the civil rights fight in the South had been carried on mostly by the National Association for the Advancement of Colored People (NAACP) and a few courageous persons. As early as 1947 Bayard Rustin had participated in a "Freedom Ride." In 1941 A. Philip Randolph, head of the Brotherhood of Sleeping Car Porters, had threatened a march on Washington of 100,000 black people and thus forced President Roosevelt to sign an executive order forbidding discrimination in defense plants. The NAACP tactics had involved mainly litigation, but this thing in Montgomery was something else. It was a nonshooting war, and the generals were men of God.

In 1954 Young had finished sorting through the women in his life. He met and married Jean Childs. They had three daughters, Andrea, Lisa, and Paula; then somewhat later, a son, Andrew J. ("Bo") Young, III. That circumstance later struck sympathetic vibes between himself and Jimmy Carter, for the President and his wife had three sons, Jack, Chip, and Jeff; then, after a similarly long interval, a girl, Amy, finally arrived.

The denomination that Young chose and into which he was ordained a minister upon graduating from the seminary was the United Church of Christ. He decided to be a missionary and applied for a post in the Portuguese colony of Angola, in southern Africa. Because of his race, the Portuguese denied permission. Young then turned his attention homeward, to the American South.

His denomination sent him to be pastor of churches in Marion, Alabama, a town of 4,000 about twenty miles northwest of Selma, and Thomasville and Beachton in Georgia, a considerable distance from Marion. Thomasville, a fair-sized town of 18,000, was ten miles northeast of the much smaller Beachton, and both lay only a few miles north of the Florida line. They were in southwest Georgia, in Ku Klux Klan country, just a little south of Albany and also south of the tiny hometowns of the Carter family, Archer and Plains.

"I wanted to be around plain, wise, black folk," Young said later of this move. "I thought, then, that poor people who knew suffering and love and God could save the world."

Following the lead of the Montgomery movement, Young spent the next two years forming his flocks into community action groups. The Ku Klux Klan kept threatening him, and he lived in fear of violence by the night riders; yet he continued to organize voter registration drives.

Meanwhile, with the success of the Montgomery bus boycott, a group of sixty black leaders, most of them ministers, met in Atlanta at the Ebenezer Baptist Church, the pastorate of Martin Luther King,

Sr. Eager to apply nonviolence elsewhere, but needing a strong organization for the purpose, on January 10 and 11, 1957, they formed the Southern Conference on Transportation and Non-Violent Integration. The next month, deciding to express their religious emphasis, they changed the name to the Southern Christian Leadership Conference (SCLC, usually pronounced "Slick") and elected Martin Luther King, Jr., president.

Other, more secular groups that would work side by side with them were in the making, notably the Congress of Racial Equality (CORE) and the Student Nonviolent Coordinating Committee (SNCC, usually pronounced "Snick"), while the NAACP would continue on its quieter path through the courts, and the Urban League would work with businessmen. Of these organizations SCLC would become the strongest and most visible, with over sixty chapters of activists across the United States.

In the same year, however, Young, still "evolving," headed north again, to New York City. By this time he had met King: the churches where Young pastored had been in areas—central Alabama and Southwest Georgia—that were soon to be the scenes of much civil rights action. At about this time King asked Young to serve as his administrative assistant, but Young felt too overwhelmed by King's stature. Instead, from 1957 until 1961, he remained one of only three black executives in the National Council of Churches.

In his position as associate director in the Department of Youth Work in the Council, he gained several kinds of experience that would stand both himself and the civil rights movement in good stead. First he sharpened his skills in working with young people, talking their language and dealing with them in such a way that they couldn't doubt their interests were his interests. At the same time, he learned how to move comfortably in the high councils of the financially and the politically powerful. He discovered the channels through which poured grants from foundations and other sources, and he learned how to keep those funds flowing. He also began to appreciate the ramifications of administration, of attending to the myriad details involved in presiding over large groups of often diverse and challenging personalities.

Later, when some said that he lacked the necessary credentials to serve as the chief American delegate to the United Nations, his supporters would point to the experience of the ten civil rights years, where he negotiated behind the scenes in dozens of personally dangerous situations. However, during those ten years with King, he was only putting a sharper edge on tools that he had picked up in this earlier period.

As the new decade turned, Young observed what was happening down South and felt increasingly misplaced. He and Jean had bought a house in Queens, he was making a good living, and he was contributing to the movement. Yet he began to fear the possible effects of serving in a predominantly white church, amidst mostly white officials. To avoid the chance of fading into what he considered white culture, he concentrated his reading on Africa and black history, and he confined his music appreciation to artists like Muddy Waters, Lightnin' Hopkins, Ray Charles, Bessie Smith, and Blind Lemon Jefferson. Still, that was not enough.

On February 1, 1960, two students from North Carolina A & T (a black college in Greensboro, N.C.), Ezell Blair and his roommate Joseph McNeill, decided that they, like any other customer, should be able to eat at Woolworth's. They took seats at the lunch counter, and were not served. They returned the next day, and again and again. Other students joined them, and the sit-ins spread, with accompanying violent reactions, to other cities.

It is interesting that so many civil rights clashes did not always start in places or at times chosen by the eventual major contestants. More than once the ministers of SCLC, in the midst of administering programs, delivering sermons, and raising money, were swept up into events by the actions of others who were not even in their organization. Blair and McNeill took their seats at the lunch counter directly after reading a pamphlet on King's exploits and philosophy, but they acted on their own initiative. Thus began the great decade of SCLC and the whole drive for civil rights.

By then King was world famous and had been instrumental in forcing passage of the Civil Rights Bill of 1957, the first such bill since Reconstruction. SCLC was growing stronger by the day, yet since Montgomery and Little Rock there hadn't been a large, dramatic confrontation. Dixie air crackled with expectation.

The sit-ins of 1960 and the Freedom Rides of the next year stirred white groups into supporting the largely black civil rights organizations. One was the Field Foundation. In 1961 it decided to back a voter-education program with $100,000. This program was to be run by Young's denomination, the United Church of Christ, in collaboration with SCLC. The church chose Young as its representative. He was sent to Atlanta.

The SCLC official chosen to work with Young was the Reverend

Wyatt Tee Walker, a bespectacled splinter of a man who was known for his diligence, forcefulness, and—sometimes—arrogance. He cracked the whip that King was loathe to handle, and bore the criticism that might otherwise have burned King. Walker allegedly said that King had to be quite a man if he (Walker) was content to work under him. He might easily have said much the same about working with Young. (To King's great chagrin, yet with his blessing, Walker left SCLC in 1964, long before the campaigns were over, to work on a research project on black history and culture; Young took over as SCLC's executive director.)

The method they chose to put the voter-education program into motion was to set up a school to train leaders who would return to their various small communities throughout the South and mobilize the voters. Young and Walker found an old academy called Dorchester Center fifty miles south of Savannah, Georgia. It had been built after the Civil War by the American Missionary Association, then during the Depression had been converted into a community center. The courses taught by SCLC workers under Young and Walker were in the areas of literacy and the techniques of voting, ranging from appraising the candidates to the niceties of registering and then actually voting. Also given were lessons on the sources of money for civic improvements and the methods by which such funds could be obtained. The students then returned to their communities and, in addition to passing this information directly to the people, also set up training schools of their own. As early as February 1962 over fifty of these schools dotted the South from Virginia to Mississippi.

At the same time Young found himself becoming closely involved with SCLC, and he finally took the job of King's administrative assistant. King was impressed by Young's personality, his thoroughness, his loyalty, and the training through which he had already put himself. As one of King's ablest biographers, David L. Lewis, describes it, the SCLC ministers, trained in philosophy and theology, were not good at dealing with sophisticated economic relationships. But Walker and Young "were capable of clinically studying the ganglion of government, business, philanthropy, and labor unions and of assigning correct values to its political and social signals. But. . .Young. . .still had much to learn."

As lieutenants, Young and Abernathy complemented each other perfectly. King could allow Abernathy to accompany him into jail, knowing he had still another lieutenant, in addition to Walker and

Hosea Williams, who was adept at holding open the lines of communication on the outside and engaging in negotiations. Yet Young and Abernathy, or in fact any two of King's top assistants, differed so much that one is reminded of the story about Lincoln. When asked how he could deal with two such different personalities as Secretary of War Edwin Stanton and Secretary of State William Seward, he answered with a story about a farmer going to market. The farmer, he said, balanced one barrel by slinging another on the other side of the horse. "Stanton and Seward will do for my two barrels." King might have said the same about Young and Abernathy, though he would not have added, as the Great Emancipator did, "till a better pair comes along."

From the civil rights point of view, the decade of the sixties appears the work of a celestial hand with a gift for symmetry. Like a great bell tolling, in each year from 1960 through 1969 central events took place, each different from the others, yet each crucial to the goal. After the sit-ins of 1960 came the Freedom Riders of 1961.

In May 1961 a group of civil rights activists set out from Washington, D.C., in buses to test the presence of segregation on interstate routes. In the upper South the trips were fairly peaceful. As they penetrated into the Deep South, instances of heckling and violence increased, until, in Anniston, Alabama, one ride came to a fiery, shattering end, and a little later another was halted in Montgomery, Alabama, in a holocaust of clubs and fists. There John Lewis of SNCC was savagely beaten for the second time on the same ride. Watching an account on television of John Lewis's activities in Nashville had helped fuel Young's eagerness to return south.

After completing the courses at Dorchester Center, two young SNCC field workers, Charles Sherrod and Cordell Reagan, found themselves in the city of Albany, in southwest Georgia, organizing the black community into protests groups. They had a plan, and after several months, when they had their organizational efforts well underway, they began the second stage.

In November 1961 some citizens of Albany and then Freedom Riders from Atlanta asked for service in the dining room of the bus station. Following their arrests, large protests and further arrests took place. The Georgia National Guard was mobilized, and so was SCLC.

On December 15 Martin Luther King and Ralph Abernathy arrived from Atlanta. Pressed into positions of leadership almost before they knew what was happening, they led a march the next day and were jailed. After three days they were released. The campaign, however, had barely begun. Soon the rest of the main body of SCLC, including the Reverend Andrew J. Young, Jr., arrived, a police chief named Laurie Pritchett began to be noticed, and it was 1962.

As far as the sixties were concerned, the first sit-ins at Greensboro compared to the firing on Fort Sumter almost 100 years earlier. Now King, Abernathy, and Young (still somewhat to the rear) stood contemplating the banks of their Bull Run.

The Lions in the Arena

RIVERS OF BLOOD

On a segregated bus in Montgomery, Alabama, on December 1, 1955, Rosa Parks refused to give up her seat.

Sixty-two years earlier, as a twenty-four-year-old fledgling lawyer, Mohandas K. Gandhi, in his first hours on the soil of South Africa, refused to give up his seat on a train and on a stagecoach.

Rosa Parks went to jail. M. K. Gandhi was thrown off the train and had to be protected on the stagecoach.

While Henry Thoreau was in prison for not paying taxes, Ralph Waldo Emerson asked him, "Why are you in jail?" And Thoreau replied, "Why are you not in jail?"

An ancient Indian emperor, Asoka, dreamed of a land awash with peace. "Truth always wins," he taught, "while violence loses." And with that, India's Golden Age began.

Tolstoy had written to Gandhi, "Only truth keeps man's spiritual forces alive. It is the only effective weapon to win a cause. Violence will never help a cause."

Mohandas K. Gandhi (1869-1948) is famous as the deviser and chief practitioner of *satyagraha* or "truth-force."

"*Satyagraha*," he taught, "is the vindication of truth by infliction of suffering not on the opponent but on one's self."

As early as 1896 he had become notorious in South Africa for resisting the system, and as he was returning from a visit to India, a mob of whites caught him in the streets and beat him. "Rivers of blood," he said, "may have to to flow before we gain our freedom, but it must be our blood."

In the Boer War at the turn of the century and again during the Zulu "Rebellion" of 1906, Gandhi served as a medic on the British side. He respected the British and always expected that before long they would see things his way. But he also had to reckon with a tough group of Dutch immigrants called the Boers, or Afrikaners, who wanted to rule South Africa's millions of nonwhites, first through warfare and then by the constant enactment of unjust laws.

Over 50,000 Indians of all faiths, languages, and castes had immigrated to South Africa. In 1906 the so-called Black Act was introduced, requiring all Indians to be fingerprinted and to carry special identification certificates. Gandhi, who had starved as a young lawyer in India because he had been too shy to argue his cases, organized a series of nonviolent protests. After a lengthy campaign Jan Smuts, the Minister of Defence, promised repeal of the act if the protests were ended. Though other Indian leaders were suspicious, Gandhi believed Smuts and complied.

The South African legislature had not taken part in the deal, refused to honor Smuts's promise, and the Black Act remained. Gandhi called another protest meeting and thousands of Indians burned their identity cards. (He never worked for the Zulus. They didn't ask for his help. In any case, he said, they would have to fight for their own freedom.)

In 1913 Gandhi led thousands of Indians on a dramatic march into the Cicero of South Africa's provinces, the Transvaal, and in the process was arrested every few hours. Eventually he negotiated repeal of a tax on indentured servants, the end of the indenture system itself, and recognition of non-Christian marriages—success coming mostly because World War I had started and the English couldn't simultaneously deal with colonial unrest.

Gandhi formed an ambulance corps to help the British in the war. (He had always supported the Empire.) Then, in 1915, after he had kept South Africa stirred up for twenty years, he returned to India and launched the project that he had been preparing all along.

For generations India's teeming millions, like a considerable part of the rest of the globe, had been ruled by a few thousand Englishmen. Gandhi felt that in South Africa he had effected changes. He felt he could do even better at home. (He couldn't anticipate how much South Africa would revert so that by 1925 conditions there were worse than when he had arrived.) For India all he asked was independence.

On April 6, 1919, after the English passed a law extending the wartime suppression of Indian civil liberties, Gandhi called for a nationwide closing of businesses. The resulting, unprecedented uproar spread all over the country. Things were especially tense in a region called the Punjab.

Gandhi, as would King, Young, and the other leaders of SCLC, had problems with associates who were not fully in tune with *satyagraha*. Later he would complain that in all of India he was the only true Gandhian. Now he set out to try to cool down his followers and was arrested.

Then, in a walled compound in the Punjab, fifty soldiers fired into an unarmed crowd until they ran out of ammunition. Almost 400 Indians died and over 1,000 were injured. The commanding general cabled London to the effect that it had been a good show.

Until that moment, Gandhi had always supported the King. Hadn't he helped carry wounded English soldiers out of danger in more than one war? But now he would serve British majesty no more.

Mohandas Gandhi, also called the Mahatma, or the Great Soul, embarked on the commitment which would lead him to jail and innumerable fasts. His many arrests resulted in a total of almost seven years spent behind bars. His wife of sixty-three years, Kasturbai—who had borne him four sons—died in prison.

Gandhi is also famous for his efforts on behalf of India's untouchables, a caste that he called the *Harijan* or "Children of God." They were closer to God than other castes, he said, because they suffered more. He adopted an untouchable child. But today in India, thirty years after Gandhi's death, to be born a "Child of God" is as onerous as ever.

After a lifetime of effort and the most careful preparation, at the climactic moment, Gandhi, like King, had to watch events snatched out of his hands with disastrous consequences.

In 1947, following Indian independence, during the partition that he had always resisted (he had worked for a united Hindu-Muslim India) fierce riots broke out. The mobs of untold millions—Muslims trying to reach Pakistan and Hindus headed toward India—kept colliding, and thousands—some say as many as a million—lost their lives.

In January 1948, when he was seventy-eight, Gandhi, the only true Gandhian, conducted the last of his fasts, this time out of jail. His aim was to halt the riots that were still in progress months after independence. But to no avail. He escaped a bomb thrown at him, but not the three bullets fired point blank by an anti-Muslim Brahman while he was conducting prayers. With his death, things finally cooled down.

At that time no one could have forecast that his legacy of non-violence would one day be represented on the world stage of the United Nations by a black man speaking for a predominantly white nation.

Chapter Two

THIS CLEAN DECISION

THE NEW YEAR'S FESTIVITIES were over and just a few hangovers lingered. Like 1976, the President of the United States, Gerald R. Ford, had already begun his slide into oblivion though the inauguration of his successor, Jimmy Carter, was still two weeks in the future.

On Sunday, January 2, President-elect Carter attended church in his hometown of Plains, Georgia. He sat in the company of a small delegation of black leaders from Atlanta, come to demonstrate their support.

The same day Mr. Carter's foremost black advocate, Andrew J. Young, himself a minister, was being interviewed on the NBC program, "Meet the Press." Slated to be the chief United States delegate to the United Nations, replacing the low profile William C. Scranton and, before him, the highly visible Daniel P. Moynihan, Young fielded tough questions about southern Africa.

"I see the United States as likely to have a very aggressive policy to move towards majority rule in southern Africa. Now, this is something we haven't really had for the last eight years," he said. ". . . When the nations of Africa realize that we are serious about majority rule, that we are moving decisively to support the British in Rhodesia, that we will back United Nations efforts to push for a resolution of the situation and achievement of majority rule in Namibia, I think we will get a new measure of cooperation from the third world that has not been there largely because they felt we didn't care. . . . I don't view the South African white community as a monolith, and I think there are forces within that country that will respond to efforts

25

and initiatives that might come both publicly and privately from the United States. . . . I have a great deal of sympathy for the white minority governments. When you talk about four million whites in South Africa, I wouldn't want them driven into the sea any more than I would want four million Israelis driven into the sea."

Interesting statements that were accepted quietly by the press and others. Even if they signaled a shift from the policy of past administrations to accommodate Africa's white minority governments, listeners would have been surprised to hear other sentiments from the delegate-to-be. After all, Andrew Young was a veteran leader of the civil rights sixties with heavy experience involving both negotiation and direct confrontation.

It was known that Young, in return for supporting Carter, had not precisely jumped at the offer of the United Nations post. As chief delegate he would be bound by government policy. And the new secretary of state, Cyrus R. Vance, would be at least nominally his boss.

Now, on "Meet the Press," eyebrows rose only slightly when the topic changed to Idi Amin. Former ambassador Daniel Moynihan had called Amin a "racist murderer" and had said that it was no accident that the president of Uganda headed the Organization of African Unity at the time.

"The tragedy of my predecessor's comments," Young answered, "was that he didn't stop there. He went on to talk about the Organization of African Unity, and by so doing demeaned an entire continent's leadership."

Then Young added a statement of intent with most provocative implications for the future. He said he "would certainly do whatever I could in countries in Africa or in the Caribbean—Haiti, for instance, or in Chile—to work for democracy and the elevation of human rights. Now, that is a difficult and touchy subject, though, and I don't think it is advanced by castigating the personalities of the leadership involved."

Early in the game, Young had picked Jimmy Carter the winner and now President. Then he had been faced with making his decision about the job that Carter wanted him to take. But making that decision in itself had taken on the proportions of a major campaign.

As previously noted, Young had entered the Carter camp long before any other well-known black figure. Though a strain of moderation had run through Georgia politics for years, Carter and

Young burst into the spotlight almost simultaneously as its brightest exponents, neatly pincering, one from the white side and the other from the black. In the same 1970 election that resulted in Carter's becoming governor, Young had made a strong bid to be the first black man to be elected to the United States Congress from the Deep South since Reconstruction, but had lost. In 1972 he ran again and won in a district that, even after the intervening reapportionment, was still less than 50 percent black.

At first Congressman Young remained somewhat wary of Carter. Though he was clearly no Lester Maddox, Carter hailed from southwest Georgia, an area that Young associated with bigotry. One story has it that during the campaign when Young called one of Carter's chief advisors, Charles Kirbo, an old "Georgia redneck," Carter deflected the comment by saying that was just Young's way of speaking, that, in fact, Young had called Carter himself "poor white trash made good."

(Kirbo, who went much farther back with Carter than Young, thought that the candidate should not try to explain away his famous "ethnic purity" *faux pas* and had said so. But in that instance Carter had heeded Young and other black leaders instead.)

In any case Carter began to look better and better to Young and he made his decision. From the Florida primary onward, Young was in Carter's camp. He worked to garner not only the black but also the liberal vote.

For a long time, the press had been reluctant to characterize any prominent black person as a leader or even a spokesman for black people. But with Carter's victory and his accompanying statements that Young was the best man in politics that he had ever known and that Young was the only man to whom he owed a political debt, the restraints were eased. "The most powerful black political figure in America," and "the most powerful black man in the United States" Andrew Young was now called.

Everybody wondered which reward he would accept. Would he become a member of the Cabinet? Or would he prefer being a close White House aide? Or would he remain cleverly content with his growing power as a Congressman, well liked and respected by all, possessor now of strong links to the Administration, with his eventual rise to the chairmanship of the House Rules Committee and even to the pinnacle of Speaker of the House clear possibilities?

Thus his acceptance of the United Nations post was, throughout this January of picking staffs and getting sworn in, still a matter of concern and genuine anguish to some. His continuity in political office was broken. What did something as lightweight as the United Nations have to do with his career-long fight for civil rights? What was going to happen to all that *power*? And take a look at what had happened to other idealists in that post: Henry Cabot Lodge, Adlai Stevenson, and Arthur Goldberg, in particular, who had been thoroughly wrung out by Lyndon Johnson's relentless conduct of the Vietnam War.

"There have been few more miserable spectacles in recent days than that of Andrew Young humbly tottering off to his new post as United States ambassador to the United Nations." Thus Alexander Cockburn and James Ridgeway expressed the dismay of the *Village Voice*, adding that he had chosen to become "little more than a speechreader beside the East River." Meanwhile, far out on the right, the arch-conservatives were already seeking grounds for his impeachment.

Young gave several answers: "I don't think we can solve the problems of blacks in America until we solve the problem of stabilizing the resources and the social structures in the Third World."

"I finally took the job after deciding that the United Nations is a good place to try to bring a little sanity to what is going on in the world. The world is on the verge of an economic crisis, and the only way to avoid that crisis is to quit killing each other and start working together. Maybe the UN is the place to do some of that."

And at another time he said that if they hadn't been assassinated, Robert F. Kennedy would have been elected president in 1968, and would have chosen King as his chief delegate to the United Nations.

This last statement suggests the key to the whole matter. Someone deeply involved with civil rights in the United States, daily and yearly feeling the anguish and pain stemming from countless marches, sit-ins, demonstrations, arrests, negotiations, beatings, and murders, occasionally looks up from both the unending ordeals and the occasional victories and makes comparisons. And what he sees is that for all the exaggerations that the exponents of the cause may find necessary to make, out there, overseas, incredibly, is something even worse! In Africa—the homeland itself—are other black people who, though in the overwhelming majority, are so oppressed that their only counterparts in America are the prisoners of Parchman Farm or Attica. And if it is essential to obliterate the injustices toward minorities in America, it is vital to erase the oppression of the majorities in southern Africa. Thus a matter of brotherhood, of true kinship, is involved, not only with the blacks in South Africa but also with those in Haiti and Uganda, imposed upon by other blacks, or the whites crushed by whites in Chile. It is a logical progression.

For all Young's testimonies to his love for the legislative give and take in Congress, what remained brightest in his heart were those broad canvases painted by Martin Luther King, Jr. The United Nations opportunity was as broad as King's Deep South of the fifties or Gandhi's India of the teens—perhaps broader.

Given the imagination and the creativity of a man still in his prime (forty-four), who had already demonstrated a readiness to take chances (and also his apparent possession of a golden tip sheet that so far had enabled him to pick the winning course—whether it involved King, Carter, or God), it is hard to see how Young could have chosen otherwise.

The Lions in the Arena

CUSTER IN A PORKPIE HAT

Daniel Patrick Moynihan knew the extremes of fire and ice, of chill and warmth, of comfort that lulls the senses and fear that hones the brain to a keen, slashing edge.

He knew abrupt dips from prosperity to welfare—how to shine shoes in Times Square, then back up to romp across the manicured lawns of suburbia, and down again. He had felt the nagging disquiet of a father who dropped out, the trials of a mother keeping things together after more than one broken marriage, always on the move, one jump ahead of the York-ville landlords, Tulsa to New York to Jersey to the Upper West Side to Westchester to Indiana and back again to New York.

Attended high school in East Harlem (a heavy mick amid 60 percent pomaded wops and 40 percent basketball-bouncing jigs), graduated first in his class.

Worked on the docks. ("I've been on this pier for forty years, and I will die before I see a nigger with a pencil. Moynihan, you're the checker.")

To show that he was no college punk, sharp, bright, fast on the draw—"The Oklahoma Kid" he'd been called—he supposedly took his entrance test at City College with a loading hook sticking out of his back pocket.

Served in the Navy, went to Tufts, traded in his previous assortment of accents for the New England prep school drawl—

And saw now what he would be some day . . .

A Harvard professor who knew something about poverty and therefore about the poor: poor Okies, poor Irishmen, and, natural-ly, poor blacks. (At Tufts he made it a point to take in a black room-mate when others had shunned him. On the docks it was black workers who dubbed him "The Oklahoma Kid.")

Picked up the final parts of the identity by which we know him so fondly today, in England, on a scholarship. Copped the bowler hat, the furled umbrella, the Savile Row suits, and the handker-chief tucked up his sleeve. Added eighteenth-century wit to his arsenal.

And back at home learned the value of political hustles—the jol-ly, funny, towering Irishman who watched Dylan Thomas die. He was a poet himself.

And speech writer, historian, publicity man, general political stagehand.

Needing brilliance in the Department of Labor, Arthur Gold-berg called him to Washington.

"I don't suppose there is any point in being Irish if you don't know the world is going to break your heart," Moynihan said after John Kennedy was shot.

And then worked for Lyndon Johnson.

Before the Vietnamese there were Negroes. In 1963 King had marched in Birmingham and on Washington, and now in St. Augustine, Florida, the police were letting white men crack black heads every night.

Since he knew about being poor and fathers who vanished, since he had counted rings in bathtubs, Moynihan became the nation's leading authority (while Martin Luther King, Jr., Ralph Abernathy, and Andrew Young looked toward Selma) on Negroes.

In spite of the civil rights successes black people were falling farther behind, and the cause, Moynihan wrote, was the black family. Two out of five lacked adult males. (Never mind the mother, working all kinds of jobs, avoiding the landlords; never mind the foremen who would die before they'd see niggers with pencils in their hands; never mind the questionable statistics.)

Black leaders were aghast. Whatever his intent, Moynihan was a wild boar crashing through the woods, about to rip through the delicate webs they had spun so painfully.

When Nixon became president, he, too, hired Moynihan. The black rioters, if not Hubert Humphrey's Johnson-stacked deck of Vietnam cards, had put Nixon into office; now it was time to cool those cities. In addition, Pat had worked for Kennedy; therefore he was a defector, bearer of a mystique that could be rubbed for luck like the head of a Negro child.

Daniel Patrick Moynihan worked hard for Johnson as an employee of Nixon. He kept a lot of the Great Society programs going and came up with the Family Assistance Program, which would give poor families cash instead of social services.

It was also while in Nixon's White House that he wrote a second memo for which he'd eventually be forgiven by everybody except the subjects themselves. It was time, he said, that the policy toward blacks be changed from government action to "benign neglect."

In 1970 Nixon tried to put him into the United Nations job, but too many foreign service pros objected: Moynihan had no experience in foreign affairs. So he settled for two quiet years as ambassador to India. Then Kissinger and Ford handed him the United Nations job.

Moynihan's stint at the United Nations was characterized by unending skirmishes and outright wars with the Third World. Idi Amin of Uganda he called a "racist murderer," and insulted African leaders like Julius Nyerere who had resisted Amin from the start by stating it was "no accident" Amin was then the chairman of the Organization of African Unity.

In bitter response to a Third World resolution equating Zionism with racism, which the United Nations passed, Moynihan tried to ram through a second, unexpected resolution urging amnesty for all political prisoners. During the debate he offered the opinion that South Africa had the only free press on the continent. Ivor Richards, the English ambassador, appalled at his tactics, indirectly called him a "King Lear raging on the blasted heath." Even Kissinger had heard enough.

Daniel P. Moynihan, who brought to the United Nations post unprecedented vigor and unorthodoxy, a Harvard/MIT professor who had served four Presidents, resigned.

A curious man whom few can fathom, whose statements do not quite sing, whose rhetoric does not quite convince, whose experiences do not quite mesh; a bulldog or a wraith, suggestive of a joker shouting "Peek-a-boo!" now in one window, now in the next; Custer in a porkpie hat setting up trick "Last Stands," then, when the Indians gather, collecting his mirrors and slipping away; the bomb-dropping United Nations brawler who grew big enough to push William Buckley's brother aside.

And now is the junior senator from New York.

What does the delegate from the Maldives think when he observes Andrew Young and remembers Daniel P. Moynihan?

United States Ambassador to the United Nations Andrew Young with his wife, Jean.

Dr. Martin Luther King, Jr., leads a voter protest march in Selma, Alabama, in 1965. Young is in front of Dr. King, Abernathy behind. Alongside Dr. King (from left) are James Farmer, Bishop John Wesley Lord, Dr. King, and James Forman. *Photograph courtesy of Wide World Photos*

The Reverend Andrew Young, then executive vice-president of SCLC at a 1968 conference called by the National Council of Churches. *Photograph courtesy of Religious News Service*

Andrew Young confers with Dr. King at a 1967 press conference at the Overseas Press Club in New York. *Photograph courtesy of Wide World Photos*

(*Above*) After winning election to the House of Representatives, Young is kissed by his wife and mother. (*Below*) At a memorial service in Atlanta for Dr. Martin Luther King, Jr. *Photographs courtesy of Religious News Service*

(*Above*) Ambassador Andrew Young meeting with members of the United Nations Correspondents Association. *Photograph courtesy of the United Nations/Y. Nagata*

(*Opposite page, top*) Then Presidential candidate Jimmy Carter confers with Rep. Andrew Young in 1976. *Photograph courtesy of Wide World Photos* (*Opposite page, bottom*) Young presents his credentials to U.N. Secretary-General Kurt Waldheim. *Photograph courtesy of the United Nations/T. Chen*

(*Below*) President Kenneth Kaunda of Zambia with Ambassador Young in Zanzibar. *Photograph courtesy of Wide World Photos*

(*Above*) Representatives of the Patriotic Front of Zimbabwe, headed by
Joshua M. Nkomo (center), attend a meeting to consider the situation in
Southern Rhodesia. *Photograph courtesy of the United Nations/Y. Nagata*
(*Below*) At the special General Assembly meeting on disarmament: Secre-
tary of State Cyrus R. Vance (left, at table), W. Averell Harriman, and
Senator George McGovern of South Dakota; Paul Newman and Andrew
Young. *Photograph courtesy of the United Nations/Y. Nagata*

Chapter Three

CONFUSIONS

OF THE TENSE MOMENTS

TO MOST AMERICANS Jimmy Carter came out of nowhere to win the presidency. Amid the Muskies, Humphreys, McGoverns, Udalls, Wallaces, and Jacksons on the Democratic lists four and eight years earlier, his name had been totally absent. When he said that Young was the only man to whom he owed a political debt, hardly anyone blinked. He seemed to have won with little help from the big city machines or any of the other vested interests.

But what about his political background? What had been his policies as governor of Georgia? How was he going to implement all those campaign promises?

His selection of a Cabinet underwent intense scrutiny. His first appointments were all white, male, and linked to the establishment. But then he named Young, and in addition gave him a number of perquisites. Young would be a member of the cabinet, and he would attend meetings of the National Security Council. In addition to his headquarters in New York, where he would preside over a staff of 125 specialists, he would soon enjoy use of a second office and a small staff installed in the middle of the State Department in Washington, the first such arrangement for a United Nations ambassador. But when Carter asked Congress for $130,000 to cover five months' expenses for this D.C. office, the House Appropriations Committee chopped $200,000 out of Young's overall $1.7 million budget instead.

The budget question was replaced in the headlines by Carter's designation of a fellow Georgian, Griffin Bell, to run the Justice Department. Many black groups opposed the appointment. Bell, a law partner of Charles Kirbo, was not known as a moderate on race. The chief sticking points were several of his decisions on civil rights cases—he was a former judge of the Fifth Circuit Court of Appeals—and his continuing membership in segregated private clubs.

According to Joseph Lelyveld, a New York writer and Young-watcher, a month or more passed after the election before Young met with Carter to talk about cabinet appointments. Young was ready to take it for granted that in any Democratic administration blacks would receive a fair number of jobs. He professed not to be concerned about numbers and said instead that he was just as interested in the quality of the white appointees.

Apparently, however, Young was not consulted about the nomination of Bell. He and Bell had worked out of offices in the same building in Atlanta, and he could anticipate the consternation that would—and did—burst out in the black community, especially since Barbara Jordan had shown an interest in the job. Bell's mediation of a busing case had angered the NAACP. (Young, however, was satisfied with the eventual compromise.)

Young pondered and finally decided that the scope of Bell's contacts with the black community made him a reasonable choice. He defended Bell, saying that he would rather have a Southerner who had struggled with the problem of race than "a Northern intellectual liberal." Stoney Cooks, his chief aide, later tried to launder this remark by saying that while white liberals were generally hiring only other white liberals, Southerners in Carter's cabinet were trying to include minorities on their staffs. Expressing a sentiment whose first part sprang directly from the civil rights struggles, while the second was the fruit of the campaign, Young said, "Liberals want to do it for you. Southerners want to do it with you."

Many black leaders were not reassured. Despite the overwhelming preference of black voters for Carter over Ford and despite the status that Young had gained, they were insisting on concrete results. Something about the expected piece of the action appeared too fragile. And Bell stuck in their craw.

An ideal compromise seemed to be black Texan, Barbara Jordan. A contemporary of Young's in Congress, she made a powerful impression on the whole country, first as a member of the House Judiciary Committee during the Watergate hearings and later as the keynote speaker at the Democratic National Convention. But when she talked to Carter about an appointment, they had not struck a harmonious note. She had publicly indicated a desire for something consistent with her background, such as the attorney general post, but

Carter stayed with Bell. Though it wasn't specifically offered, she "no-noed" the United Nations job, and friends advised her not to risk the HEW snakepit. Meanwhile, other black leaders—Vernon Jordan of the Urban League and the mayors of Detroit and Los Angeles respectively, Coleman Young and Tom Bradley—also declined those jobs in the administration which were offered to them.

However, other blacks accepted offers. Patricia Roberts Harris, a former law school dean and ambassador to Luxembourg, agreed to become head of the Housing and Urban Development department. And Ben Brown, another former civil rights activist, came on board as head of Action, the Umbrella agency that included the Peace Corps and Vista.

As for the appointments of those persons with whom Young would be working directly, things went more smoothly—perhaps because it had been planned long in advance. Cyrus R. Vance, a career diplomat and as low keyed as Kissinger was high, would be the secretary of state, and the post from which Kissinger had spread his power—national security director—would be held by Zbigniew Brzezinski. Brzezinski, like Kissinger, was born in Europe, possessed strong academic credentials, and was associated with the Rockefellers.

So on January 5, Young joined the first of what were to be a series of "cluster" meetings with his fellow designees who would later become familiar as co-executors of the United States foreign policy and the national security. Besides Carter and his vice-president, Walter Mondale, they included Vance, Brzezinski, Defense Secretary Harold Brown, Director of the CIA, Theodore Sorensen (who, however, did not survive the nomination process and was later replaced by Admiral Stansfield Turner) and the chief economic adviser, Charles Schultze.

At that time the main criticism as to the composition of the group concerned the somewhat mysterious Trilateral Commission. This was a group whose existence had only recently become generally known and which, in its elitism, suggested something close to a vast conspiracy. It had been formed a few years earlier in reaction to the American preoccupation with its adversaries, Russia and China. The commission felt obliged to redirect attention to the three-part, thus "trilateral," alliance of the United States, Japan, and Western Europe.

Brzezinski, under the auspices of David Rockefeller, directed the commission, which was said to have as many as 300 members, and one allegation was they had picked Carter to be President, then arranged to have him elected. It was noted that of Carter's top nominees, fifteen, including Vance, Brzezinski, and Young, were members of the commission.

Young, however, was involved with a more pressing matter: staffing his department. He had a broad field from which to choose, ranging from those who had served at the United Nations at some point or in the State Department, through the members of his Congressional staff, to old civil rights activists. It was expected that he would hire a representative number of women, blacks, Hispanics, and other minorities. He had promised that another black person would hold at least one of the four remaining ambassadorial jobs under him.

What Young chiefly had in mind was giving others of a persuasion similar to his an opportunity to share in the system, as close to the top as possible. After all, exactly ten years before, he and King had staged a large antiwar demonstration in front of the same United Nations building. It was he who, trying to strike the proper note of respect and conciliation, had ensured that the Viet Cong flags of the radicals were kept at a distance. Now he was serving in one of the highest posts in that government whose policies he had vigorously opposed such a short time earlier. Why couldn't the same be true for others, especially those who would be assisting him?

This was a vindication of the American Dream if there ever was one, and so there was unremarkably little outcry when he did indeed begin making a number of changes, though characteristically he fell far short of loading his domain with radicals a la Putney Swope. Some even cheered the prospect of a new outlook, a new spirit in the United Nations seat, while the chief reservation was that if he swept out too many of the old hands, he would have no one to show him the ropes or how to handle the people with whom he would have to deal. He wouldn't know where "the bodies were buried."

For his chief deputy, Young picked James F. Leonard, who was fifty-six and a career diplomat. Leonard spoke Chinese and Russian as well as French and was an authority on the Far East and disarmament. Most recently he had been head of a private group formed to promote understanding of the United Nations, the United States Association for the United Nations.

In the number three post Young placed Don McHenry, who was a member of the Carnegie Endowment Staff and had formerly worked on United Nations political affairs for the State Department. And to run his Washington bureau in the State Department, Young chose Dr. Anne Forrestal Holloway, a thirty-five-year-old Ph.D. with expertise in international relations. Holloway and McHenry were black; Leonard was white.

From his old congressional staff Young retained Tom Offenburger as his press secretary and Stoney Cooks as his chief aide. Beginning in 1965 Cooks had worked for the SCLC in conjunction with such leaders as Young and Hosca Williams. He had been particularly effective in setting up voter registration campaigns. When Young won a seat in Congress, Cooks accompanied him and performed much the same role he would have at the United Nations—as an intermediary between Young and the rest of his staff.

Young also demonstrated his influence by exercising another perquisite given him by the President. For the position of assistant secretary of state for International Organizations, he drafted Charles William Maynes who, like McHenry, was a member of the Carnegie Endowment Staff and of the Carter transition team.

A little later Young made one other important addition who, in one sudden flare of publicity, became his best-known assistant: "Andy Young's Andy Young." This was Brady Tyson, a former missionary who had been forced out of Brazil because of his humanitarian zeal. Like Cooks his loyalty to Young flew far in advance of any self-interest in holding a government post. Later, after feeding Young advice on foreign policy, Tyson became a nominee to the United Nations Human Rights Commission.

Choosing his staff was the easy part. More difficult was acquainting himself with the myriad problems of the United Nations while at the same time satisfying the public's curiosity about his motives and probable course of action. For example, Third World nations almost routinely put forth resolutions to oust South Africa from the United Nations. How would the ambassador handle that situation when it had regularly been the policy of past United States administrations (and presumably of Carter's too) to veto such resolutions? It wouldn't be hard to guess that Young himself might personally favor such a resolution. At least, as a black person, he might feel a strong pull to line up with the other black members of the United Nations.

Young answered, "No problem." In the first place he didn't think that expelling South Africa would be helpful in breaking down apartheid. And in any case he "wouldn't be sitting around waiting for [other actions by black African delegations against South Africa] to happen. I might be able to influence things so I wouldn't have to cast a veto."

In his opinion the propaganda weapon used by black Africans at the United Nations had not worked, and he was looking for more practical ways to force changes. One group that he had in mind was American and South African businessmen. He mentioned business groups in the American South who had helped bring about peaceful desegregation because violence was bad for business.

"There is going to be change in South Africa," he said, "and the only question is whether it will be rational or violent. In that kind of situation, people who have billions of dollars at stake are likely to become forces for peaceful change."

But if he hadn't been able to influence things by the time such a vote came up, he was prepared, he said, to be absent so as not to have to oppose his principles.

On January 21, one day after President Jimmy Carter's inauguration, the new administration revealed that it would waste no time in making use of its United Nations ambassador, though he had yet to be approved by the Congress. Julius Nyerere, president of Tanzania, and perhaps the most respected statesman south of the Sahara, invited Young to visit Dar es Salaam, his capital city, for a special celebration on February 5. The occasion was the anniversary of the merger in 1964 of mainland Tanganyika with the island of Zanzibar to form the present-day United Republic of Tanzania. At the same time the Second World Black and African Festival of Arts and Culture would be underway in Lagos, Nigeria, and Young was anticipating catching that on his homeward swing. These festivities, however, were only background music to the more serious purposes of his office.

Until recently sub-Saharan Africa had received the least notice by the United States foreign policy makers of any of the world's areas. Not till Ford's last months in office had Henry Kissinger taken his famous shuttle diplomacy south of Egypt. It was too late. The Cubans had beat him there, sending troops and technicians to Angola in support of Agostinho Neto's Popular Movement in the three-sided war following the sudden exodus of the Portuguese. And meanwhile in southern Rhodesia, also called Zimbabwe, the decade-long control by Ian Smith's white minority government was being challenged by stepped-up black nationalist attacks. In the territory of Southwest Africa or Namibia, under pressure by the Big Powers from without and nationalist groups from within, the Republic of South Africa's grip was slowly being pried loose, finger by finger. Back in Angola the South Africans, like the United States, had backed the losing side. And in South Africa itself, the townships, aroused by disgruntlement with the education system, were in an uproar; police had already killed over 400 protesting blacks; the jails were packed.

In regard to Angola, Kissinger had been too late, but he held what were purported to be friendly meetings with various black leaders. Then in Pretoria, South Africa, he managed to get Ian Smith to agree to an agreement whereby, in two years, rule would be peacefully transferred from Rhodesia's 270,000 whites to its 6,000,000 blacks. At first the several black nationalist groups, under Joshua Nkomo, Robert Mugabe, and others, were agreeable to discussing this plan, but after meetings in Geneva, Switzerland, the negotiations broke down, and the nationalist groups subsequently rejected the idea. Since then Britain's envoy, Ivor Richards, had been trying without success to budge either side from their positions. And meanwhile the guerilla war in Zimbabwe continued taking its toll.

Young had visited a third of Africa's fifty-five nations before he had been picked for the United Nations; his contacts there compared to those that he enjoyed in the United States; and he was known to be taking care of two children of an imprisoned South African black nationalist. It was expected, therefore, that while enjoying the celebrations in Lagos, he would make the acquaintance of the Front Line leaders. Black Africans would watch him for signs that the new administration did indeed support majority rule in Rhodesia as well as in South Africa. Meanwhile Young would also be under Ian Smith's strong scrutiny for indications that Kissinger had been accurate in forecasting that the Carter government would throw its weight behind a settlement allowing Rhodesian whites to stay.

The British had recently proposed an interim government under its influence, which the black nationalists had backed. They trusted the English. South Africa was in favor of the peaceful switch to black rule in Rhodesia, which appeared a paradox, unless one appreciated their fear that the longer guerrilla warfare lasted on their border, the greater the likelihood of Soviet intervention. After all, had not Cuban troops helped force them out of Angola?

But despite South Africa, Ian Smith rejected the plan. In desperation, both he and England were again turning to the United States, soliciting its influence in world affairs.

On January 25, Young appeared before the Senate Foreign Relations Committee for the hearings on his nomination to the United

Nations post. There he commented on this situation:

"Rhodesia cannot survive without South Africa," he said. "If South Africa says 'Negotiate,' Rhodesia will have to negotiate. . . .I think one reason Ian Smith has refused to bargain is that he believes in a crunch he will get our support." And he urged application of economic pressure by repeal of the Byrd amendment, through which the United States did not observe the economic embargo of Rhodesia practiced by other nations and continued to import chrome.

At the committee's hearings Young was praised by nearly all its members, though Young, always keeping South Africa in mind and also always giving Jimmy Carter room, tried to temper anticipation of his performance by saying that he didn't expect to stay in lock-step with the administration. "I fully expect. . .to make mistakes and, maybe, even be betrayed by the confusion of a tense moment."

Ironically, he handled a question on Vietnam as if bent on providing an example. He said that he hoped that the United States would establish normal relations with that country before it again asked to join the United Nations. On three previous occasions when Vietnam had applied, both in its two sections and in its united form, the United States had cast vetoes. Cyrus Vance, Young said, had expressed a desire for an early meeting with the Vietnamese, and the reporters gained the impression that Young forecast such a meeting to take place within ninety days.

Only Representatives Larry McDonald, Republican of Georgia, whose district bordered Young's, and Alan Ogden, a spokesman for the United States Labor Party, spoke against Young. The committee endorsed him unanimously. In the full Senate the next day he was again praised by, among others, an old-line Southerner, John J. Sparkman, Democrat from Alabama and chairman of the Foreign Relations committee; and an old-line northern liberal, Clifford P. Case, Republican of New Jersey. The vote was 89 to 3 in favor of Young, the only dissenters being conservative Republicans Carl Curtis of Nebraska, Jesse Helms of North Carolina, and William Scott of Virginia. But neither they nor any other Senator spoke in opposition.

The overwhelming vote of approval, however, was almost obscured by the storm that had broken over Young's remarks to the committee. The Vietnam War was especially fresh in the minds of those who had supported it, and there was continuing dissatisfaction with the Vietnamese accounting of the American POWs, the missing and the dead. The State Department therefore rapped Young across the knuckles by saying that it was too early to discuss a specific meeting as long as Hanoi continued to withhold such information.

"I'm learning," Young said, "that talking in this job gets you in more trouble than keeping quiet. . . .I said I hoped it would come within sixty to ninety days, but no official decision has been made. And in any such conflict as this, they [the State Department] are right, because I'm [still] just an unemployed Congressman."

On January 31, in the East Room of the White House, the Reverend Andrew Jackson Young, Jr., former Congressman from Georgia, was sworn in by Justice Thurgood Marshall as the chief United States representative to the United Nations. Andrew Young, said President Carter on that occasion, is "a very rare combination of inner strength and self-assurance. Of all the people I've ever known in public service, Andy Young is the best."

Hastening back to New York, Young was applauded by hundreds of members of the United Nations secretariat after he presented his credentials to Secretary General Kurt Waldheim. Not often had the arrival of a new ambassador aroused such enthusiasm. And on Tuesday, the first day of February, he left for London to meet with Ivor Richard, chairman of the Geneva talks on Rhodesia, before flying on to Africa. He and his people were offered a military plane, but Young wanted to avoid the image that might be created by the sight of such a large, powerful aircraft employed for his use alone. His idea was to keep everything casual and relaxed, so he took a commercial flight.

He hadn't even intended to bring along his press secretary till the Los Angeles *Times* phoned with a request to send a reporter along. Young ended up being accompanied by twenty-two reporters.

Just before leaving he was interviewed by Dan Rather of CBS. In the interview he voiced his opinion that the Cuban presence in Angola actually was bringing "a certain stability and order" to that shattered country. "The Cubans went to Angola because we were not there with a rational movement first. . . .Most colored peoples of the world are not afraid of communism. Maybe that's wrong, but communism has never been a threat to me. I have no love for communism. I could never be a communist. . .but. . .racism has always been a threat. . . That has been the enemy of all of my life and. . .everything I know about life."

THE HEAVY HITTER

Not Nixon, not Ford, but Henry Kissinger is the one person whom Cyrus Vance, Zbigniew Brzezinski, Andrew Young, and Jimmy Carter can feel breathing down their necks. The Carter administration rolled into power over Kissinger's back, yet they still consult him regularly. He looks happy and fit for a man who has lost so much power, as if he hasn't really lost it, or has the prospect of taking up just where he left off at any minute.

Born Heinz Alfred Kissinger near Nuremberg, Germany, in 1923, into a devoutly Jewish home, he was ten when Hitler took over and fifteen when he and his family finally fled from the Third Reich—in the nick of time. Like Daniel Moynihan, he graduated from a New York high school after making straight As.

As the ramrod of the National Security Council, Kissinger worked for Nixon throughout his ill-fated terms of office and accompanied Nixon on all the trips overseas. A master at the game of foreign policy, Kissinger gradually usurped the duties and then the position itself of William Rogers, the secretary of state.

In World War II he returned to Germany in an infantryman's uniform. After seeing action in the Battle of the Bulge, he became an interpreter for a general and then an interrogator for counterintelligence.

A listing of the diplomatic transactions in which Kissinger was involved would fill a small book. If he had been involved in nothing but ending the Vietnam War, the twists and turns would stupefy the mind. But there were also the trips to China, the India-Pakistan

War, the Turkish invasion of Cyprus, the SALT talks, the renunciation of biological and chemical warfare, the myriad negotiations in the Middle East, including the Yom Kippur War, the belated forays into Rhodesia and South Africa, the endless sparring with the Russians, to name only the most noticeable episodes.

After the war Kissinger earned impeccable academic credentials: Summa cum laude, Phi Beta Kappa, M.A., Ph.D., all gained at Harvard. A man of the utmost loyalty, he turned down a University of Chicago offer of a professorship, preferring to remain at Harvard as a temporary instructor. He is faithful to his school and to America, which enabled him to realize the dreams so thoroughly shattered by thudding jackboots and arrests in the night.

Kissinger is an intimidating figure, a triumph of cybernetics. Americans feel more comfortable with imperfect men at the top. It helped to know that Abe Lincoln was melancholic. Jimmy Carter confessed that in his heart he had occasionally lusted after other women besides his wife, and he won the Presidency. More people can identify with Billy Carter than with Henry Kissinger. Billy Carter is not generally believed to have gotten straight As.

As an academic at Harvard, Kissinger's specialty was foreign power politics. In 1957, in a book called Nuclear Weapons and Foreign Policy, *he offered as a substitute for John Foster Dulles's threats of massive retaliation a more sophisticated policy that he called "flexible response." He proposed that while nuclear weapons could be used for tactics, the nature of the overall strategy should determine the technology employed. Because of such work and some of his later policies, and also because of a German accent that he never lost, he has been identified with Dr. Strangelove of the Kubrick movie.*

In 1961 John Kennedy adopted his policy of flexible response.

Americans like machines that work. And Kissinger worked. But some Americans—troublemakers—also like to know *how* the machines work. Kissinger liked to negotiate in secret. He carried the vast jumble of American foreign policy around in his head. One moment he'd be seen grinning, escorting some lady—younger, taller, beautiful—to a party or some other social event. Then, a few days later, he would emerge from a plane looking grim and businesslike and intoning weighty abstractions into a microphone. Eventually, after having been divorced for some time, he married one of those tall, beautiful women. But somehow that did not soften his Strangelove image of settling the peoples of the world into their proper places for a test of the Doomsday Bomb. He had already received too many straight As.

As early as 1956 Kissinger came under the aegis of millionaire Nelson Rockefeller, who set up a project in which Kissinger continued to work out his realpolitik. Kissinger advocated maintaining a hard line against the Russians while exploring every avenue to avoid a shootout. He came up with something called detente. When Rockefeller sought the Republican presidential nomination in 1968, Kissinger helped write his platform. Later he was recruited by the winner, Richard Nixon.

While Nixon was sinking into the mire of Watergate, Kissinger, now secretary of state, had the world pretty much to himself. He was the Hammering Hank Aaron, the Jack Nicklaus, *and* the Joe Namath of foreign policy. Yet even he did not emerge from Watergate unscathed. He was under suspicion not only for having kept such bad company, but also for using questionable surveillance techniques. When leaks developed in his office, he had asked, in fury, that the telephones of his employees be tapped. He still didn't want anyone to know how the machine worked. The press called him "The Lone Ranger."

Jimmy Carter ran and won, criticizing Kissinger's secrecy. He promised to conduct foreign affairs openly. (A lot of Americans were surprised to learn that they had been lined up on the side of Pakistan against India.) Carter announced that he would emphasize human rights. (People were beginning to detect the heavy hands of Kissinger and the CIA in the rightist takeover of Chile.) For his secretary of state Carter picked a West Virginian who knew his way around his office and was not likely to let business slip from under his control. And the new director of the National Security Council was seemingly put together out of that same Blitzkrieg-forged European steel as Kissinger. But Brzezinski appeared less likely to try to do it all himself. He is the coordinator keeping everything running smoothly, applying a dab of grease here or there; he is the one who gives out the As.

For all his criss-crossing of the globe, there were some important areas that Kissinger virtually ignored. One was Japan (thus the Trilateralists). Another was sub-Saharan Africa. The good doctor turned out to be human after all. He had flaws. He was the home-run king who couldn't hit to all fields. He left voids into which

Andrew Young and Jimmy Carter found themselves flowing as naturally as water into the cracks of a parched field.

"I think," said Ambassador Young in his *Playboy* interview of July 1977, "that one of the big weaknesses in Henry Kissinger's equations was that he couldn't understand. . .that racism is one of the most powerful dynamics in the world today. . . .I think that the horrors of racism in Kissinger's childhood were so terrible that in order to function, he had to put it behind him. Otherwise he would have been so bitter and filled with hate that he could never have done anything. This is not a criticism, just an acceptance of reality. I take racism in small doses."

Chapter Four

SUFFER THE CHILDREN

AS FAR AS SCLC'S CAMPAIGN in Albany, Georgia, is concerned, history's verdict seems to be that it was disjointed. Even the time frame, based on the three occasions when Martin Luther King, Jr., and Ralph Abernathy were jailed, had an interrupted, leap-frog pattern. King and Abernathy first arrived in Albany on December 15, 1961. They were arrested on the sixteenth, released several days later, and tried in February 1962, after which their sentencing was delayed until July 10. Till that summer they stayed mostly in Atlanta. SCLC's role in the Albany campaign therefore centered chiefly on the events of July and August of 1962, when King and Abernathy returned for sentencing and spent two other, more substantial periods behind bars.

Young, only recently involved with SCLC, played only a small role at Albany. He would not get into actual confrontation until Birmingham the following year. The Albany campaign, however, was a first for everyone in that it was the first time that organized blacks stood toe to toe with the forces of discrimination in a single pitched battle lasting for months.

Andrew Young commuted to Albany from the Dorchester Center, about a 150-mile drive. Except for Wyatt Tee Walker, all of the SCLC officials exerted efforts in Albany with intermittent frequency. The price of this was one of the many lessons that Young took from that town.

Young knew the area. Thomasville and Beachton, the two Georgia towns in which he had pastored back in the mid-fifties, were only a short distance south of Albany. Until the Carters came along he had never expected much from that Black Belt region. One had only to think "voter registration" and in minutes, seemingly, the KKK would come charging out of the pines. In Albany no more than

10 percent of the black people were making even a marginally decent living, and this in a city of 56,000 having a black state college inside its limits and an integrated army base just outside.

Members of SNCC as well, the two young men who laid the groundwork for the Albany movement, Charles Sherrod and Cordell Reagan, were both graduates of Young's Dorchester Center. SNCC, however, wasn't overjoyed when SCLC came in at the invitation of Dr. William G. Anderson, an old schoolmate of Abernathy's and the guiding spirit behind the Albany movement. Certain members of the movement appreciated SCLC's resources but not the accompanying national attention. They thought things would move more effectively if the control remained local. SCLC's Wyatt Walker was accused of "throwing Reverend King's weight around."

These were only a few of the things that went wrong at Albany. But one learns from one's losses. Young and the other SCLC strategists learned from Albany.

Once the ministers of SCLC arrived and looked around, they saw so much evil and received so much support from ordinary citizens, even children, that they went after everything.

As in Montgomery, they went after the bus lines. The result was that in a short time the bus line folded completely which wasn't really the aim. But they didn't go after only the buses. They wanted to desegregate the bus and train terminals as well. They wanted blacks on the police force. They wanted Albany's black citizens to be admitted to the libraries, movies, parks, and other places of entertainment. They wanted the city to form a biracial committee to handle subsequent grievances.

Their approach was morally justified, but in retrospect it would have been better strategy to concentrate on just one or maybe two goals. SCLC was trying—in vain—to get the Justice Department to act. The FBI would say that it was keeping things under observation and that would be all. A lawyer could be assaulted in a sheriff's office, a pregnant woman inquiring after a prisoner could be beaten badly enough to suffer a miscarriage—such incidents would only mean the writing and filing away of two more FBI reports.

King and his young co-workers were also up against shrewd opposition. The city fathers would cool down demonstrations by agreeing to parleys, then deliberately let the negotiations break down. Laurie Pritchett, the chief of the Albany police, was the star of this show. He never used dogs, fire hoses, or tear gas. During the moments of prayer he would bow his head. Then he would arrest the demonstrators and send them, not to his jail, but to those in the outlying counties where the actual brutality was practiced.

Young perfected small techniques in Albany. Twice each day he visited King and Abernathy in jail. The first day the chief guard called out, "Here's a little nigger wants to visit the big nigger." The next day Young said, "Good morning, Sergeant Hamilton, how are you?" "I'm okay," the guard said, before he had a chance to turn to see who it was. Every time Young visited he worked on the officer, using courtesy, inquiring after his family, his interests. Eventually the guard's hostility buckled.

The real glory of Albany was the black townspeople. Even back in December, before King's arrival, 500 had been jailed, and by the time SCLC withdrew, several thousand, or about 5 percent of the black population, had been imprisoned. A large proportion were children or teenagers.

But finally they had had enough. When King and Abernathy were jailed for the third time, on July 27, neither Sherrod nor Reverend Samuel Wells, pastor of Albany's Shiloh Baptist Church, nor Andrew Young could get the crowd to move out of the church.

"Now friends," Young said, "we have the names and addresses of those who have signed their names as being ready to go. Now is the time to get our affairs in order." Sherrod was less diplomatic. "You ought to be ashamed of yourselves for sitting on your chairs while our leaders are sitting in a filthy jail!"

But they would not go.

When SCLC left Albany at the end of the year, with Birmingham ahead, the only change effected was the desegregation of the terminals, and that had come about through an ICC ruling not directly related to the movement. Dozens of demonstrators had been beaten. Countless acts of violence had taken place over the surrounding countryside. And to the particular distress of the ministers, nightriders had burned down four black churches.

More than anything else, to Young and the other leaders, Albany had been a bitter learning experience.

The Birmingham campaign, it might be said, really started on May 17, 1962, when King sent a letter to President Kennedy asking him to put the powers of his office squarely behind advancing "human rights in America." Without giving dates and places, he telegraphed the backing that SCLC expected. With the one hundredth anniversary of the Emancipation Proclamation approaching, it was time for the federal government to clean up its act.

Birmingham was important because it was undoubtedly the South's toughest big city: the black inhabitants called it "Bombingham." The police force was under the control of the public safety commissioner, an amazing individual named "Bull" Connor. For about a generation he had played a big part in seeing that Birmingham's reputation was secure. As a result, every black family was reputed to own an arsenal. Roy Wilkins warned SCLC that it would have trouble maintaining nonviolence with the people there; he called them some of "the roughest Negroes in the United States."

King, Young, and the others planned for Birmingham in all the big and little ways that they had overlooked in Albany. Since 1956 Birmingham had been the territory of the Alabama Christian Movement for Civil Rights, which was vigorously led by the Reverend Fred Shuttlesworth. King called ACHMR the "strongest affiliate" of SCLC, and he was pleased when Shuttlesworth said he would be more than happy to see SCLC come into Birmingham for its next campaign. At that moment he was leading a boycott of the stores, started by students at Miles College, and it was 95 percent effective.

SCLC had already decided to hold its 1962 convention in Birmingham, in September. It might have started its drive that fall, for things were happening. During the boycott the store owners had been prevailed upon to take down the "white" and "colored" signs. Then, under pressure from the city government, in particular Bull Connor, the merchants had put them up again. However, the Birmingham city government was changing; instead of three city commissioners there would be a mayor and a city council. Elections under the new system were being held that fall. Though Albert Boutwell, one of the candidates for mayor, was no prize, King didn't want to increase the chances of Boutwell's chief opponent in the election, the same Bull Connor. Therefore King held up the campaign for six months, till April 1963.

For three days King, Abernathy, Young, Walker, and the others met at Dorchester Center to work out their strategy. In the end they came up with four goals, a number that they considered workable in view of the broad support that they could expect, thanks to the Reverend Shuttlesworth. They would push for the desegregation of the various public facilities in the department stores, the hiring and promoting of blacks in stores and industry, the forming of a biracial committee to work on future desegregation measures, and the freeing of demonstrators.

Afterwards many would say that SCLC benefited from large doses of luck in Birmingham, ranging from Bull Connor's character to the fact that they were able to get thousands of children not only to march but also to behave nonviolently when assaulted. But as Young later pointed out, the results came through hard work. While waiting for the outcome of a run-off election between Boutwell and Connor, and in preparation for the sit-ins, Wyatt Walker scouted the whole of Birmingham's downtown, taking note of such things as the numbers of seats at the lunch counters, the entrances and exits, the nearby landmarks. In the meantime Young and several others conducted workshops on nonviolence, and later they went into schools all around the city, talking to the students.

King was busy too, swinging around the country to raise cash for bail, and following that, he put himself in especially close contact with the movement, spending his mornings, for instance, with black business leaders, briefing them on the goals and techniques of nonviolent action, then in the evenings, accompanying Andrew Young or Bernard Lee or Dorothy Cotton to the meetings with the students, to whom he gave similar talks.

Young saw that the leaders faced considerable skepticism, that there was a strong undercurrent of violence running through the black population, and that it had the potential to undo the plan at the first instance of brutality against the demonstrators. But Young was convinced then and has restated his conviction many times since that in Birmingham in 1963 nonviolence was the only tool that stood a chance of working.

On April 2, as Easter approached, Boutwell defeated Bull Connor for mayor. Connor bitterly blamed the defeat on the black vote, and he and the other two commissioners insisted that their terms had not yet ended. As a result, the demonstrators would set out into a city that was being contested by two rival governments.

On April 3 the sit-ins started. On the sixth the demonstrations began, as Shuttlesworth marched on City Hall. And on the next day, a Sunday, King's brother, A.D., who had a church in Birmingham, led a prayer pilgrimage downtown, during which the police dogs made their first appearance.

The following week King decided that the moment had arrived when a renewed boycott should be launched against the stores and that he, Ralph Abernathy, and Al Hibbler, a famous blind singer, should go to jail. For the first time in his life he was going to disobey a court order, an injunction obtained by the city fathers against further protests. Finally they were combining Gandhi's civil disobedience with nonviolence. They went in on Good Friday, charged with parading without a permit.

It was Easter, and Andrew Young marked the occasion well. Left on the outside as usual, he had decided to test the city's spirit of Christian fellowship on the occasion of the celebration of Christ's resurrection.

He had no problems. Accompanying two young women, he went to one of six white churches that SCLC had selected for morning worship. It was the First Baptist Church, pastored by the Reverend Earl Stallings. Reverend Stallings shook hands with Young and his companions and assured them that they would be welcomed; Young enjoyed the services. His assistant in the action workshop was also welcomed at the First Presbyterian Church, and at a third church, though they were admitted to the services, four of the elders, two of them in tears, prayed with SCLC's three women representatives. At the other three churches Young's people were refused entry.

That afternoon, as A.D. King was leading another march toward the City Hall, his group was arrested. Hundreds of black spectators arrived to watch the loading of the patrol wagons. The expected happened. One woman resisted arrest, the police manhandled her, the rocks started flying, and the police waded in and called up the dogs.

By this time, to the rest of the country, Birmingham presented the spectacle of a boiling cauldron, yet the real action hadn't started. Many celebrities were sending telegrams to John and Robert Kennedy, but in the meantime behind-the-scenes negotiations had started. With others in the movement, Young was meeting with Boutwell and the store owners, setting forth the movement's goals and trying to reach an accommodation. But the store owners were reluctant to move without the backing of the big businessmen and industrialists in that major coal and steel town.

In Young's estimation this was the low point of the campaign. So far Bull Connor, following the example of Laurie Pritchett, had not really slipped up. He had brought in the dogs, but mainly he had kept shoveling people into the jails, and now hundreds were imprisoned and SCLC had run out of money for bail bonds. On April 20 King and Abernathy allowed themselves to be released from jail so that they could raise more money.

Together with James Bevel, Dorothy Cotton, and Bernard Lee, Young suggested that they could desegregate the public libraries and parks by sending in children. He didn't think that Bull Connor would arrest them. SCLC, he and his co-workers suggested, might also send children to integrate white schools merely by standing around or sitting. King agreed, but wanted it done quickly; the demonstrations were no longer on the front pages.

Young, Cotton, Bevel, and Lee, with about a dozen others, went around to the schools, into the libraries, and even into the classrooms. If police were called, they would leave and then come back after the police left. They asked the children to come to the church to see SCLC's films and to hear what nonviolence was all about.

Young sent one of the first groups of recruits to the white library. "You won't get arrested there, and you might learn something," he told them. They went, and it worked. The children sat and read without lifting their eyes to observe the shocked expressions.

It was decided to unload the school system and load the jail system, on an *en masse* basis. D-Day was May 2, by which time they had instructed and mobilized 6,000 children. That afternoon they fed the children in waves out from the main staging center, the 16th Street Baptist Church. The police arrested them as fast as possible, running out of patrol wagons and using school buses, but still two or three waves reached downtown where most knelt and prayed. Almost a thousand were jailed. The next day the police barricaded the church, but not before 500 more children got out.

Finally, under Connor's orders, the police attacked the children with dogs and fire hoses at pressures of up to 100 pounds. They handled the dogs badly. It was just as if the police were inviting a riot, Young said. Instead of using the dogs to contain the crowd, the police unleashed them upon the demonstrators. At least five people were bitten, and in addition, one Wallace man deliberately tried to swerve his car into the crowd, whereupon black spectators on the rooftops started throwing rocks and bottles.

Through the next few days these marches continued without letup, while the nation recoiled at the photos of the dogs ripping at nonviolent demonstrators and the blasts of water washing brave, nonresisting young people up against curbs and buildings like so many dead leaves. Andrew Young led one group of over 3,000 children downtown, using several different routes. They trooped in and out of the stores, singing "Ain't gonna let nobody turn me 'round" and "I'm on my way to Freedom Land." They returned to the church, regrouped, and headed downtown again. Young himself was impressed, and he saw that the children's courage made an equally big impact on the store owners.

The Kennedys finally moved. The assistant attorney general in charge of the Civil Rights Division of the Justice Department, Burke Marshall, made his presence felt in Birmingham. Roger Blough, the board chairman of U.S. Steel, had been contacted, and he in turn had put pressure on his associates in Birmingham, the same "Better Business" people whom Young in turn had met through church contacts. With this kind of pressure at work, Young and the other protest leaders finally worked out a settlement.

SCLC had achieved its goals, but the battle was not over. Bull Connor called for a white boycott of the stores that had agreed to desegregate facilities and to place blacks, by promotion or hiring, in previously all-white positions. On May 11 the KKK held a rally at the edge of town, and that night, two charges of dynamite wrecked A.D. King's house and another put a hole in the Gaston Motel, SCLC's headquarters. The ghetto exploded into a night-long riot, and Kennedy put army units on alert at nearby bases. But the next day King and Abernathy managed to cool things down.

In the next months sporadic violence continued, culminating in September when someone heaved a bomb through the windows of the 16th Street Baptist Church during Sunday School classes. Four little girls died and twenty other children were injured. At the funeral services, a well-known black writer suggested that nonviolence had had its say and now guns were in order. Christopher McNair, one of the bereaved fathers, answered, "What good would Denise have done with a machine gun in her hand?"

That was the lesson of Birmingham.

Birmingham, with the bombs, the dogs, the fire hoses, and black children praying in the streets, established what Young liked to call the "Coalition of Conscience" that lasted through the next several years, till the Vietnam protests of 1966 and 1967. It led to a new awareness by white America of the injustices of segregation and discrimination. And it confirmed the effectiveness of nonviolence.

Naturally Young knew that violence was almost a corollary of nonviolence, but it would not be SCLC's violence. The SCLC leaders were aware that at any moment it might be used to end their lives; in fact, they were sometimes surprised that it hadn't already.

Birmingham wasn't the only scene of civil rights activity. On June 13 President Kennedy sent to Congress a far-reaching civil rights bill. And two days later Medgar Evers, a leading NAACP figure, was killed by an assassin at his home in Jackson, Mississippi. That very day some of SCLC's workers tried to use the rest room at the bus station in Winona, Mississippi, and were arrested and beaten. The same thing happened to the people who tried to bail them out.

Young and James Bevel decided to try to secure their comrades' release. Their reasoning was that, as Southerners, they could deal with the white Mississippi mentality.

(Young, in a 1977 *Playboy* interview, described how Northern activists, like those who worked with SNCC, would pull up at a service station, ask for gas, and then sit with the windows rolled up, "scared to death," while the attendant would call ahead and say something like, "Hey, Sheriff, I got some more outside agitators headed your way."

(Young recalled that he, King, and the other SCLC people would pull up, get out of the car, and talk to the attendant about the weather, road conditions, anything. They would walk around, buy an RC Cola and a moon pie, lean against a fender, and relax, as if they had all the time in the world.)

That day, however, they were in a hurry. Young and Bevel asked Dorothy Cotton if they could borrow her car.

"If Anell and Mrs. Hamer got beat up, I can get beat up too," she answered.

They tried to tell her that what they had in mind was going to Mississippi to keep people from getting beat up, not getting beat up themselves. "We don't want you to go," Young said, "not because you're a woman but because you're a masochist."

Why did he say that?

Enraged, Cotton jumped in and took them out of there at about ninety miles an hour. On the highway they zoomed around a curve and found themselves face to face with a large Mack truck, passing on their side. Cotton barely escaped to the shoulder and on to the highway again.

Then and there, Young said, he decided that if he had to die soon, it would have to be for a cause rather than for nothing. With that thought, working in civil rights was easier, especially when one was employing such a beautiful, endlessly subtle, and effective means as nonviolence.

That perception was most severely tested in 1964 in St. Augustine, Florida. Young, and SCLC, were brought there when, on Easter Sunday of 1964, Mrs. Malcolm Peabody, seventy-two years old and the mother of the governor of Massachusetts, was arrested for taking part in a sit-in.

St. Augustine was much smaller even than Albany, with only

15,000 people, one-third of them black. With its four hundredth anniversary coming up the next year, it was the oldest city in the United States. "The Ancient City," as it called itself, was a tourist town located on the ocean about fifty miles south of the Georgia border. One of its chief attractions was a picturesque open-sided building with a cupola, the old slave market.

Twenty-five years earlier the town had had black policemen, black salespeople in its largest store, and a black doctor with numerous white patients. But now local blacks trying to better their condition met with extreme violence.

In response to the publicity generated by Mrs. Peabody's arrest, by early June civil rights leaders, including Young, were mounting daily marches. Their goals were desegregation of public facilities and increased black representation on the police force and in the fire department. In St. Augustine they also intended to refine further their techniques of nonviolence, at the same time that organizations like SNCC, in reaction to the pressures they felt, were moving in other directions.

St. Augustine was in many respects an incredible place. It was, more than most towns Andrew Young saw, like the setting of one of those cowboy or motorcycle movies in which the so-called leading citizens have completely handed over control to a band of drunken, leering, cynical rowdies who have ridden in from nowhere. The police chief, Virgil Stuart, was hardly a factor, and the sheriff, L. O. Davis, was a heavyset, genial observer with a cigar, dedicated to protecting the white citizenry, large numbers of whom were likely at any time to be armed with clubs, guns, and phials of sulfuric acid.

St. Augustine, in effect, belonged to terrorists who were variously Klansmen and members of a group called the Ancient City Gun Club. The gun club was headed by a professional redneck named Hoss Manucy. Ol' Hoss didn't smoke, drink, or chase after women; his only hobby, he said, was beating and killing niggers. (This teetotaler, however, had been arrested for moonshining, and it was said that he had a "forty-barrel farm.") He and his brother Bubber had put together a gang called "Manucy's Raiders." Their hobby was to ride through town with Confederate flags tied to their whip antennas, coordinating their activities with CB radios, threatening and beating people, and discharging firearms.

To avoid the stifling heat, most of SCLC's marches took place at night, and an eerie pattern soon set in. By day the demonstrators were harassed and beaten on the beaches; at night they would march to the slave market, the focus of their operations, where Manucy's men would be waiting, with scarcely any restraint set by the police on their ferocity.

Until a federal judge stopped it, some of Manucy's men were sworn in by the sheriff as "volunteer special deputies." "It's one thing to oppose the Klan," Young said. ". . . But when you have one man, wearing civilian clothes, beating you while another, wearing a badge, stands waiting to arrest you when the first one gets tired, well, that makes you think."

The sheriff tried to use his authority to block the marches, but a federal judge overturned his orders. Then King and Abernathy tried to enter a motel and were arrested and stayed in jail for two days. By that time, as if Manucy weren't enough, J. B. Stoner, a lawyer for the Klan, had arrived from Atlanta. Stoner organized three white marches, two through black neighborhoods, where the people greeted them with singing and placards urging "Equality for All in '64."

In the meantime Kennedy's civil rights bill, which had been shamed out of the congressional committees by his assassination in November 1963, and which Lyndon Johnson had helped conduct through Congress, looked as if it would imminently become law. St. Augustine's "leading" citizens again began to consider a biracial committee.

On the night of June 25, the climax came. Connie Lynch, a Klan organizer from California, led a "White Citizens Rally" at the slave market. "If it takes violence to preserve the Constitution, I say all right," he preached. "I favor violence to preserve the white race anytime, any place, anywhere. Now it may be some niggers are gonna get killed in the process, but when war's on, that's what happens."

Fred Shuttlesworth, leading the marchers that evening, took them up the side of the plaza, past the police, past hundreds of whites gathered on either side. Then the whites attacked, criss-crossing the plaza and beating anyone they missed in the initial assault, until heaps of black bodies littered the ground.

Somebody hit Andrew Young in the jaw, and he went down, unconscious. He didn't really know what happened until he saw it on a newsreel several years later. The people charging back and forth kicked and stomped, and only luck kept him from being seriously hurt. Dozens were injured, and nineteen of the marchers had to be hospitalized.

After that the Florida governor, Farris Bryant, banned night marches, and without federal marshalls, the demonstrators couldn't move. The civil rights lawyers took their case to U.S. District Judge Bryan Simpson in Jacksonville, in an attempt to keep the sheriff, the police chief, the governor, and others from interfering with the night marches, which had been permitted by the judge.

During the testimony, as reported by the *Pittsburgh Courier*, Young stated that he had been attacked so many times by the same men that they were on speaking terms. He particularly remembered one who always wore overalls and a railroad cap.

As the *Courier*'s reporter, Snow James, put it, "Florida Attorney General Kynes made the mistake of cross-examining the Reverend Mr. Young."

"Don't you feel it was an unreasonable protest, to go marching through residential sections after eleven o'clock at night, singing songs?" the attorney general asked.

"Well, sir, when you take into consideration all the centuries of unreasonable discrimination to which the Negro has been subjected, and the fact that he has so often fought for the freedom of this country, and is now fighting for the right to survive in America, the singing of prayerful songs does not seem at all an unreasonable form of protest."

"Well, what is your purpose to staging all these 'nonviolent' demonstrations? Are you trying to bring the city of St. Augustine to a crisis?"

"You might say we are trying to bring it to a crisis of conscience."

Just before July 2, the day that Lyndon Johnson signed the strong new Civil Rights Law of 1964 on public accommodations, SCLC left St. Augustine, with King feeling that they had won. From his own experiences, Young might not have stated it so positively. When blacks in St. Augustine later tried to enter the motels and restaurants under the protection of the new law, some were beaten and King had to return briefly.

Finally, a federal injunction was issued under the new law that outlawed Manucy's raiding and forced restaurants and motels to admit black patrons.

It was time to go back to Alabama. Selma awaited.

The Lions in the Arena

REDEMPTIVE FORCE

Bull Connor had a glass eye.

Martin Luther King, Jr., was a black man in a segregated land.

Connor, as a young man, developed the power in his vocal cords by being employed to read the baseball ticker tape aloud in a pool hall. Though his proper name was Theosophilus Eugene, "Bull" was what his friends called him, and he was listed as "Bull" in the phone book.

King, following in his father's footsteps, developed his oratorical skill by interpreting the gospel from Baptist pulpits. His co-workers called him "Doc" and, before SNCC started using it derisively, "De Lawd."

Bull Connor got into politics and became Birmingham's Commissioner for Public Safety, Health, Education, and Welfare.

Martin Luther King, Jr., became the president of the Southern Christian Leadership Conference, the strongest, most dynamic civil rights organization of the 60s.

Bull Connor was the man most responsible for Birmingham's reputation as a segregated city. For over twenty years he kept the lid clamped shut through the vacuum of fear.

Though he was coming off a "defeat," King could not resist being drawn to Birmingham because of that reputation. Twice he tried to avoid Connor, but then it was Easter, the season of redemption, and that auspiciousness overrode circumspect strategies.

Though he'd been voted out of power, Bull Connor stayed for the confrontation. He believed in Birmingham, in Alabama, and in himself. He believed in white supremacy.

King argued that whites would gain their salvation through the suffering of the blacks.

Bull Connor was pleased to provide the suffering.

Repeatedly King sent marchers to City Hall. Bull Connor scooped them up by the hundreds.

King had spent months swinging around the country raising bond money; in days Bull Connor took it all. The first time that King himself led a march, Connor arrested him.

King had always shared a cell with Ralph Abernathy. Bull Connor separated them. King kept the walls from closing in by leaning on one and writing his famous "Letter from the Birmingham Jail," which refuted Billy Graham and others who were urging him to go slow.

Bull Connor wondered why there was still so much muttering when he had done such a good job. Heretofore he had been using the tactics of another man, Laurie Pritchett, and he had won.

While he was in jail, King had his able young lieutenants devise new strategies and open negotiations.

Bull Connor, sitting encased in his armored car in the spring days, was not invited to the meetings attended by the people who had wanted him out to begin with, to revive Birmingham's sagging economy. Nor had the niggers shown any sign of wanting to salute his patience. When the children broke out of the church and gathered in Kelly Ingram Park on May 2, Bull Connor had had enough of ingratitude.

It is time now for a good word about Bull Connor.

He was consistent. He was reliable. He lived up to advance billing. He did not lighten up. When Fred Shuttlesworth was injured by a blast from the hoses and carried off in an ambulance, Bull Connor regretted that Shuttlesworth wasn't leaving in a hearse. He did not lighten up. He was everything that everybody said he was. President Kennedy credited him with doing more for civil rights than anyone since Lincoln.

It was not his fault that the moment arrived when he could order his firemen to loose yet another blast of water and they would not obey. It was not his fault that in one day he could order King's arrest so many times that everyone lost count and still King went free.

He had done all he could.

Martin Luther King, Jr., believed in achieving social justice through the dynamic use of nonviolence and civil disobedience. His chief tool was subtlety.

Bull Connor believed in the usefulness of fear and instilling obedience through sheer force.

In Birmingham Martin Luther King achieved something less than a complete victory, but time was on his side.

Bull Connor's time had run out. He had done everything he could, short of death—and the bomb hurled into the Sunday school sealed the impossibility of his redemption through nostalgia.

From Birmingham Martin Luther King's world kept expanding as surely as an exploding nova, and the next year he was awarded the Nobel Peace Prize.

For his efforts Bull Connor was pleased to receive a gilded hard-hat inscribed "Battle of Ingram Park." Forced at last to step down, he said he believed the city owed him a year and a half in back pay.

Chapter Five

THE FRONT LINE

AS HIS PLANE DESCENDED for its landing on February 2, 1977, at London, on the first stop of his first diplomatic tour, Andrew Young personally was fogged in by clouds of controversy swirling up from three of his recent remarks.

First there had been his prediction about the impending United States accommodation with Vietnam. Second, he had implied that the white minority government in Rhodesia would have to negotiate with the black majority if that was the desire of the South Africans. (Having already chided Young gently about the Vietnam remark, Secretary of State Vance responded to the Rhodesia statement by saying that matters were "not quite that simple.") Finally, he had said the unthinkable—that Fidel Castro's Cuban troops had brought a certain measure of "stability" to Angola. It didn't matter that in the same interview Young had tried hard to clarify his remark and to make it more palatable. "The Cubans went to Angola because we were not there with a rational movement first," he had tried to explain. And he had not backed away from his contention that the presence of the South Africans was as undesirable on one side of Angola's borders as that of the Cubans on the other side.

The problem was that all this was consistent to Andrew Young but not to those for whom racism was a lesser evil than the Cold War. For the latter group, the gospel was still preached by the great Harvard thinker, the old pro, Henry Kissinger, to whom this obviously biased, lightweight amateur, Andrew Young, was not to be compared. No one recognized that Young's judgment would eventually be vindicated.

Meanwhile, from Young's two target states came chortles of glee. "The new boy is getting his lumps early," a South African official said, and the Rhodesia *Herald* called him "a strolling player for the theatre of the absurd."

Young was unperturbed. Just before leaving the United States, he had again set out his concept of serving in the United Nations post as a "point man." In the infantry this is the lead soldier in a patrol probing dangerous territory, the one who is most likely to expose the enemy positions and also the likeliest to become the first casualty. Young was willing to go along with the State Department's efforts to present a united stand by repudiating his most disputed remarks. Nevertheless, he had told Vance that to retain "the right to say what I really believe, I'd be willing to take whatever flak came and I'd be willing to be repudiated by him whenever it was officially necessary. I got no ego problems about that whatsoever." Yet, he told the press, "Everything I said there is gonna happen. I'd stake my life on this. You know it's gonna happen on all of them."

Young further explained his position: "I mentioned [to Vance] that there were a number of things the American people were thinking about. I told him that if he did not mind, I would raise controversial points and talk about them. I said to Cy, 'You can refute and modify what I say,' [but] I told him that Vietnam was the one thing I would like not to have to modify my views on. Martin Luther King's life was deeply imbued with concern over what Vietnam was doing to us. It would be a repudiation of him if I did not continue to take a position."

Young had done nothing more than repeat what Vance had said about Vietnam at his own confirmation hearings earlier, except to add that the United States-Vietnam accommodation would begin in ninety days or less. In fact, somewhat less than ninety days elapsed before Vance sent a mission to Vietnam. Two months later, in May, United States and Vietnamese officials met in Paris. The meeting would result in a United States pledge not to veto Vietnam's next application to join the United Nations. On July 19, less than six months after Young's statement, Vietnam was admitted to the United Nations.

As for the Cubans in Angola, a high-ranking State Department official who knew something about Africa said a few weeks after Young's comment: "The fact is that without Cuban technicians in Angola it would be an awful mess. There would be more fighting and total chaos. Young's choice of words may have been unfortunate, but in substance he was right."

Which left Rhodesia . . .

The new United States ambassador to the United Nations left the country with anticipations that extended quite a bit beyond attending two large celebrations in Tanzania and Nigeria. Young expected to meet with the presidents of fifteen African nations. He wanted to show them the new moral force in United States diplomacy that he embodied as well as represented, and he wanted to hear their thoughts on what should be done about Rhodesia. "I came here to listen," he said.

Unfortunately, between the time he stepped on one plane in New York on February 1 and the moment he stepped out of another in Zanzibar on February 3, several things happened that threatened even that modest a goal.

In Ethiopia, Brigadier General Teferi Bante, the chairman of the military council and the head of state, was one of the leaders who had planned to enjoy Tanzanian President Nyerere's hospitality and to talk with Young. But on February 3 he was shot and killed in an attempted coup.

Secondly, Kenya, President Nyerere charged, had broken up the East African community that included Kenya, Tanzania, and, to some extent, Uganda. Kenya had shut down the headquarters of the East African Railways System, the East African Airways had suffered a financial collapse for which Kenya and Tanzania were blaming each other, and the border between the two countries was about to be closed. Thus Young was visiting a president whose country, despite the anniversary, was not at all in a happy state.

Also, in a development aimed most directly at Young's reasons for coming, the prime minister of Rhodesia, Ian Smith, rejected the plan offered by British emissary Ivor Richard in place of Kissinger's original proposal.

Kissinger's idea had been to set up a transitional governing council consisting of a balanced number of blacks and whites. At the end of two years, power would be transferred, peacefully it was expected, into the hands of the black majority. Behind Smith's acceptance of this plan were probably two principal thoughts.

One was that during those two years, with national security under "European" control, whites would still be effectively at the helm, with the power to determine the nature of the changeover. In addition, those who weren't staying would have all the time they needed and the means to leave the country with all the assets that they cared to take. In any case they wouldn't have to contemplate a long, difficult trip to some other, probably indifferent country. They had only to drive across the border into the welcoming arms of South Africa, where their presence would strengthen that bastion of minority rule.

The premier's other idea was that the transfer of power would thus be a responsibility of the United States, obliging it to protect white interests under the new regime. Smith always calculated that dismay at the growing Soviet and Cuban presence in neighboring Mozambique would sooner or later drive the United States into taking a strong position on the side of an anti-Communist or white minority government in Rhodesia.

The Carter administration, through Andrew Young, had lost little time in warning Smith that reliance on that notion was risky. Before leaving New York, Young had accused Smith of trying to bait the Cubans and Russians into moving into Mozambique so as to draw the United States to his side. The United States, said Young, would not let itself fall into any trap requiring it to send troops to Southern Africa. "I think we've had more than our share of trying to get in and run other people's affairs."

Ivor Richard, the chairman of the Geneva Conference, had put together a plan setting up a Rhodesian government of thirty-two blacks and whites. At their head would sit a British commissioner who would have the power not only to shift the racial composition of this governing council but also to cast the decisive vote. Richard had obtained approval to some degree from everybody on the one side—the leaders of the five black front-line countries, Zambia, Mozambique, Botswana, Tanzania, and Angola; the two black hard-liners of the Patriotic Front, Joshua Nkomo and Robert Mugabe; and the matching pair of more moderate nationalists, Bishop Abel Muzorewa and the Reverend Ndabaningi Sithole.

But now Ian Smith had said no to all of Ivor Richard's hard work, and instead was holding fast to the Kissinger plan, which the black leaders had long regarded as only a jumping-off spot for further negotiations. This meant that Young, who had hoped to be able to apply a little grease to the gears, would alight in the midst of a once more tragically stalled situation. The guerrilla war that had caused 2,500 deaths in 1976 was likely to spread—in Mozambique 500 Cuban and Russian experts were already training the Zimbabwean guerrillas, while in Rhodesia mercenaries of many nationalities were flocking to the call.

These developments stole the thunder from the arrival in Africa of America's first black chief delegate to the United Nations. In Zanzibar, the large island off mainland Tanzania, the delegations from the various foreign countries were greeted by a guard of honor and over 200 people singing, dancing, and playing instruments. Waiting to greet Young were only the deputy Tanzanian foreign minister, Isaac Sepetu, and the United States ambassador to Tanzania, James Spain.

In the interests of diplomacy the Tanzanians suggested that they had something special lined up for Young, but nothing materialized. He cooled his heels in Zanzibar while the situation in Rhodesia worsened. He exuded patience, saying: "I can always see hope where there is none. I think we are two-thirds of the way toward developing a scenario that both blacks and whites can live with." It was a rephrasing of the lessons learned in his movement negotiations.

Ian Smith was about to announce that he would go it alone, without any external help, when Rhodesia had broken away from the British twelve years earlier. He would follow the Kissinger plan, but Nkomo, Mugabe, and their Patriotic Front were out. He would deal only with Muzorewa and Sithole. The next day, in Mozambique, Nkomo and Mugabe embraced at a public rally, declaring that they were perfectly satisfied to carry on guerrilla warfare, and that, indeed, continued violence was the only answer short of Rhodesia's immediate unconditional surrender. And spirits sank, as this seemed to ensure not only more immediate waste of human life, but also the same kind of continued warfare afterward that was still ravaging Angola.

Finally (actually, after not so long a time), when Young had had a chance to become settled and collect his thoughts, the talks began. On February 4, he met with the host, Tanzanian President Julius Nyerere, and later made the acquaintance of President Juvenal Habyalimanda of Rwanda. The next day he conferred with Presidents Kenneth Kaunda of Zambia, Siad Barre of Somalia, and Jean Baptiste Bagaza of Burundi. All the meetings were brief, with the longest probably being the seventy minutes he spent with Kaunda. Those two bright spirits, Kaunda and Young, then commented on the talks.

Kaunda spoke of his pleasure at seeing Young in the post of the United Nations ambassador "not because he is black but because of his principles and beliefs, which we think are in agreement with his leader President Jimmy Carter." And Kaunda expressed the confidence of the Africans in Carter's administration, and he predicted this confidence would be borne out eventually. In fact, he thought it would be a good idea if the United States took the lead in trying to bring majority rule not only to Zimbabwe (Rhodesia), but also to Namibia (South-West Africa) and to South Africa itself.

Young said that the talks had contained far more substance and "even moderation" than he had expected, and his only regret was the absence of the other liberation groups.

Then he returned to a theme that he had first brought to public attention with his "Cuban" statement and which he would continue to develop whenever he got the chance. This was his attempt to demote the bug-a-boo of communism to second place behind the more important spectre of racism. In fact, this would soon be one of his personal crusades, reminiscent of King's efforts to do away with the Vietnam War, in part because that war diverted an almost fatal portion of the spiritual and material resources that had been going into the drive for civil rights. Similarly, to Young the obsession with communism was like a veil that people seemed almost to delight in holding before their eyes, so that they could not grasp the full extent of the primary evil, at least where southern Africa was concerned.

Young was sparked by his desire to pass on Nyerere's assurance that no African country would become communist. They had in mind not only Angola but also Mozambique, the most critically situated of all the front-line countries and whose president, Samora Machel, like Angola's Agostinho Neto, was absent. "He [Nyerere] said there may be intellectual Marxists among the leaders but that didn't mean they were going to set up communist states." And this was in line with the Carter administration thinking, which, Young said, wouldn't be paranoid about communism.

Less highly placed members of the African delegations came up with more pointed appraisals of Young himself as he eased through two more days of socializing before flying on to his other stop in Africa, Nigeria. He seems to have been a hit personally. One of Kaunda's Zambians described him as "open, easy to talk to." A delegate from SWAPO, the South-West Africa People's Organization of Namibia, said he was "a man with principle and integrity." Another delegate said, "I think Andy Young is different. It's surprising he isn't pushing some line. It's so refreshing it almost makes you suspicious." In other words, Young had yet to pass the test. This man expressed the common African complaint that while most Americans would hear Africans out, "it doesn't seem to make much difference how we feel or what we say. Americans . . . always think they're right, even if it's our affair."

("I came here to listen," Young kept repeating.)

A Somali said, "I hope he isn't being used. We won't be tricked by one black face." "You Americans," another official told reporters, ". . .think things are going to change overnight just because you send a black over here. Ambassador Young may have gotten Jimmy Carter elected President, but that doesn't mean he's going to work miracles in Africa." A third delegate was more specific about what was bothering them—the difference between Young's statements and the official line taken by the State Department. This, of course, involved Young's Cuban remark. "So what does that mean about what he is telling us? Are they personal views or do they really reflect what the Carter administration wants to do?" And a Zambian said, bluntly, "All his good actions and intentions cannot change the basic fact that the economic ties of your country help perpetuate white minority government in Africa. And that's a fact of life. I can't see any administration in a capitalist society like yours changing very much."

Before he left, Young held one more meeting with President Nyerere. Apparently speaking for all five front-line countries while Young listened, Nyerere, a true elder statesman and one of the most respected, presented some rather sharp positions. At first he seemed to contradict Kaunda by urging that the United States continue to lie low in the Rhodesian affair. He said that it was still the business principally of the British, and that even though Ian Smith had rejected Richards's proposals, talks should go on—not between Smith and Richards but between the British and the Nationalists. But then, when Richards, Nkomo, and the others had reached an agreement, the United States should step in and get Smith "out of the way" by tightening the economic embargo. The main thing he wanted to see for now was a repeal of the Byrd Amendment which allowed the United States to continue importing chrome from Rhodesia when other countries were observing an economic embargo. In fact, Young himself had already as much as promised to deliver the repeal of the Byrd Amendment sometime in March.

A month later, as the amendment was indeed about to be repealed, columnists Rowland Evans and Robert Novak reported this talk between Young and the Tanzanian president in a somewhat darker light. If their account is reliable, Young, back in the United States and acting essentially as a spokesman for black Africa but with the full backing of the administration, passed on to R. F. Botha, the South Africa ambassador, the following hard-hitting warnings from Nyerere:

The current military struggle in Zimbabwe could have only one end: victory for the black nationalists and the obliteration of any subsequent white influence. Meanwhile Namibia's independence, as ordered by the United Nations, must be granted *now*. Eventually South Africa, like Rhodesia, would be dealt with, but for the time being it was of no immediate interest to black Africa and would be left to stew for a while. Sooner or later, however, the white South Africans would be "destroyed."

After four days in Tanzania, Young stopped over in Nairobi, Kenya, where he was particularly impressed with the sight of a Colonel Sanders Fried Chicken place in the middle of town. Then he flew on to Lagos, Nigeria. Nigeria, one of the two black African members of OPEC, was supplying 18 percent of the oil imported into the United States. Only Saudi Arabia was sending more. (Gabon was the other black member, and Angola also had oil.) Also, it was expected that by 1977 or 1978 at the latest, Nigeria's gross national product would surpass that of gold-rich South Africa.

The country was populated by 70 million vigorous people, and it has a well-trained army of 250,000 men. It was radically anti-South Africa. Nigeria had contributed over $50 million to liberation movements in the south. In the Angolan Civil War Nigeria had been neutral—till South Africa came in. Then Nigeria had joined the Russians in supporting Agostinho Neto's Popular Front. "The moment one single South African ant crosses the border, the whole picture changes," was the way one Cabinet minister put it. Nigeria's foreign relations with the United States had lagged drastically behind trade relations, a matter made more acute by America's deepening dependence on foreign oil. Henry Kissinger had tried three times to visit Nigeria and had failed.

By the time Young arrived in Lagos, Festac, the Second World Black and African Festival of Arts and Culture, had been in progress for three weeks. It was about to reach a climax in a spectacular *durbar,* a display of military horsemanship combined with religious pageantry. Black achievements in culture, music, and dance had been celebrated by over 15,000 participants from fifty-seven countries. The American delegation had gotten bogged down in politics, one dispute

centering on whether white participants should be included. Finally
the U.S., in its group of 500, sent no whites—though Cuba and Brazil
did—and the American representation generally disappointed, for, of
the many promised superstars, only singer Stevie Wonder appeared.
The festival was also marred when, during the opening ceremonies,
the vigilante spirit that was sweeping Nigeria erupted in the stands.
Several people, apparently pickpockets, were snatched up by the
crowd in the upper decks, passed head over head, and tossed over the
rail. "Please stop throwing human beings! Will you please stop
throwing human beings!" an official begged through the public address system after several were killed.

Shortly after Young arrived the spectacle shifted from Lagos to
Kaduna, a city in Nigeria's Moslem north. Here Young was seated in
the first row of the reviewing stand, in the presence of eight African
heads of state and one seat away from the Sultan of Sokoto, Sir
Abubakar, the most powerful spiritual leader in Nigeria. The next
day the Nigerian press would bubble over Young's bowing when he
met the sultan. Just a matter of good breeding, Young explained. "I
had seen the power of the sultan as a Moslem authority for 50 million
people, and as a good politician, to anybody who leads 50 million
people you owe a certain amount of deference."

(The same day, in distant Atlanta, along with two whites, Wych
Fowler, the vice-mayor and president of the City Council, and Paul
Coverdell, a state senator, both John Lewis and the Reverend Ralph
David Abernathy filed to run for Young's vacated Fifth District
Congressional seat. Many in the black community were distressed at
the prospect of Lewis and Abernathy running head to head. Julian
Bond and the King family supported Lewis.)

"Drummers sitting on camels pounded a steady beat," wrote John
Darnton of the *New York Times*, "golden stallions charged through
the dust, and stately emirs, fanned by worshipers under multicolored
parasols, raised their spears to cries of adulation from the crowd."
Before the 40,000 spectators gathered at the racecourse in Kaduna,
3,500 horsemen, 500 camel drivers, and 20,000 dancers paraded for
five hours. At the climax, waves of the tribesmen charged across the
field toward the reviewing stand with their spears posed before, at the
last moment, stopping short and throwing up their fists in salutes.

The Nigerians called it the greatest *durbar* ever to take place.

Among the heads of state enjoying the hospitality of Nigeria's
leader, Lieutenant General Olusegun Obasanjo, was Angola's Marxist president, Agostinho Neto. That name had begun to loom large in
Young's career, along with the Cuban remark. The United States,

which opposed Neto's Popular Front and thus with South Africa ended up aligned with the losers, had established no relations with Angola and officially had no intention of doing so. Therefore Young came with no instructions concerning Neto or Angola from his government.

Now General Obasanjo suggested that Young talk with Neto, and that night after the *durbar* Young obliged. Later he told critics: "If I had not met Neto, it would have been insulting to Nigeria to snub one of their friends."

The State Department said they weren't surprised at the Neto meeting since the purpose of the trip had been for Young to contact as many leaders as possible. What was said between Neto and Young? Reportedly, Neto did most of the talking, touching several times on the subject of establishing relations with the United States. Young then experienced the first disagreement of his trip. When Neto insisted that only military force would free Rhodesia, Young differed, saying that the nationalists' negotiating position was stronger than their military position.

The next day Young was toasted by Obasanjo, who pledged support to Young's "great and important task of bridging the wide gulf between the United States and Africa."

Young's trip to Nigeria was both a success and an important icebreaker. He summed it up: "The Nigerians know I respect them and come as a friend and equal. Nigeria did not want Kissinger to come and play god in African politics. The problem is Nigeria is arrogant and Kissinger is arrogant and so there was a clash. I may be just as arrogant but I can control it better."

Young met with other African leaders, so that he had pushed his total up to twenty by the time he sat down again with General Obasanjo, on February 10. It turned out to be his longest talk by far, three hours, and afterward the general, who seldom held news conferences, joined Young in reporting the outcome. They called it "unusually frank" and announced that it had opened up a new era of cooperation between Nigeria and the United States.

Young was surprised at the conciliatory tones with which Obasanjo and the other Nigerian officials had approached him. "Nigeria," he said, "has the reputation of being the big bad boy of Africa and traditionally anti-United States. I frankly expected to receive a short lecture, if not a long one, on the past sins of the United States in Africa." It was the best example of a phenomenon that he had begun to notice. "With governments that were supposed to be the most militant I've been able to be the most conservative and get away with it."

Then Young, who till then had said he had just come to listen, unveiled a new Rhodesian proposal that Obasanjo and he had devised and that he would recommend to the administration. It would involve holding a conference from which Ian Smith's government would be barred, but which would include the United States, Nigeria, Great Britain, Zaire, the front-line countries, which were defined as those five black states on Rhodesia's borders, and the Zimbabwean nationalists. The general, who had seen what had happened in Angola and in Zaire, as well as in Nigeria itself, was concerned about the feuding between the several liberation groups. The conference would try to unite them against the minority Rhodesian and South African governments. "If you can get all these guys in one place, united on something, it would be very hard for Smith and Vorster to buck." (As Young spoke, those two gentlemen were huddling together in Capetown, with Smith trying to get Vorster's backing.)

As for the communists, Obasanjo had told Young, turning directly to the most recent issue that had separated his country and Young's, the Cubans were no problem. They were still present in Angola only because South Africa was supporting a rival nationalist group. Displaying Nigeria's strong pro-African sentiments, he referred to the Cuban troops as a blemish on black Africa, and he assured the United States that their removal could be easily negotiated. Events could not have proved him more in error.

General Obasanjo praised the United States—and, indirectly, Kissinger—by pointing out that Smith's government had not moved toward black majority rule until the United States had stepped in. He said United States involvement was necessary for a Zimbabwe settlement, and he joined Nyerere in recommending economic pressure.

Ending his tour as he had begun it, Young stopped over in London to brief Ivor Richards. In the meantime he took another step toward exorcising the former secretary of state while trying to enlist support for the ideas that he had picked up in Africa, as well as for any future initiatives. Referring to the Geneva conference on Rhodesia, he said that Kissinger had put a burden on Britain's back with his plan, then unintentionally had left Britain in the lurch through Ford's loss of the election.

Young was satisfied with the trip. He thought he had collected enough facts to start work on a dynamic African policy. Somebody asked him about the "dynamic new American initiative on Rhodesia," referring to his and Obasanjo's idea for the conference, and Young promptly pulled his cards close to his chest, saying "I don't know anything about the 'dynamic New American initiative.' . . . I think that was just some headline writer trying to sell news-papers." And Richards backed him up. "Nothing dramatic will hap-pen in the near future."

By the time Young returned from his first African tour, after hav-ing served in his post for barely two weeks, a pattern had been set. The general public usually would receive only his juicier comments from the media. He had opened up vital new channels between the United States and its second largest supplier of oil, which also hap-pened to be Africa's most populous country. Yet, with the Cuban re-mark still echoing, the headlines stressed his latest anti-Kissinger statement.

But that was not all of the pattern. Certain professionals recog-nized the substance of what he had done.

"Andy Young has gone into an absolute disaster area for Ameri-can foreign policy—sub-Saharan Africa—and it appears to me that we've finally begun to show some motion," said one of Jimmy Carter's high White House men. "The ironic thing is that the folks who helped design that disaster, which Andy found in his lap, were taking potshots at him while he was over there trying to wrestle and struggle with the problem. This is not only unfair but also dumb, be-cause it indicates a profound misunderstanding about the way the President reacts to things like that. The net result has been that with every little snotty shot from anonymous folks over at State, their in-fluence and esteem has declined and Andy's has gone up."

While Young was still in Nigeria, in New Orleans—his home-town—the International House, a group of businessmen, profession-als, and other top citizens dedicated to world peace, trade, and under-standing, voted to delay proceeding with a proposal to invite the am-bassador for a speech. The only black member, a Dr. Henry Braden, said he believed the denial was racially motivated. Indignation swept the nation. The vote's overturn became inevitable the moment the news het the street. Young himself saw no reason to get excited over an invitation that he hadn't received yet. A white member, George Ormond, called the affair "a damn disgrace. It was just a plain vote against someone they didn't want." George Healy, a former news-paper editor, who had put forth the proposal, said he didn't believe race had been involved.

Some members just didn't like what Mr. Young had done in Africa.

The Lions in the Arena

THE GENTLE GIANT

Kenneth Kaunda, the President of black-ruled Zambia, and Ian Smith, the Prime Minister of white-ruled Rhodesia, sit facing each other across the Zambezi, by which their two countries are joined as naturally as two slices of an orange. They also happen to be joint owners of the Kariba Dam which generates enough electricity to light every bulb in central Africa.

"I would like to assure you that Rhodesia has no desire for anything but friendly relations and non-interference by one in the internal affairs of the other," Ian Smith wrote to Kaunda in July 1965 after Zambia's independence. But in November of that year he rebelled against Britain's policies of transferring the colonies to black rule and declared Rhodesia's independence under the rule of the white minority.

One of the leading exponents of Gandhi's principles of non-violence and *satyagraha*, Kenneth David Kaunda is often called "Africa's Gentle Giant," or the "Conscience of the Continent." In Zambia's struggle for independence he put Gandhi's ideas to work. "It is no good trying to lead my people to the land of their dreams," he said, "if I get them killed on the way."

Kenneth Kaunda is accomplished on the guitar and has a fine voice. Sometimes he sings to his countrymen. He does not smoke, drink, or eat meat, having intentionally lost such tastes in prison to lessen the ordeal. Every day he jogs a mile around his palace grounds. He has large, warm eyes and a ready smile. The youngest of eight children, he arrived so late in his parents' married life that they dubbed him "The Unexpected One." He has seven sons and two daughters.

Kaunda is most deeply pained by the lack of humanity shown by his neighbors to the south and by his inability to bring those governments to a level of decency. He had hoped that his country, with its multiracial society, would serve as encouragement to those around him. But the nearby minority governments so far have heeded only the force of arms.

Zambia sits at the center of southern Africa like the cracked hub of a furiously spinning pinwheel. Round and round revolves black and white Africa, first Tanzania, Malawi, Mozambique, Botswana, Namibia, Angola, Zaire; next, Nigeria, then Rhodesia, geographic companion-piece to Zambia; and beyond, the Republic of South Africa.

Formerly the northern half of Rhodesia, Zambia, together with Nyasaland, now Malawi, formed a British colonial conglomerate called the Central African Federation. Because there were far fewer colonists, British colonialism with its natural adjunct of white supremacy was not practiced with the same fervor in northern Rhodesia as in its southern counterpart. In addition, the occult is said never to have ceased being a strong force in the area.

Whatever the factors, Zambia did not experience many of the usual agonies in achieving its independence. Starting in 1960 with a series of moves resembling a political shell game, spurred on by threats and acts of passive resistance and civil disobedience, the Zambians strained the leashes of Britain and southern Rhodesia progressively, until in January 1964 they broke free of both. Kaunda had had to go to jail only twice.

However, no sooner did Zambia become independent than the occasion was marred by a revolt in the north led by a religious fanatic. To Kaunda's distress, before he could bring it under control, 500 persons had been killed. Since then, tribalism has continually threatened to splinter the country. Finally, Kaunda found it necessary to outlaw the small tribal political parties, so that today only his party is legal in Zambia. By idealist standards, this is questionable democracy.

It hurts Kaunda that he has had to spend all the subsequent years in an endless series of maneuvers so that he can continue working for majority rule while at the same time resisting the efforts of the minority governments to choke off his country. Facing the break of vital trade links with Rhodesia, he joined with Tanzania in having the Chinese build for them, in record time, a railroad from Zambia to the sea. In January 1973 Ian Smith, trying to humiliate Kaunda, closed the border with Zambia. Less than a month later, embarrassed, he reopened it. Kaunda kept his side of the border closed. "Let them eat their blankets," he had already advised his countrymen.

It hurts Kaunda that he has had to mobilize his tiny army in an effort to keep Smith from pursuing guerrillas into his territory as they have in Mozambique, after he prevented for so long the operation of the guerrillas out of Zambia, and that in fact he has had to declare war on Rhodesia and has even had to lob a few shells in that direction. "Nonviolence is the only way to win your enemies to your way of thinking." Thus he had long ago expressed his belief in the practices of King and Gandhi.

But now he faces something else, against which the sweet reason with which he is so familiar appears to be of no avail.

Visitors to South Africa have wept upon noting the conditions which, as Andrew Young has pointed out, are far worse than they were in the Deep South where black people at least retained the right to own land and to move about freely. Because of such flaws in these segments of mankind over which he has no control, Kenneth Kaunda similarly weeps. In fact his tears flow more easily than those of any world figure.

On one occasion a session of the United Nations had to be delayed until he could compose himself.

Then the Conscience of the Continent went home to pressure the British some more.

Chapter Six

MARCHES THROUGH TEARS

"SCLC's approach was radically different [from SNCC's]. Instead of remaining in a community to develop autonomous organizations, it would organize dramatic demonstrations to get the attention of the nation. After getting that attention, as was the case in St. Augustine, Albany, and Birmingham, SCLC would submit a list of demands to the local power structure, win minor concessions, proclaim a great moral victory, and leave town."

The River of No Return,
Cleveland Sellers (of SNCC), p. 117.

UNTIL 1965 BLACKS IN SELMA, ALABAMA, fifty miles west of the state capital of Montgomery and a hundred miles south of Birmingham, constituted one percent of the voter rolls, although they amounted to slightly over half the population of 30,000. In the whole of Dallas County, of which Selma was the county seat, there were only 130 registered black voters; adjoining Lowndes and Wilcox counties, both 80 percent black, had none at all.

The first of the white citizens councils, formed to combat the drive for civil rights, was organized in Selma in 1954.

Selma was the headquarters of Sheriff Jim Clark who, not satisfied with the ability of his regular deputy force to crush the rising expectations, had put together a large, allied group of vigilantes called a "posse."

Selma was, coincidentally, the hometown of Bull Connor.

Andrew Young was familiar with the area. Marion was Young's first pastorate, twenty miles to the northwest, and the hometown of his wife, Jean. Not wanting to patronize the local movie in Marion, where blacks were confined to the balcony or the "Buzzard's Roost," they had their first date at a recreation center in Selma instead.

In St. Augustine, Birmingham, and Albany, SCLC had worked mainly to desegregate public accommodations, and those and countless other demonstrations, including the Freedom Rides and the sitins, had resulted in the 1964 Civil Rights Bill. When it was drafted, King had delegated Andrew Young as one of the advisers from SCLC. But now it was time to focus more directly on the key prerogative of the American citizen, the right to vote. The ballot was the linchpin; grasping that should bring the whole system of segregation tumbling down.

To the extent that any area was the territory of a particular civil rights organization, Selma was SNCC country. Reverend and Mrs. Bernard Lafayette, two SNCC workers, had come into Selma as early as February 1963, but their efforts had been severely hampered by Sheriff Jim Clark, his deputies, and his posse. Soon any gathering having over three blacks in it was likely to invite arrests, and church services were invaded by deputies listening for mentions of voter registration.

SCLC had stated several times its intent to put the spotlight on Selma, and finally, a few weeks before King spoke at his first rally there, on January 2, 1965, the conference held another three or four day session in Birmingham to map out its strategy. Unfortunately, a briefcase containing these plans was stolen from King in Anniston, Alabama, and before long every police chief in the area, including Selma's Wilson Baker, had a copy.

Nevertheless, Dr. King sent James Bevel ahead to announce SCLC's coming, and on the second day of the new year, King kicked things off with a rally at the chief staging point, the Brown Chapel A.M.E. Church. His action was in defiance of an injunction issued the previous July by Judge James Hare, Clark's friend, against mass meetings.

By this time King's life was so full of speaking engagements and accepting awards that for long periods it was left to Young, Hosea Williams, James Bevel, Bernard Lee, and others to keep things going. Not till January 18 did King return to Selma, where he was the first black to register at the ornate Hotel Albert, and then he led a march of 400 to the county courthouse to register. On this, the first of many such encounters, Clark told the SCLC people that no registrars were on duty; they would have to come back another day. And so they did, day after day, in columns.

One of the unique things about Selma is that Young and his associates had to cope with both a Laurie Pritchett-type police chief and a Bull Connor-variety sheriff. At first, dealing with the demonstrators was mainly in the hands of the chief, Wilson Baker. During that first January rally Clark was far away in Miami, not having returned from watching Joe Namath in the annual Orange Bowl game. Wilson Baker had been appointed by a progressive city government headed by thirty-five-year-old Mayor Joe Smitherman. Together they were determined to carry Selma farther along into the twentieth century. To keep the town relatively peaceful and to avoid eventual bloodshed as much as possible required measures that Baker tried to provide.

Unfortunately for Baker, Sheriff Clark had free rein around the courthouse, and he enjoyed the confidence of high Alabama officials, including Governor George Wallace. He and his posse had been traveling all over Alabama looking for civil rights trouble spots.

On January 22, SCLC varied its tactics by mounting a demonstration of 125 school teachers. The contrast between these customarily reserved, polished professionals and the hardened deputies barring the way on the courthouse steps was striking. That night, back at the Brown Chapel church, Young told the people how proud he was. "This is the first time in the history of the movement that so well organized and dramatic a protest has been made by any professional group in the Negro community."

The Selma black community, notwithstanding the reservations of some SNCC officials, was solidly behind the protests, and the campaign began to get national attention that was unprecedented even by Birmingham standards. On February 1, SLCL started saturating the courthouse area. That day 770 people were arrested, including Abernathy and King. The next day Clark shoved 550, mostly children, into the jails.

During the five days that King and Abernathy stayed in prison, Malcolm X, at SNCC's invitation, came to Selma. This presaged an escalation which made Young feel uneasy. Of course, by then Malcolm X had split off from the Black Muslims, but Andrew Young couldn't be certain of what would happen with the volatile Malcolm in Selma.

Speaking at Brown Chapel, Malcolm X suggested that the

demonstrators take their case to the White House and if that didn't work, then go on to the United Nations. He was a powerful speaker. The people were becoming stirred. Young's anxieties increased.

Then Coretta King and Juanita Abernathy, in town to see their jailed husbands, pulled up in a car. Young ran over to Mrs. King. "You're going to have to come inside and greet the people," he said, "because Malcolm X is here and he's really roused them. They want to hear from you."

Mrs. Abernathy spoke first and then Coretta King finished the job of shifting the crowd into what was to Young and the other worried SCLC lieutenants a less truculent mood. Malcolm X later talked with Mrs. King and assured her that he had come not to interfere in the campaign, but as a reminder of the alternative to King. Just over two weeks later, in New York, he was assassinated.

The day of Malcolm's departure an injunction was issued that was supposed to facilitate black voter registration. Young was hopeful. "In every battle there are many rounds," he told the people at Brown Chapel just before it came out, "and this round may have come to an end. We may have a little breather."

But when the injunction emerged, Young realized that it was quite inadequate. He announced that it was "pitiful and disappointing." The main problem was that though it called for the registrars to meet "more often than twice monthly," they would still convene so infrequently and enroll so few people each time that years would pass before all of Dallas County's 15,000 eligible black voters could register.

King demanded a new and stronger federal voting rights bill. The marches from Brown Chapel A.M.E. to the Dallas County courthouse with further indignities at the hands of Jim Clark continued. Finally he saw a few too many approaching black faces; he had roared once too often into his bullhorn. He suffered a mild coronary and collapsed. "These niggers have given me a heart attack," he gasped. But he recovered.

On February 15 King sparked another giant demonstration. Hosea Williams led a crowd of nearly 3,000 down to the courthouse where the SCLC people had been told that this time blacks would be allowed to register. But before they went in, something strange happened. Jim Clark left the courthouse and drove away; always before he had stayed for the fun. Then a black youth came out and told Williams that the courthouse was packed with 500 whites, all armed with ax handles, pitchforks, and other tools.

Meanwhile the FBI felt that there were three different spots where the assassination of Dr. King would be attempted that day. They said they knew two of the spots but not the third.

Young kept holding up the march so they would have time to find the third place. But King insisted on continuing down to the court-house with Williams. And he insisted he was going to go into the courthouse.

Young drove up and told Dr. King, "Get in the car." But King said no, he would walk. And he marched straight toward the waiting mob, which parted for him like the waters of the Red Sea.

Meanwhile, in Marion, which was Coretta King's hometown as well as Jean Young's, SCLC was conducting parallel demonstrations under the leadership of the Reverend James Orange. In one night march a state trooper shot a demonstrator, Jimmie Lee Jackson, a young pulp cutter, in the stomach. A few days later he died—the first of the three martyrs of this campaign.

The daily marches were beginning to suffer from attrition. Why not break loose from Selma and take the case to the Alabama state capital and thus fully into the national eye? The SCLC leaders made plans for a Selma to Montgomery march.

The history of SCLC's campaign in Selma is also the story of its tangled relations with SNCC, especially to Andrew Young, who negotiated with them so often. James Forman and most of the others at SNCC had opposed SCLC's entering Selma, as they thought the demonstrations would only disrupt their activities and harden white attitudes still further. But John Lewis, the SNCC chairman, thought the march to Montgomery was a fine idea: it would greatly help the black people of the state. He was from Alabama, and he flatly told his associates that he intended to take part. SNCC then said all right, but Lewis could participate only as an individual. Officially, however, SNCC would sit it out, and come in later "to pick up the pieces."

On Sunday, March 7, as King and Abernathy ministered to their congregations in Atlanta, Young was readying people for the march. Although he had no specific foreknowledge of what was to happen, along with the other lieutenants, he was concerned about the risks. For one thing, George Wallace had issued a directive forbidding the march.

John Lewis would be one of the leaders, and Young, Bevel, and Williams flipped a coin to see who would represent Dr. King as the SCLC leader in the first wave. It came up Williams.

So it was Williams and Lewis in the vanguard of the 600 marchers to the Edmund Pettus Bridge leading out of Selma. And there, waiting on the other side, was a wall of state troopers.

Behind the marchers came Sheriff Clark's deputies.

The state troopers halted the marchers. Then Clark's men attacked from horseback, swinging clubs and cattle prods. They chased the marchers back across the bridge and through the streets past cheering white onlookers to the church. At one point some of the demonstrators abandoned nonviolence long enough to retaliate with rocks and bricks, inciting the police and the state troopers to fire tear gas. Clark's men kept charging. Only Wilson Baker's intervention allowed the demonstrators to reach the security of the church. Among the dozens of injured, Hosea Williams was knocked down and teargassed, and John Lewis suffered a fractured skull.

Enraged, the SNCC leaders changed their minds. Now they were ready to march. But the SCLC people wanted to hold up trying again until they got a court order authorizing it. SNCC felt that they didn't need such permission. As the angry Forman said later, "We would ram the march down the throat of anyone who tried to stop us."

Willie Ricks of SNCC marched a large group of schoolchildren up and down, trying to break through the cordon of state troopers. Young felt this would only incite more violence, and he tried to talk to him, but to no avail. Finally, he and the other SCLC leaders had a showdown with the SNCC officials in a back room of the Brown Chapel church, where King asserted himself. SNCC went on to Montgomery with the intention of opening a second front there.

King was agonizing over whether to defy the federal injunction against resuming the march. Young's advice was that they shouldn't. After all, the whole point was to get the federal government to act *affirmatively* on SCLC's initiatives. Finally, the head of the new Community Relations Service (CRS), former Florida governor Leroy Collins, flew down and helped work out a compromise.

That Tuesday SCLC had three thousand people on hand ready to march, with King in the lead. James Forman of SNCC and James Farmer of CORE were in the front ranks. As before, the troopers were waiting on the other side of the Pettus Bridge. The marchers crossed the bridge and approached the troopers. After kneeling for a moment of prayer the marchers rose—the troopers moved aside—and King directed the marchers to turn and go back to the church.

There is still some controversy surrounding this move. Did Dr. King chicken out, or had he agreed to this maneuver through Andrew Young, who handled the negotiations? One CRS man insisted that he gave Young a map detailing the route and exactly how far the marchers should go before turning back.

Fortunately, the rush of events made such arguments irrelevant. After returning from the bridge and taking a meal in a black restaurant, three white Unitarian ministers were jumped by white thugs. One, the Reverend James Reeb, was beaten so badly that two days later he died.

Such incidents steadily increased the pressure on President Lyndon Johnson to act. On March 15 he announced that in two days he would be sending a strong voting rights bill to Congress. The same day that the bill went in, the federal courts permitted the Selma-Montgomery march and barred Clark, Lingo, and Wallace from interfering.

Andrew Young's focus was the unity of the march. SNCC didn't appreciate the presence of so many outsiders, and it was dissatisfied with SCLC's way of doing things, especially King's turning back on the previous attempt. For four days Young, Bevel, and Williams negotiated with Forman and others. Finally, echoing the earlier John Lewis compromise, the SNCC leaders agreed to take part as individuals but not as an organization.

Two thousand strong, the demonstrators crossed over the Pettus Bridge without incident on Sunday, March 21. That afternoon and through the next three days they marched eastward, covering the fifty-mile distance in segments of various lengths and camping overnight at black-owned farms. After penetrating dangerous Lowndes County, Stokely Carmichael's turf, on Wednesday, March 24, they pulled up three miles outside of Montgomery. Thursday morning, in the rain, 30,000 demonstrators streamed into Montgomery and on up to the capitol, where at last they presented their demands.

Victory turned bitter with a third murder. While driving back to Selma from Montgomery with a young black man in her car, Mrs. Viola Liuzzo, a white Detroit housewife, mother of five, and one of the volunteer transportation workers, was spotted by a bunch of Klansmen. They pulled alongside and fired into the car, killing Mrs. Liuzzo.

Perhaps in reaction to the Selma martyrdoms, the Voting Rights Act of 1965 proceeded through Congress in a remarkably short time. On August 6 the SCLC leaders were present when Johnson signed it into law. Seven years later Andrew Young was serving in the United States Congress, the first black member from the Deep South in over seventy years, as a result of that Act he had helped to write.

Between those two events there was an important shift in focus. Watts occurred. Other cities rioted. King and Young and their associates looked northward.

The fact was that for some time the South had meant more in the way of emphasis than of exclusivity. At least ever since Young had been aboard he had known it would be only a matter of time before SCLC turned toward the North and its terrible conditions, particularly in housing and the job market. And he was highly disturbed by the apathy toward civil rights shown by northern blacks. As far back as July 1963 he had told a congregation in New York that there was no real nonviolent leadership in the North.

"The Negro is just beginning to understand nonviolence as a means of freedom, and is the only one preaching nonviolence in a violent world. . . . Although we've tried to avoid interfering, the time has come for some real leadership." And Young predicted that Dr. King would come north to provide that leadership.

Two years, it was true, had passed without that happening, with conditions growing worse, and with Watts exemplifying a full-scale explosion. Yet even then, securing adherence to the new voting rights laws in the South was tugging at the SCLC ministers, as were other matters, such as the major campaign that they were considering mounting in Natchez, Mississippi.

Wyatt Tee Walker had left SCLC, and in September 1965, having succeeded him as SCLC's executive director, Young checked out Natchez and the possibilities there of drawing attention to the need for a law making it a federal crime to kill civil rights workers. When the three young Mississippi Summer Project workers, Andrew Goodman, Michael Schwerner, and James Chaney, had been killed near Philadelphia, Mississippi, in the St. Augustine days, it had been possible to prosecute their accused murderers—unsuccessfully—only on the grounds of depriving them of their civil rights. "The report I'm going to take back," Young told a large black audience in Natchez, "is there's some bad white folks over here. Dr. King will be glad to hear that. . . . It was bad white folks like Jim Clark and Al Lingo in Alabama that gave us the right to vote."

Natchez, legendary as a tough town even within Mississippi, was a natural SCLC target but Chicago, the refuge of so many black Mississippians, was also a bastion of discrimination. It was home to over one million blacks, more than in all of Mississippi, concentrated in pockets of varying degrees of wretchedness on the west and south sides. Hosea Williams said that he had never seen such hopelessness. "They don't participate in the governmental process because they're beaten down psychologically. We're used to working with people who want to be freed."

Observers kept telling Young and the others that Chicago would waste them, that they weren't ready for the resourcefulness of the Daley machine. Also, though other civil rights organizations were operating in Chicago—SNCC, CORE, the NAACP, and the Urban League were all united with some local movements under the banner of the Coordinating Council of Community Organizations (CCCO), headed by the capable Reverend Albert Raby—the unity was illusory. There was no agreement on what should be done.

A federal man told Young that Chicago might be King's Waterloo. (A better analogy might have been General Robert E. Lee's foray into Gettysburg.) "The Lord will provide," Young replied.

What the Lord did provide cannot tidily be presented here. Briefly, there were two phases. The SCLC people were later accused of not doing their homework, but they were in Chicago for quite a long time before they tried to launch any sizable marches or other demonstrations. The first phase really was mostly a period of studying the conditions and exploring of tactics such as rent strikes and boycotts. "You've got to hit those cats where it hurts the most—in the pocketbooks," Young, Lee, and the others told the tenants.

Finally, with the promise of a long hot summer "not of racial violence but of peaceful nonviolence," Dr. King promised to present the demands that his people had put together in a march on City Hall on June 26, 1966. But on June 6, James Meredith, the hero of the integration of the University of Mississippi, was sprayed with buckshot just after beginning his March Through Mississippi. King, along with SNCC and other groups—but particularly SNCC—felt an obligation to finish what Meredith had started.

That not only delayed the second phase in Chicago by several weeks, but also infused it with added urgencies. This stage began at last with a rally at Soldiers Field on July 10, 1966, and continued with a series of marches, some fully as dangerous as anything SCLC had ever undertaken in the Deep South, if not more so. These protests were to have culminated with a march into perhaps the epitome of northern racial intransigence: Cicero. Though Young felt that it was the kind of gamble that events made them take, he was nervous. "We're not too hopeful," he said. "We haven't been able to put on enough pressure yet. In Birmingham and Selma we almost needed martial law before we could get anywhere." But on August 26, King obtained what was called the "Summit Agreement." Though the concessions in the area of housing that thereby had been wrung from the city and federal governments and from businessmen appeared far-reaching, they still fell short of what King had hoped to accomplish. Nevertheless, he cancelled SCLC's participation in the marches and took time to study the various situations.

But the march into Cicero, which Young had managed to get postponed, took place anyway. On September 4, 205 angry and defiant militants, including members of SNCC and CORE, having thrust nonviolence behind them for good, paraded through a steady rain of rocks and bottles, under the protection of 3,500 police and National Guardsmen. Subsequently, King, Young, and the others left the "Windy City" increasingly in the hands of a fast-rising young star, the Reverend Jesse Jackson, and were glad that the intervals when they didn't have to return to that project lengthened.

Chicago was a clash of ideas as much as it was a contest of wills between the men of Martin Luther King and those of Mayor Richard Daley, or between the civil rights groups and the thousands of hecklers and the Nazis in Marquette Park and the Gage, Bogan, and Belmont-Cragin neighborhoods. Equally on trial with the real estate companies, the lending agencies, the landlords, the private employers, and the city government was the concept of nonviolence. Though the triumph of the Selma-Montgomery march and the passage of the 1965 Voting Rights Act was fresh in SCLC's minds when they came to Chicago, they knew, from Watts and the riots at Harlem and Rochester, that a new tide was threatening to rise. Though SCLC thought they had proved that nonviolence was an effective and the only really feasible technique, they knew that experiences in the Mississippi Summer Project, Lowndes County, Alabama, and other places had led Stokely Carmichael, James Forman, and others to reach different conclusions. "We have got to deliver results—nonviolent results in a Northern city—to protect the nonviolent movement," was the way Young expressed it.

During SCLC's early efforts in Chicago, in February 1966, a three-day riot broke out on the west side. Amid suggestions that their activities were at least partly to blame, the SCLC people worked feverishly to try to get things cooled down. Chicago's youth gangs were an important part of the population; they were considerably less apathetic than other segments, but they were also prime riot material. King's assistants, James Bevel, James Orange, and Young, had been working to establish lines of communication to them.

One day members of one of these gangs dropped in at King's apartment while he was in a rear room asleep. Coretta King talked to them but she was frightened. Then Young, Lee, and another SCLC worker, Al Sampson, arrived. The gang objected to the presence of white staff members, but Sampson pointed out that many whites had helped the movement and some had died for it. Though some of the gang members left, Young talked the leaders into staying. He asked Coretta to make them some sandwiches and kept them entertained until King woke up and came out, whereupon they were impressed at finding themselves talking and sharing some barbecue with him. More lines were opened.

However, these were all small, almost isolated strokes. The leadership whose absence Young had lamented in 1963 was present in Chicago in 1966, but it was hard to stir the populace, at least to SCLC's kind of tactics. And then, as if to put the point to the SCLC leaders more clearly, James Meredith was shot. King and Young, with Stokely Carmichael, had to take that hot, shimmering road to Jackson.

The SCLC ministers felt obligated to finish Meredith's march, but it was not their show. Stokely Carmichael liked King, and the other SNCC officials generally respected him, but the continually fermenting politics inside SNCC had finally bubbled over. John Lewis, as firmly committed to nonviolence as anybody in SNCC (he had numerous beatings to show for it), had been replaced in April by Carmichael as SNCC's chairman, and now, on this march, endlessly repeated all the way to Jackson, Young and King would hear the cry that signaled the repudiation of nonviolence, "Black Power!"

They were guests on this Meredith march, his March Against Fear, tolerated because of the past but subjected to hearing numerous threats uttered against the Mississippi state troopers and others that they suspected would never be implemented, though they never knew what might be tried. It was a debate they were conducting, with their feet and with the presenting of their persons to grievous harm by actions as well as by words—on into Philadelphia, where, far from chastened and repentant over the deaths of Chaney, Schwerner, and

Goodman, resentful instead, enraged, the white spectators attacked with cherry bombs and fists. Some of the marchers retaliated in kind and were getting the better of it till the police intervened. That night the Philadelphians fired into the marchers' campsite four times.

Nevertheless the debate continued, with King suggesting that the slogan "Black Power!" be replaced with "Black Equality!" In the town of Canton, eighteen miles from Jackson, they had intended to pitch their tents at a black elementary school, but the police would not permit it. Carmichael and some others decided that they would set up camp on the school grounds anyway. The Mississippi police fired tear gas and then charged into the demonstrators with clubs and whips—

In Chicago Andrew Young had tried to explain that SCLC's conception of nonviolence was far from passive. King himself, Young said, had never rejected the idea of vigorous defense in extreme cases. "Even Gandhi preached that he would rather a man be violent than be a coward," Young pointed out. "Dr. King has never said that a man didn't have the duty to defend his person or home against attack. But we insist on nonviolence in demonstrations because it works."

In Canton the police attacked while about 500 of the demonstrators were kneeling and praying. It was Young's first experience with tear gas. He climbed up on a truck with a bullhorn and tried to shout instructions on where to run, but then the gas reached him and he had to jump off. He was vomiting, and he thought he might die. As he ran, not upwind as he had been advising the demonstrators, but downwind, having completely lost his cool (like Carmichael and nearly everyone else), he was thinking, "If I had a machine gun I'd show these——"

Then, as now, Andrew Young had almost never permitted himself the luxury of anger, which he regarded as a sign of weakness. And in the whole movement, including St. Augustine, this was the closest he came to outright hatred and the urge to retaliate.

Meredith himself and others completed the march and held a modest rally in Mississippi's capital, Jackson. King returned as he had vowed for a sort of grudge march through Philadelphia. Then King and Young returned to Chicago, too, and after a giant rally attended by 60,000 at Soldiers Field, began the excursions into the white suburbs, climaxed by a five-mile march in the rain on August 21.

But it was Canton, Mississippi, that crystallized the tenor of the March Against Fear and also perhaps everything that SCLC faced in Chicago. The attack by the troopers was all that those who had been so disposed needed to lose the last vestiges of faith in the redemptive value of nonviolence. From then on, while more cities had their hearts burned out and while the nation began to indulge itself more heavily in other violences thousands of miles across the sea, Andrew Young found himself a member of an increasingly small group that was the sole guardian of a tool that seemed to them still serviceable, in fact, the only one that could be used to repair the house without wrecking it: nonviolence. The alternative was barbarism.

The Lions in the Arena

THE MAGNIFICENT BARBARIANS

Stokely Carmichael loved Martin Luther King, Jr. Yet he, Willie Ricks, and the other young people of SNCC deeply wounded the SCLC leader spiritually with their cries of Black Power. Carmichael and Ricks took on *De Lawd* in the dust and the heat of Mississippi's fields, but word of the encounter took a long time to sail around America. By the time James Earl Ray's bullet destroyed King's temporal being, Black Power had proved itself antithetical to nonviolence. Violence ricocheted through 130 American cities and towns before spending itself. It was in the fading coals of the last burned liquor store in D.C., the last looted grocery in Chicago, the last stripped TV shop in Oakland that the seemingly fatal rebuke to nonviolence were delivered. . .

Until the Resurrection!

The day King was killed, Stokely was in D.C. getting ready for the Poor Peoples Campaign.

Stokely himself, allegedly carrying a gun in his pocket, led a band of youths down 14th Street, trying to get store owners to close, out of respect, and was alarmed when, instead, glass began to break and hands reached in. . .

"Brothers!" he screamed. "This is not the way!"

But what was the way?

Stokely, left behind in Trinidad while his parents assessed their prospects in the United States, received an early, proper British education, memorized Kipling's "The White Man's Burden,"

Stokely, taken to Harlem when he was eleven and then to the East Bronx, integrated a white gang, the Morris Park Dukes, became a war counsellor, learned to steal automobile radios and hubcaps,

At the Bronx High School of Science for the bright and the quick, Stokely—bright, quick, and wild—read Karl Marx, met white liberals,

Dated white girls, became a showpiece in Park Avenue salons and the bohemian haunts of Greenwich Village, like a piece of African sculpture on an elegant plaster mantel, the Nubian prince,

Wondered if niggers weren't passé.

Consigned his father to an early grave with disdain, because good old Adolphus had worked too hard for a dream he couldn't grasp, had glimpsed good in too many things, a cupboard, a door cunningly crafted and hung by his own hands. . .

Stokely, thumbing through his college scholarship offers, viewed the first sit-ins as publicity stunts, "Nigger see, nigger do," until the night he saw the princes like himself getting ketchup poured in their hair, being slapped off their stools, climbing back up into the seats with dignity, without violence.

The young people of SNCC, the nonviolent godchildren of M. L. King, Jr., who had attended its birth, who had seen it was allocated funds; Julian Bond was there, but not Stokely, not yet.

Stokely, looking for the way, made the same decision as Andrew Young, passed up the mostly white schools and went to mostly black Howard, spent his freshman vacation on a Freedom Ride into Mississippi, and forty-nine days at Parchman Farm, where for generations black convicts in striped suits chopped and hoed and sweated their lives away, roaring till they were hoarse in the searing sun about bald-headed women and thirty-eight specials that would make them dangerous again.

Took a degree in philosophy, became a field organizer for SNCC, marched through Lowndes County to Montgomery in 1965 with King, the father,

Discovered an odd Alabama law, that any group of at least 20 percent of the voters in a country could call itself a party,

Planted himself in the 80 percent black Lowndes soil, formed the Lowndes County Freedom Organization with a leaping black panther for its symbol. . .

Stokely Carmichael, the tall, loose, hawk-nosed youth in overalls. And when they found out what he had done, white landlords evicted black tenants by the dozens.

Stokely brought in tents and raised black registration till he had 300 more than the whites, put in a slate of black candidates. And lost in the elections by an average of 400 votes. Stokely

Strolled through Mississippi in 1966 with King, a gigantic middle finger lifted, laughing and joking with the ghost of the father,

Succeeded nonviolence-loving John Lewis as chairman of SNCC. He was moving fast now, Stokely,

Dubbed "The Magnificent Barbarian" by his co-workers because of his controlled wildness,

Odysseus, driven half mad by the song of the violent sirens,

Wondered if he was old enough for the job, confessed to confusion,

Traveled without SNCC's okay to Cuba and talked of arming urban guerrillas,

Dropped his chairmanship after one year, then was kicked out of SNCC for emphasizing the evils of race to the exclusion of those of class and because of fears of a cult of personality.

Became Prime Minister of the Black Panthers, but they too fell short, his ship was driving hard now for the ultimate shore,

Dropped the gun-toting, bullet-riddled Black Panthers because they were too ready to join forces with the white radicals, the bomb-makers.

Stokely Carmichael, the only son, with five sisters,

The sharpest, most finely honed of those keen leading edges—Huey Newton, Eldridge Cleaver, Angela Davis, George Jackson, H. Rap Brown—all of them blunted against the stone wall that the American public chose to erect against the human spirit with the election of Richard M. Nixon. The gun waved in the sixties made them completely unfit for the seventies, when only the children who did not deny their fathers, the Andrew Youngs, the Hosea Williams's, the John Lewis's, the Walter Fauntroys, found a place.

In the Lowndes County cotton fields, toting little black babies piggy-back and talking with the ineffably dignified old share-croppers about the weather and the vote, Stokely was essentially alone. SNCC had its front office, its reassuring James Formans and Ruby Doris Robinsons, but the field workers were alone out there with their courage, their ulcers.

Andrew Young, Ralph Abernathy, and Martin Luther King always had each other and their devotion—Jesus in the vanguard and the Almighty at their backs,

And did not have to switch ideologies in mid-stream, for their tool had been tempered and honed by the centuries,

The knowledge of ancient Freedom Fighters!

Nonviolence, a weapon so substantial that maybe it required religious training to lift and hold it,

While Stokely and the others relied only on their own experiences to lead them on,

Making it up as they went along,

And stumbling everywhere they went—Rap . . . Angela . . . Huey . . . Malcolm . . . and Stokely . . .

Stokely who, with King's death, jumped from the father figure to the mother, became the fourth husband of Miriam Makeba, the South African singer, began speaking of Pan-Africanism and an end to capitalism, journeyed to Guinea. . .

And disappeared.

Chapter Seven

"MOTOR MOUTH"

ON FEBRUARY 16, 1977, while Andrew Young was reporting on the success of his first African tour, in Uganda Anglican Archbishop Janani Luwum was detained for questioning, accused of being a member of a plot against President Idi Amin. Archbishop Luwum was the spiritual leader of 3 million Christians in three other countries besides Uganda. Charged with him were two cabinet ministers. On the way to the place of questioning all three prisoners were killed, it was reported, in an auto wreck, from which the driver emerged alive. President Amin was "shocked and stunned."

Meanwhile, in South Africa, other blacks' deaths were unexplained. The previous October, before the United States election and Young's subsequent participation in a conference in Lesotho that influenced his decision to take the United Nations job, the tenth such instance within a year had occurred. A student named Jacob Mashabane, although he didn't drive, had been arrested on a charge of attempted car theft. In prison, which was crowded and closely supervised, Mashabane somehow contrived to fashion a noose out of his shirt and hang himself.

Andrew Young reacted. Pushing human rights was a new ingredient of American foreign policy, and many thought it quixotic and hopeless, especially when dealing with countries as intractable as Russia, South Africa, or Uganda. Nevertheless, Young called his first press conference since arriving at the United Nations.

The deaths in Uganda of the Archbishop and of Ministers Oboth-Ofumbe and Oryema were, he charged, "assassinations in the guise of an auto accident." They were "sadistic and malicious actions that need to be condemned." And he saw it as of a piece with the "suicides" in South African prisons, which had risen to eighteen in a year.

Black majority rule, Young continued, could come to South Africa in as little as five years. In fact, "I'm probably being too conservative when I talk of five years in which South African blacks ought to be prepared to run businesses and administer the society. The events of time will probably move faster than that."

Shortly after this statement was made, financial statements on the cabinet officers were released. They revealed that Young was low man. Almost all the others possessed, in addition to real estate and other resources, stock in sizable amounts; Young owned little except two homes, one in Washington and the other in Atlanta. Deadpan, he reported that he needed to take no action to avoid conflicts of interest.

Nevertheless, he had landed in a position of some affluence. In addition to a salary of $57,500, he was getting travel expenses, and $42,000 was available for entertainment each year. At his disposal was a third home, an eleven-room suite in the Waldorf Towers in New York, paid for by the government, with a butler and catered food included. However, he felt uncomfortable with the luxury and the lack of open spaces, trees, and the amenities of nature that children especially could enjoy. By the end of the month he still had not moved his family there.

At this time his three daughters, Andrea, Lisa, and Paula, were grown, or nearly so, while his son "Bo" was still a small child. And after the practice of his parents, he and Jean usually had someone living with them—students, civil rights workers, and others. For almost two years, they had been extending hospitality, help, and advice to the two older children of Robert M. Sobukwe, a South African activist.

Sobukwe was the leader of the Pan-African Congress, an outlawed nationalist group. In 1960 he had been arrested on the same day that the South African police in Sharpeville fired into a crowd of black demonstrators and killed sixty-nine. Since his release from prison in 1969, Sobukwe had been confined to the mining town of Kimberly and had not been allowed to speak publicly.

Young met Sobukwe in 1974 and saw in him the South African equivalent of Martin Luther King, Jr. With majority rule,

Sobukwe—Young was certain—would be the South African prime minister. A few weeks later Sobukwe wrote Young, asking for help regarding his two older children, both in their early twenties, attending college in the United States. Young, then a congressman, contacted the South African ambassador and got visas. Nobody quarreled with such private kindnesses. But Young's official dealings, after his return from Africa, were not to be quite so free from reproach. The rumblings grew with his selection of staff.

He had decided that when one was speaking of human rights, as the Carter Administration was, experience in protest movements was a valuable qualification. So he had chosen Allard Lowenstein to be the delegate to the United Nations Human Rights Commission. Lowenstein had been the first white to serve as a board member of SCLC. Later he had been in the forefront of the antiwar movement, and he had served a term in Congress.

Other Carter appointees were also bringing in large numbers of outsiders, but to the career foreign service people, Young was one of the worst offenders. They approved his choosing James Leonard for the second-ranking ambassador, but the replacing of all the ranking members of the United States mission, as well as making at least ten changes in his staff, left the old hands extremely disturbed. Against their argument for experience, Young set the notion that good representation of the minorities that made up so much of the United States and that corresponded to the composition of the rest of the world could only be an asset at the United Nations. While other agencies were reporting to Carter the trouble they were having in finding qualified blacks, Young was reporting, tongue in cheek, "We've had great trouble in finding competent whites."

Some of the media were attacking Young on other grounds. *Time* magazine and the *Washington Post* had challenged him from the first. Now they were disturbed by the proposal of Young and General Obasanjo concerning the conference on Rhodesia that would include all interested parties except Smith himself. They thought Young should have returned with background, not suggestions.

(It is remarkable how the media can misread history. They should know by instinct that the final verdict always falls on the side of men like Young, regardless of the opposition. When a Hubert Humphrey or a Senator Philip Hart of Michigan dies, great pools of previously unsuspected love are discovered. In contrast, a James Eastland faces a vast, stony desert. Humanity, having gold-plated the memory of

Martin Luther King and Albert John Luthuli, is waiting to ask Ian Smith and John Vorster, "Well, what did you do for me?")

From the black community, too, came criticism of Young. Bayard Rustin felt that Young's rebuke of Amin had been far too mild. Rustin, an earlier associate of King's in the civil rights struggle than Young himself, had also worked in four African liberation movements, and to him the Uganda president had become almost a personal affront.

With its 10 million people, its large, active army, and its large, active leader, Uganda, like Nigeria, should have been one of the stalwarts behind the front-line states in bringing majority rule to southern Africa. Instead, it was engaged in the liquidation of large parts of its own population, harboring hijackers, playing international pranks, and shooting coffee smugglers. Amin, who controlled only the most noticeable of several such regimes in black Africa (Equatorial Guinea and the Central African Empire were others), was tailor-made for men like Ian Smith and John Vorster when they wanted to point to examples of black irresponsibility. Young, for now and for some time to come, was studiously omitting Uganda from his itineraries. Amin was what black people used to call a "disgrace to the race." He was like an ice-cold shadow that Young couldn't ignore and couldn't lose.

The last bone that people found to pick was the ambassador's continued absence from his headquarters. When he had appeared at the United Nations to present his credentials, staff members of the various delegations, those who normally would hardly turn their heads to look at a king, had stood on chairs to see better. Since then he had spent almost all his time on the road or in Washington. Envoys from the European, Latin American, and Asian countries were disturbed, since he had clearly marked out southern Africa as his "corner." He had made only one speech at the United Nations, and that not a major one, delivered without notes, as was his custom. Speaking to the board of the United Nations Development Program on the subject of foreign aid, he ended by saying that he was grateful for their attention "when I don't really know what I'm talking about."

At last, on March 1, it was his turn to preside over the Security Council for a month, and the delegates were especially looking forward to his presence during sessions on southern African affairs. Sooner or later a vote on economic sanctions against South Africa would come up, and he would have to face the old question of what he would do.

Yet, even after March set in, Young was still not often seen at the United Nations. One reason was that he was busy in Washington lobbying for the repeal of the Byrd Amendment (to observe an economic embargo of Rhodesia by no longer importing chrome), which was crucial to his African policy and his credibility. But in the second week of that month he gave another interview in which he served up a veritable platterful of the kind of comments that guaranteed him front page coverage.

He suggested that United States troops might be used as part of a United Nations peace-keeping force (not for combat) in Rhodesia. As for South Africa, he said that country was currently able to meet all external and internal threats, and he revised his estimate for the advent of majority rule upward to ten years. If that government should be attacked, however, "I see no situation in which we would have to come in on the side of the South Africans. . . . You'd have civil war at home. Maybe I ought not to say that, but I really believe it. An armed forces that is 30 percent black isn't going to fight on the side of the South Africans. This President has too much understanding . . . of white racism ever to align himself with it."

Once more Young attacked the Red preoccupation. The Cubans and the Soviets might help rebel groups to win, but once they were in power there wasn't one that wouldn't turn to the United States for trade dealings. In any case, in Angola Cuba was finding its Vietnam. "It's a huge country. The Cubans don't have the forces to stabilize it. - . . . A dozen or so bodies are going back to Cuba every week—maybe more—and people are asking, "What are we doing, dying over there?' "

Young pointed out that his efforts in southern Africa were already bearing fruit. Israel was one beneficiary. The African states had softened their hostility toward that isolated country. He had always thought that those attitudes were black Africa's way of pointing out American neglect of their own countries.

Another benefit was practical: "If we don't take an interest in human rights in southern Africa, we can't count on Nigeria to supply oil. We have a bloc of forty-seven nations automatically against us in every forum. They can't destroy us, but they can be very disruptive of our initiatives, say, in the Middle East."

He also figured out strategies on the South African veto. He could either soften it so that it wouldn't totally destroy the South African government, or he could get the vote postponed.

On the ever-present issue of Rhodesia, he added that if full-scale war did break out there, all the United States could do would be to stand around and pick up the pieces or back up a United Nations or British Commonwealth peace-keeping force.

Two days later Young and Vance were attacked by Rhodesian Prime Minister R.K. van der Byl. "There they are," he said, "having a hell of a meeting, and not a single one of them knows a thing about it, or has set foot here, or has talked to our moderate blacks, who constitute the majority." He was angry because of American insistence on the inclusion of the guerrillas, the Patriotic Front, in any settlement. "It has the atmosphere of staggering absurdity," van der Byl sneered.

Then, as if following the pace Young had set, in Geneva, Switzerland, Brady Tyson, Young's deputy chief delegate to the United Nations Human Rights Commission, expressed "profoundest regrets for the role that some [United States] government officials, agencies, and private groups played in the subversion of the previously democratically elected government of Chile."

Again the shock waves hit the doors of Young's United Nations mission. Tyson called Young. "Take it in stride," the ambassador told him. (The *Washington Post* promptly dubbed Tyson "Andy Young's Andy Young.") "It's nothing to panic about." Young tried to cool things by telling Vance that it was another case of "someone trying to make a headline out of something." But the uproar persisted. Tyson was called back to the States and Young had to join him in the "chat" with Vance at the State Department. Young said he hadn't taken into sufficient account Tyson's emotional involvement in Chilean issues, such as torture. Meanwhile Carter was calling the comment inappropriate, and Tyson later said that it had been only a "personal view." "We are not here to listen to each other's personal views," responded a European delegate.

And so Young's second month on the job was half over and still he had seldom been seen in the U.N.'s hallowed halls. Instead, he seemed to be maintaining his involvement in nonglobal politics. In the race for his old congressional seat in Georgia, Young endorsed John Lewis over Abernathy, his fellow King lieutenant of so many years. Abernathy, the president of SCLC after King's death, had quit that post specifically to run in this race. Yet Young backed Lewis with this statement: "We are not going to have a black congressman unless we can develop a consensus around one person whom we can support and trust and who also has support and trust in the white community." It was the kind of political decision that Young had made before, puzzling and even angering such colleagues as Hosea Williams.

But Young's most noticeable foray into areas having little if anything to do with the United Nations came with the taking of some hostages in Washington, D.C., and it had the healthy effect of provoking fresh debate on a subject in which he had reason to be extremely interested and in which he could now claim some expertise: freedom of the press.

Several years earlier, in a dispute over ideology, a gang had broken into a home purchased for a group called the Hanafi Muslims and had brutally murdered six members of the family of the group's leader, Hamaas Abdul Khaalis. Though the killers were caught, prosecuted, and found guilty, Khaalis was not satisfied.

On March 9 he and his men took control at gunpoint the District Building, the B'nai Brith Building, and the Islamic Center Mosque in Washington. In the process they shot a black member of the D.C. City Council, and they killed a radio reporter who also chanced to be black. Along with some other demands, they ordered that the government immediately hand over to them the murderers of Khaalis's family.

For several days they held 130 persons hostage before ambassadors from various Islamic countries persuaded Khaalis to surrender. In the meantime Khaalis had been in frequent phone contact with a number of reporters, and the event had been saturated with media coverage.

An incident more directly counter to what Andrew Young was trying to do can scarcely be imagined. Here, at the center of world and national attention, were American blacks beating and holding hostage not only other American blacks (and killing one), but also Moslems and Jews. Young, having just returned from Nigeria, had observed at first hand the grandeur and power of black Moslems, and he could recall vividly the contributions of Jews, in money and human life, to the civil rights movement. He had been going to great lengths to demonstrate to the Israelis, who were showing signs of moving closer to South Africa, the stake that they, too, had in the liberation of blacks in southern Africa.

Young reacted with an early statement: "We create a lot of these phenomena for ourselves, for we have so glorified and publicized events. In a sense we're advertising to neurotic people that when you want a lot of attention, do something suicidal and ridiculous. . . .The First Amendment has got to be clarified by the Supreme Court in light of the power of the mass media."

Some newsmen didn't think it proper for the U.N. ambassador to make such a statement. They complained to President Carter. He backed Young to the extent of saying newsmen should attack the problem themselves.

Fred Friendly, a former CBS news director, replied to Young directly. "It's obvious," he said, "that reporters and editors are going to have to give the entire problem more thought and discussion. Because if they don't, then somebody is going to start playing around with the First Amendment, and if that happens. . .the terrorists will have really won and we will have lost."

However, the constitutional question was set aside when the news spotlight shifted to other events.

On March 17, after meeting the public in Clinton, Massachusetts, in the first of what would be a series of "town meetings," the President was scheduled to speak at the United Nations. This, together with the imminent Security Council debate on South Africa, caused Young to have to stick closer to the United Nations through the next few weeks.

In the meantime, his credibility had received an important boost. Congress had repealed the Byrd Amendment, thus cutting off imports of chrome from Rhodesia. Carter signed the bill on March 18.

Young and President Carter were in a limousine on their way to the United Nations when the following conversation took place:

"I hope you're going to stick with me," the President of the United States said to the man whom some were betting he would fire before summer.

Young was astonished. But now he was about to learn more about Jimmy Carter. "What do you mean?"

"It gets awfully rough out there because people aren't used to discussing foreign policy with the American people in advance. I don't intend to shut up, and I hope you won't let them intimidate you either."

Carter went on to illustrate how they couldn't help but be on the right track. He mentioned how at Clinton he had been almost embarrassed by the enormous applause after he had said the Americans had a right to know ahead of time about decisions and commitments made beyond the borders that would affect not only the citizens of today but also those of future generations.

Young answered that he had every intention of continuing to speak openly, but he wondered if he hadn't spread himself out too thin. "There are so many battles," he said. "You have to know which ones you can fight and which ones you can win."

"I know. People tell me I should be more sensitive to that. But I hope you won't let it discourage you. I think we've got to keep speaking out."

Young did, which a short time later led *Time* to hang on him the heavy-handed appellation: "Motor Mouth."

In an interview with *Playboy* conducted not long after Carter's speech, but not published until the summer, Young suggested that the apparent slipups were not much more serious in his case than they were in Carter's. He pointed out that at this time there were still two administrations, the one that was being brought in and that knew what the President wanted with respect to open diplomacy and human rights, and a second consisting of the old hands, the bureaucrats, who as yet did not understand the changes or agree with them. Much of the criticism was coming from the latter group, aided by what Young called the "old Cold Warriors in the press." In his view they were as isolated as they might earlier have accused President Nixon of being, reading mostly each other's stuff and not getting out to see what the nation was discussing.

The strongest resistance to Young's policies within the State Department came from the Bureau of African Affairs, where Vance had retained most of Kissinger's people. Since under the Kissinger plan, John Vorster was regarded as crucial to any Rhodesian settlement, they were disturbed at how he might react to Young's comments.

It was also partly a problem of differences in style. "When you have a State Department where for eight years only one man speaks and thinks for everyone," Young said, "my kind of statement is a problem."

No matter. To these "old Cold Warriors," used to the diet served up by Henry Kissinger, Carter and Young were amateurs. Calling for the observance of human rights in the Soviet Union as well as in friendly countries (up to 10,000 political prisoners in Iran and another 1,000 killed by the rightists in Chile, torture and rule by decree in the

Philippines, widespread jailings for dissent in South Korea, as many as 60,000 interrogated or jailed in Uruguay in five years) sounded good, but aside from withholding foreign aid, the United States had little leverage. And foreign aid was not a good weapon. Kissinger had known that and had instead made trade-offs based on mutual self-interest. This was the attitude Young was up against.

As for open diplomacy, according to Young there was no alternative. "Once the Xerox copier was invented," he told *Playboy,* "private diplomacy died. There's no such thing as secrecy. It's just a question of whether it's leaked or revealed openly." And he told *Time,* "If you're going to wait until something becomes official United States policy before it is discussed in public, then, in a way, the people are being dictated to." He admitted that that did run the risk of confusion as to exactly what the policy was, but that was nothing compared to the risk of forming policy behind closed doors. "That got this country in trouble in the past. Open mistakes can be corrected very easily."

Some of Young's friends were not so confident. A diplomat from Western Europe said, "He is so clearly a nice man, a good man, an intelligent man who has moved into a new world. It's a minefield requiring very careful treading."

"Andy's never been in a position where people were hanging on every word he said," Julian Bond offered, and he proferred some advice that Young at this or any other point could not easily have taken. He was, after all, a preacher with twenty years of experience in spinning off fully structured sermons or talks before all kinds of gatherings, from pre-teen demonstrators in Birmingham to crusty septuagenarians in the United States Congress. Bond recommended that Young write down what he was going to say. "The quick response is fine for a politician who is representing 460,000 people, but it's not the right thing for an ambassador." In the face of all the comments, Young remained unflappable. Brady Tyson wouldn't repeat the kind of mistake he had made, Young said, "but that is not true of me. I'll probably make more mistakes, because I'm more exposed."

After Carter's half-hour speech to the United Nations, Young flew back to Washington with him on Air Force One. Young talked with Zbigniew Brzezinski, not about geopolitics or John Vorster, but about problems on a more human scale, such as the trouble they were both having sleeping. Young, whose habit had always been to work long hours, was finding that no matter how late he went to bed, he was so keyed-up that he would automatically pop awake at six in the morning. He had previously kept himself in shape with jogging and tennis, but now he was finding little time for that, and he had gained ten pounds.

A few days later, on March 21, the Security Council began its debate on South Africa. Young's presiding over the session marked his initiation proper, after almost two months in the post, into the United Nations. He was given a warm welcome by African diplomats who referred to him as "Brother"—another of those gratifying moments before more serious business set in. In this case it involved what the United Nations should be doing about South Africa, and what could be done about avoiding a possible veto in case of a vote.

Aside from the fact that this was the first time that activities at United Nations headquarters had actually required his sustained personal attention, one gets the impression that Young did not gladly fling himself into attending the lengthy debates and the other day-to-day functions that were part of the routine.

As far as the people were concerned, Young was excited. The United Nations reminded him of the jigsaw puzzles that Jean was so fond of putting together but for which he never had the patience. People puzzles were another matter. He felt that he was good at fitting people together so that their activities made sense. He had done it in the civil rights movement, in Atlanta, and in Congress, but the United Nations had some of the biggest, brightest people puzzles of all.

He was not so excited about the trappings that went with the job. He had moved into his Waldorf Towers suite, but his family still had not, and soon he would be suggesting that the Government would be doing considerably better if it could get some New York good samaritan to donate to the United Nations ambassador a more modest, closer-to-the-earth townhouse in place of the rarefaction of the forty-second floor. He disposed of the two Cadillac limousines that had belonged to the mission and substituted a Ford. And riding in the right rear, the status seat, was "crap." He sat in the front with his driver and shared breakfast with him in the suite. At first the driver couldn't believe it. "No one ever included me before," he said. "You work with me, you gotta be part of the family," Young answered. He also liked to introduce visitors to the butler.

In his conduct of official United Nations business, Andrew Young was equally unorthodox. Adlai Stevenson had described the job as a mixture of "protocol, alcohol, and Geritol." Young, on the other hand, tried to approach his duties as he had approached his work in Congress. Maneuvering on the House floor had been one thing, but it hadn't taken him long to discover that the most important work of assembling a majority was always accomplished earlier, in the cloak-room or the gym, "digging, scratching, and communicating."

In the United Nations he found no cloakrooms, but there were plenty of meeting rooms, offices, and lounges scattered around the city, and he began to call on delegates. After he visited Ambassador Lai Ya-Li, the head of the Chinese delegation, one of his political officers admonished him: "You gave them some important information."

"Is that bad?"

"And we got nothing."

Young shrugged. "I still believe it is best to be open with people," he replied. "Their suspicions are far worse than reality. I figure the more people know about us, the better they like us."

On another occasion Young talked West German Ambassador, Rudiger von Wechmar, into arranging a luncheon attended by important Western delegates. The ambassador had to cable home for permission before he could do it. Young was surprised to find a delegate tied to such a short leash. Instead of calling his people into his office, he visited them in theirs. "I want to know what everybody does," he said. He arranged meetings of his staff members in his suite. He urged his people to speak out.

In the meantime, while the debate on South Africa continued and Young and the other delegates in the United Nations pressed the flesh and took each other's measure, other developments of vital interest to him were in progress. On April 5, in Georgia's Fifth District, Young's candidate, John Lewis, lost by over 20,000 votes to Wych Fowler, whom Young had beaten in 1972. Both candidates had been careful not to campaign along racial lines; nevertheless, that was the division of the electorate.

That night Young appeared on a British TV interview, and he was asked about the forthcoming South Africa vote. He said he favored the economic sanctions that black African states were urging against that nation of apartheid. Once more, though Africans weren't always comfortable with the comparison, he saw similarities between the Deep South of the fifties and sixties and present-day Rhodesia and South Africa, and he considered the sanctions to be the same kind of nonviolent weapon as the sit-ins used by King.

"The United States might not use its veto," he suggested, when the vote came up. "It would depend, I'd have a big hassle about it." But he wouldn't want England or France to use their vetoes, thus taking him off the hook. Clearly he hoped for favorable instructions.

"I would think that at some point we're going to have to realize that we are not going to be able to do business with black Africa on one set of principles and then deny that set of principles totally in doing business with white Africa. All of us are going to have to make a choice."

In this same interview, goaded by interviewer's insinuations regarding American racial troubles, he countered with the opinion that Britain was "a little chicken" on racial matters both in southern Africa and at home. Sometimes, he said, he almost thought that the British had "invented racism." In any case, "they institutionalized it certainly more than anyone else in the history of the earth. . . .I think it would be in Britain's self-interest to have a little more backbone in facing up to race at home and abroad."

Some thought that Young had taken leave of his senses. How could a United Nations chief delegate so blatantly insult America's closest ally and furthermore one that was bearing the major burden of arranging majority rule in Rhodesia? Didn't he know that sympathizers for black suffrage were far more likely to be found among the 40 percent of English descent among white South Africans than within the 60 percent who were of Boer lineage?

Ivor Richard, the British chief delegate, sent a note objecting to the remarks, and Young promptly apologized. While he told the public that he had responded to the interviewer's implication that race was purely a United States problem, somewhat awkwardly he explained to Richard that he had not intended to malign or single out Britain, since race problems were to be found everywhere. He had been unfair:"Britain has struggled as gallantly with the problems of cultural and racial diversity as any people." And he asked the British ambassador to reprimand him whenever he overextended himself."

Richard wasn't all that upset. "I see a lot of Andy Young, and I enjoy working with him," he said. "I would not dream of doing anything so magisterial as trying to reprimand him."

"It was the worst day of my life," Young told Richard privately.

"Was it really?" Richard told Young that he could sympathize, after having suffered himself for being too outspoken after ten years in the House of Commons.

On the basis of this incident, one is tempted to award Andrew

Young high marks as a politician, or to give the credit to his personality. After all, who can imagine Richard or anyone else consoling Daniel P. Moynihan in this manner?

However, judging by the lengths to which he went in apologizing and explaining it away, Young was not at all certain about the ineptness of British influence in Africa. His uncertainty surely increased when the new British foreign secretary met with militant African leaders like Nkomo and Mugabe, stopped off unexpectedly in Angola, and also inspected Rhodesia and South Africa.

The Lions in the Arena

AT

MY TEACHER'S FEET

Bull Connor shrugged and may have let a ghost of a smile escape when he heard that Martin Luther King, Jr., had won the Nobel Peace Prize. "They're scraping the bottom of the barrel," he said.

To many citizens King was a rabble-rouser, inducing conditions exactly contrary to peace wherever he went. Thus somehow they transferred the load of his adversaries' violence onto his shoulders.

In King's eyes, however, the prize seems to have been a mandate for the future fully as much as recognition of past accomplishments. He took the term "Peace Prize" seriously.

But much earlier he had already expressed his belief that nonviolence could also be used to bring peace among nations.

Andrew Young started noticing.

In 1965 the hostilities in Vietnam were not strongly impressed on the country's consciousness. LBJ said some of our ships had been attacked, and only two senators voted against giving him his head. No problem. For years the United States had been shipping troops to countries around the world—Korea, Lebanon, the Dominican Republic, Haiti—Teddy Roosevelt had started it all. They were mostly maneuvers anyway, noting to get excited about.

But people like King and his wife, Coretta, and Dr. Benjamin Spock, author of the most popular baby book in history, were watching as more and more American soldiers and material were dropped into Vietnam's fields, jungles, and highlands, and the destruction, defoliation, and deaths mounted. Daily, in the name of dominoes, the United States was squandering ever-increasing resources on the unpopular and probably losing side of a civil war in a distant country, while at home the injustices of decades were being allowed to persist.

On May 11, 1965, following the Selma-to-Montgomery march, King announced his participation in a new cause. "It is worthless to talk about integrating," he said, "if there is no world to integrate in-
. . . .The war in Vietnam must be stopped."

Andrew Young listened, and so did other black civil rights leaders. . . .And Lyndon Johnson.

Roy Wilkins of the NAACP, Whitney Young of the Urban League, Bayard Rustin, and even King's father advised King to stick to civil rights, and in September 1965, the president arranged for him to talk it over with Arthur Goldberg, the United Nations ambassador.

Andrew Young accompanied King, as did Bernard Lee and Rustin. Goldberg told them the United States was indeed trying to begin negotiations, working through neutral governments. Any protests in the meantime, however, would only hurt the process and might keep the United States involved in the war for years.

A few days later Johnson rolled out another big gun. Vice-President Hubert H. Humphrey, who had been pushing for black civil rights for over twenty years, took King and Andrew Young, plus others from the Urban League, CORE, and the NAACP, on an evening cruise down the Potomac in the presidential yacht, the *Honey Fitz.* Reminding them of the contributions that the Administration had already made to the cause of blacks with promises of more to come, Humphrey's intent was to cement the bond between the government and the civil rights leaders. But the glue wouldn't hold. Floyd McKissick, the new director of CORE, was, like King, firmly committed to ending the war, and they couldn't see how buying more guns was compatible with really pressing matters like the anti-poverty budgets.

In June 1966 Johnson, still nearly as committed to ending domestic injustices as he was to winning the war, convened a White House conference on civil rights. While the head of one of SCLC's local chapters was given a vice-presidential position in the conference, Martin Luther King, Jr., the foremost civil rights leader, was invited to attend only as a guest. And meanwhile he suffered attack from numerous blacks, who found it as convenient to be proud of the disproportionate participation of black soldiers as they did later to lament the higher casualties.

All this Andrew Young absorbed.

By the end of 1966 and into 1967, matters had become difficult for Dr. King and SCLC beyond anything that Bull Connor or Jim Clark could ever have conjured up. The riots and the ever-increasing calls for Black Power were combining with the adverse reaction to King's antiwar activities to decrease his influence. Yet he pressed on, and in the spring of 1967 temporarily set aside civil rights to concentrate on the war. The high point was a gigantic rally and march on April 15, 1967, from Central Park to the plaza in front of the United Nations buildings in New York City. Though the police would go no higher than 125,000, King estimated the crowd at 400,000.

Andrew Young was there.

In prominent positions in the organization of this Spring Mobilization were persons associated with the Communist Party and other suspect groups. Several months later black disapproval was clearly articulated in a column written by Carl Rowan, formerly the director of the U.S. Information Agency. Dr. King, he said, had created "doubt about the Negro's loyalty to his country." And old questions about communist influence had been revived. "I report this not to endorse what King and many others will consider a 'guilt by association' smear, but because of the threat that these allegations represent to the civil rights movement." A national survey, Rowan said, showed that close to one of every two blacks believed that King was wrong, and of the others, 27 percent were undecided.

Andrew Young was outraged. "It was not his speaking out

against the war but the war itself that disrupted Congress, created the reactionary moves, and really imperiled our entire nation," Young—in a rare event—then lost his temper. "Carl Rowan is almost the worst kind of sophisticated Uncle Tom, and I don't think that white Americans appreciate Negroes catering to the worst-element, red-baiting, snide-innuendo approach to problems."

King's speech at the Spring Mobilization was not one of his most memorable. Someone remarked that it had been "written with a slide rule." But speaking to the SCLC ten days earlier, he had already clearly struck the tone of his resistance to the war. Dealing simultaneously with the cries for black retaliation and for the war, King mentioned the young men who had asked, when he advised them to be nonviolent, " 'What about Vietnam?' Their question hit home, and I knew that I could never again raise my voice against the violence of the oppressed in the ghettos without having first spoken clearly to the greatest purveyor of violence in the world today—my own government."

Andrew Young remembered.

Chapter Eight

POINT MAN

UNTIL THE UNITED NATIONS LIMELIGHT, it had not been easy to characterize Andrew Young. In the civil rights days, some regarded him as one of King's most militant advisers, while others considered him the quickest of the lieutenants to begin negotiations and work for compromises. (King himself had fondly nicknamed him "Tom".) During the 1968 Poor Peoples Campaign, Young had issued statements threatening to shut down the whole of Washington, D.C., whereas during some 1964 picketing at a fair housing protest in New York City, he had protested the signs reading "Segregation Isn't Kosher" on the grounds that such a slogan would offend Jewish tenants. Tact was a quality that a Wyatt Walker or a Ralph Abernathy had been satisfied to leave in Young's hands. After four years in Congress and before that two years of moving through Atlanta's higher circles, Young had arrived in the United Nations with a reputation solidly based on always saying the right thing.

Things had changed.

Now, at the same time that he felt the compulsion to present his views, more and more he was being obliged to deal with the shock waves that resulted. Even before the British remark, he had begun to complain that he could not get out of the newspapers. He tried repeatedly to explain that he was trying not to make policy but to incite the American people into thinking about the world creatively.

Feeling the necessity to explain himself following the disastrous BBC-TV interview, he called the press to the State Department building in Washington. There he attempted, unsuccessfully, to speak off the record. He pointed out that if his African trip had been successful, it was because of his credibility, which was established by his public statements. Even though he had asked the White House to muzzle him if they thought his comments were becoming harmful, they were, on the contrary, continuing to encourage him to speak out.

Had the State Department encouraged him?

"They don't discourage me."

The sessions were formally ended by the State Department spokesman, Hodding Carter III, when someone again brought up the subject of the continuing presence of Cuban troops in Angola.

"I should never answer these extra questions," Young sighed. But he was the man who had said that he hated to look another human being in the eye and say, "No comment."

The United States shouldn't, he felt, "get all paranoid about a few communists, or even a few thousand communists." Sometime earlier he had put this same point to *Newsweek* in even more forceful language. When Americans react as if "the presence of twenty Cubans anywhere in the world is a threat to peace, I say that's stupid. It *is* stupid, and if the Americans stop to think, they'll realize it's stupid." In any case a large number of the Cubans weren't soldiers at all but technicians, doctors, and engineers who were desperately needed in war-ravaged Angola.

The whole thing reminded him of the uproar when the Chinese built the railroad in Zambia and Tanzania in the 1960s. The railroad had been completed quickly without Tanzania or Zambia turning communist.

He brought up another pet point, that no matter what the communist forces attempted, it would be the West to whom the Africans would turn in the end because of technological superiority.

Having thus tried to come to terms with the press in something resembling an act of contrition, three days later Young was in trouble again. He was being interviewed by an Associate Press reporter one night at the United Nations when they started talking about majority rule. Young said that he thought the shift to majority rule in South Africa ought to start at once.

"Do you think the South African government is illegitimate?" the reporter asked.

"Yeah," Young answered.

The next day, in Capetown, South African Foreign Minister R.F. Botha called in United States Ambassador William Bowdler to find out if the report about Young's answer was true. "We are awaiting the reaction of the United States government," Botha rumbled.

In Washington, Hodding Carter answered that Young had been told by Secretary of State Vance that his statement was "incorrect," and that later South Africa would be told just that in a more formal statement. Botha replied that his government accepted this assurance that the remark did not reflect official United States thinking, but he would make a formal protest anyway. Considered a moderate, Botha felt that Young's latest "remark" had hardened the reluctance of conservatives like Vorster to make any concessions to the blacks.

To the average black person, this whole episode appeared bizarre, if not surreal. Indeed, one would probably have been hard-pressed to find even a few blacks in the United States, not to mention South Africa, who would have called that government legitimate. And they found it hard to understand how any white person could, when the only participants in that government were representatives of the 4 million people of one color bent on keeping the 18 million of another color completely disenfranchised or otherwise sealed off in a series of reservations covering a fraction of the total land area.

Representative James G. Martin, Republican of North Carolina, called for Young's resignation because of his statements. Typifying the criticism, Martin said that Young "terrified our allies and insulted the British." Young "misunderstood the rebellion in Zaire, incited revolution in South Africa and Rhodesia, and accused the minority government in South Africa of being illegitimate while endorsing the minority government in Angola. . . .When he spoke in Congress, we listened. Now, we cringe. . . . I had high hopes he would make us proud, but enough's enough."

Young lashed back at Martin.

"He and I never got along when we were in Congress together. . . .And I don't think it's his business to tell me that I should resign."

And on TV Ms. Lillian Carter, the President's mother, was asked about reports that there were some windbags in the Cabinet. "One of the windbags," she said, "must be Andy Young."

A few days later, President Carter himself said he agreed that Cuban troops "bring a certain stability and order" to Angola. (He also said that Neto's government was likely to remain in power and that the Cubans should get out. Furthermore South Africa "has a legally constituted government" and, using the same word that he and Young had applied to the Cubans, Carter described that government as a "stabilizing" influence in southern Africa.)

Increasingly, one of the most interesting things about Andrew

Young was turning out to be his backing by Jimmy Carter. "Our friendship is very interesting," Young told *Newsweek*. "It's like people who have similar backgrounds and similar experience but who don't have to talk to each other to be friends. . . .It's not me programming him, nor is he doing it to me. We hardly communicate at all, and we didn't during the campaign. When the 'ethnic purity' thing came up, I didn't have to ask him what was said and how he got into it. I felt it was necessary for me to criticize him very harshly because there was a constituency that was terribly concerned, and he was not upset by that."

About this time it was made public that Carter had assigned Vice-President Walter Mondale a role in shaping African policy. Actually, Mondale had already been working in that area for a month and had been meeting with various Africa experts, including Young and some of his staff. "Finally it's happened," thought Young's adherents as well as his critics. "He has gone too far and is now about to be pushed into the background, confined to the more routine, prosaic duties of his position." Young assured one and all that was not the case. "There's enough work there for anyone who wants to do it," he said, after listing the crises that were afoot in Ethiopia, Zaire, Rhodesia, and Namibia.

On the contrary, Young was so far from being nudged out of position that another trip to Africa was in the air, this time involving a visit to South Africa. "I can hardly see the South African representative speaking to a man who questions our legitimacy," Botha reacted.

"Beautiful," Young thought. Such a remark helped both of them, Botha because he was running for reelection and Young because it strengthened his credibility with the black African delegates. It made little difference that Botha couldn't see how South Africa could deal with him. "He couldn't deal with me before that statement. . . .My whole approach to South Africa has been extremely moderate—too moderate."

It was the confident talk of a man who felt that his position had been strengthened, not weakened, yet Young temporized. He said that the South African government was illegitimate morally if not legally. He still thought that change to black rule in South Africa could be made nonviolently, and he was disturbed by some of the big American companies who were more cynical and were doing nothing to avoid eventual violence.

"All my life, everything I have done has been controversial and naive and people have advised me against it," he told a meeting of the United Nations Association. He said he had patterned his whole life on being "terribly optimistic. These impossible dreams are worthwhile and I wouldn't trade them for any amount of realism, caution, and protocol. . . .Perhaps in the past we have been too timid, perhaps we have asked too little of ourselves, of our nation, of the United Nations. Before the massive problems of racism, torture, and famine we dare not be timid."

In the meantime, on the Rhodesian question, developments continued to unfold. London came up with a new plan, though there was no great optimism that it would find acceptance any more easily than had its predecessors. It consisted of two stages. In the first there would be meetings between the rival white and black leaders to work on the main points of a constitution providing black majority rule. Following that, a conference would be held to ratify the constitution and to work out the details of the elections.

The main sticking points were the rival black nationalist figures, Nkomo and Mugabe, and Ian Smith. But there were factors that might bring both sides around. If Nkomo and Mugabe insisted on waging guerrilla warfare, they would eventually win, but their military machine was inefficient and it could take as long as five years. In that time one or both, being politicians rather than military men, might easily be replaced by other guerrilla leaders in the Patriotic Front, so it was to their personal interest to work out a faster deal. Smith, on the other hand, also had a stake in avoiding the many white deaths and the destruction of property that would result from a protracted war.

England was interested in having the United States co-sponsor the conference, but that would depend on whether the nationalists objected. In any case it looked like a long, sticky affair whether it was resolved by negotiation or by war.

It was against this background—the situation in Rhodesia and his distinct lack of popularity among South African leaders—that, on May 9, Young set out on his second African trip. This was actually part of a two-pronged operation, for, simultaneously, Mondale was leaving for Vienna, Austria, to meet with John Vorster.

Young announced that he wanted to stop over in South Africa for a one-day private trip, but when he left the United States, whether or not he would be able to do so was still highly in doubt. The Afrikaners were still burning about the "illegitimate" charge, and Young had fanned the flames by adding that he "hated" anything to do with the

South African government. "And yet I know that it is in our interest and in the interest of the majority of the people in that country to maintain some kind of relationship and influence."

On April 6, three days before Young left, the South Africans announced that it might not be convenient to receive him. The purpose of his visit was not clear, and Young's office had not gone through "normal channels." But Young said that he had been invited to speak to South African businessmen and to white students at Witwatersrand University and that the United States had cleared it with the South African government through its ambassador there. Botha responded that a South African industrialist had indeed inquired as to whether there would be any objections to such an invitation. "We replied that in principle there would be no objections, provided Ambassador Young approached us through the normal channels."

The industrialist was Harry Oppenheimer, a diamond millionaire and the kind of friend Young valued most, for himself and for blacks. Oppenheimer was one of the main props of the South African Progressive Reform Party, a white group that opposed apartheid, and he was already in trouble with the South African authorities for having donated $3 million to causes that helped blacks.

As his plane flew toward the Ivory Coast, Ambassador Young was the one least worried by the developing diplomatic crisis. He knew that he had the South Africans over a barrel. As far as public relations were concerned, they stood to lose whether or not he was admitted.

By this time he was far and away the figure most feared and despised by the South African and Rhodesian minority governments, more because of the influence he was believed to have on American policy than because of what he said. In fact, his statements were far from the only reasons why the South Africans were trying to deny him entry. He would be coming to South Africa directly from a United Nations conference in Mozambique that would be attended by delegates from the Pan-African Congress and the African National Congress, the two big nationalist groups that the government had outlawed, and it was expected that he would try to visit his friend, Robert Sobukwe, the exiled leader of the Pan-African Congress. Adding to the South Africans' difficulties was the timing, brilliant on Carter's part, that would split the South African forces. While Vorster would be diverted to Vienna to see what Mondale wanted, Young would be trying to enter by the front door.

Attempting to avoid being outmaneuvered, Botha was outraged. "We are an independent country," he fumed. "We are a proud nation. We are going to be dictated to by no force, and by no power, not even the United States. We are not prepared to crawl before them, least of all Mr. Andrew Young." Young had added to his itinerary the intention to meet with black leaders, and Botha said he had done that entirely through unofficial channels. "Forget about color," the South African foreign minister said. "It's just a question of good manners. I mean, what would the United States government think if I simply announced that I was proceeding to visit the Indians of Maine, to deliver an outrageous speech, and ignoring altogether the officials in Washington? It would not be acceptable to them and it isn't to us."

Andrew Young, the original blithe spirit, said that he still planned to keep his speaking engagements in Johannesburg, unless, of course, the invitations were withdrawn or the government barred him.

Young arrived in Abidjan, the capital of the Ivory Coast, on May 10. It had been expected that he would go on to Nigeria, but that depended on whether Nigerian Foreign Minister Joseph Garba would be there. Ghana, Gabon, and the Sudan were other possible but not certain stops. But attending the conference in Mozambique was set, as was a weekend side trip to Lisbon, Portugal, to coordinate strategies with Vice-President Mondale.

The occasion in the Ivory Coast was a week-long meeting of thirty-three American ambassadors to African countries, held in a large hotel called the Ivory Tower. It would be important for the not yet fully formulated African policy. Again Young had come chiefly to listen.

There was a lot to hear. The ambassadors were uneasy over the apparently unbraided strands of policy variously personified by Mondale, Vance, and Young. The existing policy had also been conducted too passively. The United States had not yet taken a big role in the Rhodesian negotiations, and the passivity was further reflected in the soft-pedaling of Soviet and Cuban influence. In March Zaire's Shaba province had been invaded from Angola by Katangan rebels thought to be backed by the Russians and Cubans. Joseph Mobutu had asked for military help but the United States had declined, and while Egypt and Morocco had sent substantial aid, the United States had dispatched only a cargo plane loaded, at Mobutu's request—there was some problem about contaminated water—with Coca-Cola. "It's better for Africans to deal with African problems than having us come in with the 101st Airborne," Young said.

Young's view that the leftist states would have no choice but to go to the West for trade could well turn out to be naive and mistaken, thought many moderate Africans. A high Ivory Coast official, Philip Yae, the president of the National Assembly, said: "Once the Soviets are firmly ensconced in Africa, the West will be cut off from its source of raw materials. You'll pay for it."

On May 11, a day after Young arrived in Africa, Vorster and his men decided they would admit Young. They probably didn't want to endanger the meeting with Mondale. But they changed the date. Young had intended to visit on May 19 and 20. They said he couldn't come till the twenty-first. On the nineteenth Mondale would be meeting with Vorster.

Meanwhile the American ambassadors sat discussing four steps that the Administration envisioned in a new, tougher policy toward South Africa. They included withdrawing the American military attache, tightening up visa requirements for South Africans wanting to visit the United States, cutting the connections between American and South African intelligence agencies, and ending Export-Import Bank credits to South Africa.

On the thirteenth, word came from Johannesburg that the South Africans were thinking of setting Young's day back again, to the twenty-third, so that he would not be in the country while Vorster and Botha were away in Vienna.

On the fourteenth, Stoney Cooks, Young's aide, said they might not go to South Africa after all. The South African government was trying to impose a series of conditions that were nettling Young.

But Young would go not as an "honorary white man" but with the "proper respect due a cabinet officer." Cooks announced this on the plane to Lisbon where Mondale and Young conferred.

Young continued on to Maputo, Mozambique. Despite the presence of an unusual number of Western nations, this United Nations-sponsored conference on Zimbabwe and Namibia was distinctly radical in tone. Among the representatives from over eighty countries were delegates from Southern Africa's Marxist states and from various liberation groups, as well as from Cuba and the two communist superpowers that were competing bitterly for influence on the continent, Russia and China. Young's influence was responsible for the presence of delegates from Canada, Britain, West Germany, and France.

As usual, Young did not spend much time sitting through the interminable speeches and debates, which here often carried strongly anti-Western sentiments. Instead, he promptly sprang into action in his "cloakroom" style. The first day he had lunch with Sam Nujoma, the leader of SWAPO, and later he met with the host, Samora Machel, the Marxist president of Mozambique.

South-West Africa, called Namibia by the nationalists, was a large territory on the Atlantic coast between South Africa and Angola. Technically, Namibia was not a part of South Africa, but that country had been administering the territory since the Germans lost control of it in World War I. Naturally the South Africans infected Namibia with a brand of apartheid, but the United Nations strongly demanded that South Africa release its hold. South Africa appeared to be on the point of doing just that, but it was trying to attach a series of conditions. They were highly resentful of SWAPO, which was waging guerrilla warfare while having been recognized by the United Nations as the sole legitimate representative of the 800,-000 black Namibians (compared to 100,000 whites).

But Nujoma and Machel had histories of bitter opposition to the United States. Nujoma looked upon the presence of the American and other Western representatives in Namibia as support for South Africa. Now he called his luncheon with Young a "very useful exploratory contact" and he told Young, "If the United States can exert pressure on South Africa we would be most grateful."

That same day, Jimmy Carter appeared on television and said that South Africa would face "strong action" by the United States in the United Nations, involving economic sanctions, unless it ended minority rule in Namibia.

Machel in earlier times had maintained that the United States had no useful role to play in solving the problems of southern Africa, and waving his finger, he lectured Young good-naturedly. To solve these problems, he said, "is not an act of charity but the duty of the whole of humanity."

"President Carter," Young said, "has decided the United States should be with the people of the world."

"I am not saying the United States has a solution," Machel said, "but it has a contribution to make. That is why I say welcome."

The next day, while the Russians were accusing the Western powers of being "the most active protectors of colonial and racist regimes in southern Africa," and while the Chinese were attacking the Russians, saying they had "spared no effort to sow discord among African states and among national liberation movements," Young was still buttonholing people and changing minds, this time winning over another critic of the United States, the chairman of the Organization of African Unity, William Eteki.

On May 19, the day when Young originally planned to arrive in South Africa, the South African police suddenly descended upon Mrs. Winnie Mandela, a vigorous black nationalist and the wife of Nelson Mandela, the leader of the African National Congress and now a political prisoner on Robben Island, out in the Atlantic Ocean. With her furniture, her other possessions, and her youngest child, aged sixteen, she was taken from Soweto to the Orange Free State, 200 miles sway, where she would be banned, like Robert Sobukwe. The South Africans said that this move had nothing to do with Young's visit. Still, in this period of exquisite timings, it looked like one more message for Andrew Young—and for the blacks of South Africa.

In the meantime, Young was finally addressing the delegates in Maputo. "The question," he said, "is not what we are going to do. The question is not what are the policies we discussed. The question is how believable are those policies. I say that we are not immune to the struggles that Africa faces, that we have known these struggles ourselves, and it is because of this that you see a determination on the part of this Administration to bring about changes around the world that are consistent with the new spirit of America that was brought on by a silent and nonviolent revolution."

"Silent" sounded strange here, but he went on. The new political freedom of American blacks had not only freed whites, he said, but it had also put the South in charge of the country today. "We say the hands that used to pick cotton had now picked the President."

He then pulled out the stops, with the observation that the racism of southern Africa was totally familiar to him, and that his awareness of it had come to him with his mother's milk. He anticipated his hearers' uneasiness with his theme: "And so, while I respect your skepticism and even your cynicism, there is in fact a change in America that makes me extremely hopeful about the proceedings that are going on here.

"I would remind you respectfully that the history of freedom in Africa has not just been a history of victory through armed struggle. The majority of nations of Africa achieved their independence through negotiated settlements, and where there was a possibility of settlements those countries moved much more rapidly in their development. It is only when negotiated settlements have been totally refuted and rejected that armed struggle becomes inevitable."

These sentiments did not sit well with the militants. The desires of these delegates were as specific as could be. They wanted to hear only one thing: what would the United States do to light a fire under South Africa?

Robert Mugabe, one of the co-leaders of the Patriotic Front in Zimbabwe, was incensed. Ian Smith had set up his white minority government back in 1965. Mugabe said they had already been through strikes, sit-ins, civil disobedience, and the rest; they *knew* that in their case only the force of arms would work.

The Nigerian ambassador to the United Nations, Leslie Harriman, was one of Young's closest friends in Africa, but now he said, "One could have hoped that Andrew Young would contribute to the conference and not lecture us on civil rights. In Atlanta I would have listened ten years ago with some patience, but instead I listened today with considerable irritation." Then he drew a distinction that would not have come easily to an apostle of nonviolence. "We are not talking about improving the lot of Africans. We are talking about *liberation.*"

Meanwhile, Walter Mondale was bluntly telling John Vorster in Vienna that if South Africa didn't start moving faster on getting out of Namibia, as well as prodding Ian Smith into an agreement acceptable to the nationalists and decreasing the withholding of black social, economic, and political rights in his own country, he could expect not only increased violence but also worsened relations with the United States. Hearing this, Vorster could think back fondly to Henry Kissinger, who regarded South Africa as an important ally in containing communism in southern Africa.

Mondale similarly presented his terms within the framework of the success of civil rights in the United States. Vorster rejected the idea as vehemently as had the black Africans. "Knowingly or unknowingly, the United States wants to equate the position of the American Negro with the South African black man." This, Vorster insisted, was a mistake. In the United States, he said, the black man had lost all vestiges of his African culture and was "an American in every sense of the word," whereas the black people in South Africa were not South Africans at all but members of several tribal nations, who couldn't possibly be absorbed into the small white population.

Andrew Young flew into Johannesburg on May 21, 1977. His plane was shunted off into a far corner of the airport. A cordon of grim-faced South African police stood waiting. Leaving the plane,

Young shook hands with about a dozen of the white policemen and customs officers and he exchanged the Black Power handshake with twice that number of smiling black chauffeurs and airport workers.

A motorcade took him to the Carlton Hotel in the center of town. Only two Secret Service men had come with him, but they were augmented by twelve South African cops on motorcycles. The procession veered off the usual motorcade routes. The hotel was swarming with security men, in and out of uniform. Tracker dogs roamed the hotel basement. The police grabbed a young white man who was caught littering the street with small slips of paper on which was written: "Young insulted us—kick him out. Hated Young is our enemy."

In the next thirty hours, the duration of his stay in South Africa, Young didn't lose much time. First he went straight to members of a group that he had always maintained held the key to South Africa's troubles, the businessmen. "I have myself lived through some experiences that I believe could have some meaning for you." And once again he described his experiences in the American South, of the role that business had played in making transformations behind the scenes. He asked them to ponder on certain facts, such as that the United States volume of trade with Nigeria had grown to twice that with South Africa.

"One of the good things about South Africa is that nobody has anywhere to go, and you have no choice but to work it out or fight it out." Only 4 or 5 million blacks needed to be brought in initially to ensure the eventual full participation in the economy. He mentioned the recent student riots in Soweto, the black township just outside Johannesburg, where the police had killed over 300 protestors. "Soweto," he said, "may indeed have provided the means for the redemption of the soul of South Africa and with it the soul of the system." (Tass, the Soviet news agency, that day called Young "a zealous defender of the interests of the imperialist monopolies in southern Africa.")

Young went on to meet other small groups of whites and blacks, who were able to hear him by invitation only. His presence was widely reported, especially by the black newspaper, *The World,* whose editor, Percy Qoboza, would soon be imprisoned. Crowds even gathered in the streets near his hotel for a glimpse of him.

He told a group of liberal white students that to leave the country would be a cop-out. It would be better to stay and help the blacks. One of the conditions of his admission, the South African officials said later, was that he not say anything controversial or inflammatory. To a group of black students he described nonviolent techniques of protest that he had used in the South. After he left they would follow his recommendations to the letter. "Jimmy Carter is an Afrikaner!" Ambassador Young told a group of editors. "He comes out of that same rural, hardnosed stock. He's been dealing with folks like Vorster all his life. I think you've met your match."

The climax of his visit was a session with about seventy activists, including Chief Gatha Buthelezi, leader of South Africa's largest black group, the 5.8 million Zulus. He brought them to tears speaking of the changes he had seen in his lifetime. "That's when I realized a nigger can be somebody!" he concluded while they stood and cheered. He and chief Buthelezi embraced. "I have stated to many fellow South Africans that you are this country's best friend," Buthelezi testified. "I have said that all your efforts on the international scene are geared toward the peaceful settlement of our problems. This is what tends to be forgotten in the anger that overcomes them."

Young left, amid cheers and the singing of the African national anthem, "Nkosi Sikelel' i-Afrika," ("God Save Africa").

"There is no doubt in my mind that over a period of time Andy Young will become a hero to the Third World," Jimmy Carter said, during a bill-signing ceremony in the White House Rose Garden.

The South African government however, accused Young of violating the conditions of his visit. This did not stop Young from sending Winnie Mandela a personal note. Young ended his second African tour by visiting the Sudan.

En route home, Young grabbed more headlines. He remarked of British foreign secretary David Owen, "I hope he is not trapped by that old colonial mentality. I think it is very strong throughout that island."

Actually, Young observed, everybody was racist, including himself. It was a consequence of being born in this century. The Russians were the worst, because they had no experience at solving the problems.

In Sweden, he said in reply to another question, people were humanitarian and liberal, yet blacks there were still treated as badly as they were in the New York City borough of Queens, where he had once lived. The United States had accomplished the most in matters of race, though the Israelis had done wonders in combining widely varying cultures. But as for the Swedes, who had brought the Turks in to do the menial jobs that they no longer wanted to do themselves and then had turned on them, yes indeed, "The Swedes are terrible racists."

Why was the traditional mediator now suddenly antagonizing so many people? The question had been asked before about another man from the South.

The Lions in the Arena

FROM LYNDON, WITH LOVE

LBJ first came to our attention
    Sometime in the 1950s; he was the floor leader, the majority whip, something big in the Senate, somebody who could boot other big somebodies into line,

A Texan, associated with Sam Rayburn, who was also reputed to be big—a protege

Of Franklin Delano Roosevelt and all those New Deal programs to give the poor and the downtrodden

A better break.

Maybe it was in those debates in the late fifties, for those two civil rights bills that most people forgot later,

Though they were big then, the first since Reconstruction—

Yes, that's when it was, in 1957, and all those long nights and days under the Capitol Dome, for thirteen days of the filibuster by the Eastlands and the Russells and the Thurmonds against a bill that nobody thinks much about now, and Lyndon, LBJ, a Southerner himself, a Texan, who had not been famous for backing civil rights measures, who had voted against the Fair Employment Practices Commission,

Genially and resolutely forcing his fellow Confederates to talk about it day and night till at last everybody was exhausted and this tall Texan, Lyndon Baines Johnson, got this first bill passed—

Hosannas!

And also refused to sign the Southern Manifesto,

Suffered a heart attack and almost died,

Was recognized as one of the real ramrods of the country, the strong man of principle and stratagem,

Mountain-mover,

LBJ, the Texas shit-kicker,

Whom JFK beat out for the nomination in 1960—the year of the second civil rights bill, which he also helped push through—and everybody was surprised

When he accepted the invitation to be John Kennedy's running mate.

By then LBJ was much better known—

He had something up his sleeve—

Why would he give up all that Senate power for four, possibly eight years of near invisibility?

For three strange years Johnson stayed in that deep shadow, noble inn his humility, never pushing—

LBJ had almost been forgotten again when the rifle poked out of the window of the schoolbooks repository

In his home state

And blew John Kennedy into eternity. The new President

LBJ grabbed the reins, his work cut out for him, held the bereaved country together, toughed out the suspicions, kept more of the Kennedy men than was good for him,

And in 1964 gleamed so brightly compared to that militaristic throwback, Barry Goldwater, that he won by a

Landslide,

and

escalated

the war.

The war was in a place called Vietnam.

Some of those fellows (he said) had fired at our ships in a place called the Tonkin Gulf. At *American* ships.

Kennedy had already sent in a few advisers—

LBJ decided to teach something about America to Ho Chi Minh, the old-line Commie who had dreams of his own (into which he had never factored a Johnson City bronco-buster)

To unite Indochina.

LBJ, the first member of the House to get into uniform in World War II, recipient of a Silver Star for hopping planes that got ripped by flak,

LBJ, a veteran of that great epic when American had come galloping in on a thundering steed of manpower and machines to rescue the world,

The same old folksy president (who during his thirty-odd years as a Federal servant had somehow managed to amass a personal fortune of at least $3 million, with a TV station and a 400-acre ranch), horrifying true dog lovers by picking up his beagle by the ears, scandalizing the genteel by flashing the surgical scars on his belly on the White House lawn,

And who, despairing of sacking J. Edgar Hoover, finally said, "Well, maybe it's better to have him inside the tent pissing out than outside the tent pissing in."

Flew to the Nam to encourage his brave troops, the flower of American manhood (except those who had fled to Canada or Sweden)

Five hundred thousand Unknown Soldiers suffering injury and death at the hands of tough little dudes in black pajamas floating through the jungles with rice cakes, AK-47s, and their own notion of body counts.

"Boys," LBJ said, "let's nail that coonskin to the wall!"

He didn't notice how Korea had pointed the way,

How the war of his Silver Star had been the last of the great clean epics,

Didn't notice

The absence of heroes.

So when the grumbling started he went out searching for consensus, delivered the greatest presidential civil rights speech ever (suspected to have actually been the inspiration of Daniel P. Moynihan) at Howard University in 1965, pushed ahead with new civil rights laws that made 1957 and 1960 look like pussyfooting, started massive anti-poverty programs, Project Head Start, and the like,

Replaced Kennedy's New Frontier with the Great Society.

America, he believed, the land of plenty, the land of excess (he knew something about excess), was capable of producing enough to feed and clothe the poor, provide jobs, lift everybody by their boot-straps. . .and win a war.

(He couldn't explain how deeply America believed that its destiny, its very nature, was always to win,

(Couldn't explain how Martin Luther King, Jr. believed it no less than Barry Goldwater, else how could he have marched so far and for so long?

(Couldn't explain that Abe Lincoln had already queered the game

(With those unfortunate words, "Shall not have died in vain.")

LBJ wanted to be loved

And instead black people, tantalized by the still too narrow wedges of the pie he offered, kept stretching out their hands for more—through shop windows in one city after another,

And college students demonstrated on their campuses and arrived in Washington by the thousands,

And eventually Lyndon Johnson, who had tried to give all Americans so much, couldn't dare a trip to much of America, was almost literally trapped inside the White House behind barricades of charter buses, began to feel new flutterings from the heart, and, deep in lonely nights,

Communed with the portrait of Woodrow Wilson, the last southern-born President, the one who set up the League of Nations, then couldn't drag his own country into it.

In 1968 LBJ declined to run again. Instead he packed in all his 10 million papers, built his memorial library down in Austin, printed up the picture postcards, then sat back and waited for time's fairer verdict—and for death.

"Every question of social and political justice raised by the [civil rights] movement, President Johnson translated into legislative action," Andrew Young eulogized. "Let God judge him for the war in Vietnam. . . .Thank God for what he did."

Lyndon Baines Johnson, a tall, big-eared, salty-mouthed man, who would have stood every chance of being remembered as one of the three or four greatest Presidents

Had he and his countrymen not been so much in the habit

Of nailing coonskins to the wall.

Chapter Nine

NIGHTMARES

FOR THE FIRST TIME the center had not held. The march of 6,000 in support of the striking black sanitation workers and against recalcitrant Memphis mayor Henry Loeb had turned into disaster. Dignity and order for three blocks, then thirty or forty young militants broke to the front ahead of Dr. King, shouting, "King is not our leader! We want Carmichael!" Then the sounds of the first windows shattering, the march leaders climbing into cars and leaving quickly, dozens of display windows looted, a sixteen-year-old shot dead by police in the debris of a Sears store, LBJ appearing on national television to deplore "mindless violence," and Adam Clayton Powell, the congressman from Harlem, speaking of Martin "Loser" King.

The warp and woof of nightmares! The visit to Memphis in March and April 1968 was not even scheduled. They were supposed to be pushing ahead with an entirely different campaign, something brand new and radical, a gigantic movement on behalf of the poor, with caravans from all over the country converging at last on Washington, D.C. The plans were firm and the kickoff date was set, April 22. An alliance had even been sealed with Stokely and his Black United Front in Washington.

Then what was SCLC doing in Memphis?

Back in Atlanta, while trying to collect himself and prepare for a renewed Memphis drive, King criticized Young and others of the staff who had not joined him, Abernathy, and Lee in that first, abortive march.

Young defended himself and the others. "We were trying to

organize the Poor People's March," he said later. "We felt [King] didn't have any business going to Memphis. We were kind of mad that in the midst of our big thing Doc would let himself get distracted by some little march in Memphis. Since the Reverends James Lawson and H. Ralph Jackson were in charge, we figured his staff could handle things."

But to King, Memphis looked like an opportunity—and a venture onto new ground. The issues were recognition of the sanitation workers' union, a wage increase, and a checkoff of union dues. The elements for the success of a nonviolent campaign seemed to be at hand: a large black population almost totally opposed to the mayor, a strong ministerial leadership, and a relative lack of competition from Black Power advocates, notwithstanding a street gang called the Invaders.

So SCLC was back in Memphis. King met with the Invaders and secured a pledge of their cooperation in a second march set for Friday, April 5. This march would be better planned. The chief obstacle was an injunction that the city had obtained against further demonstrations. In the past, defying court orders had brought King almost more success than obeying them, but now he was already under attack from too many other quarters. So it became Andrew Young's job to attend all-day court hearings in an attempt to lift the injunction. Each evening he had to report, to King's considerable dismay, no success as yet.

On April 4 he was asked by U.S. District Judge Bailey Brown about the effect on King of any violence in the proposed march. "I would say that Dr. King would consider it a repudiation of his philosophy and his whole way of life," Young answered. "I don't know when I've seen him as discouraged and depressed."

Six hours later, at about 6:00 P.M., Andrew Young was standing in the courtyard of the Lorraine Motel near the right rear wheel of a white Cadillac limousine lent to them by a local undertaker. Along with several others—James Bevel, Bernard Lee, Jesse Jackson, and King's attorney, Chauncey Eskridge—he was waiting to go to dinner at the home of the Reverend Samuel Kyles, pastor of the Monumental Baptist Church. Everyone was ready except Ralph and Martin, who were still noodling around up there on the balcony. Everything was set . . .

In Memphis (Dallas, New York, Los Angeles) . . .

To Andrew Young it sounded like a firecracker or backfire from a passing car.

He sprinted up onto the balcony, the first one there behind Ralph.

To the hordes of police who came pouring out incredibly from everywhere, they pointed out the direction from which the shot had been fired. In the blood at their feet lay King with a large hole in his neck.

Young searched for a pulse, believed he found one, but there was that hole.

Now, in the most shattering moment thus far of his life, all that he could grasp to steady himself was facts.

"Oh Lord," he murmured, "it's all over."

"Don't say that!" Abernathy snapped.

The ambulance was slow to arrive. Young phoned Coretta, saying he thought Doc might still be alive. Remembering something he had said to King earlier that day, worrying that it might have been taken the wrong way, he asked Ralph if Doc had mentioned it. Abernathy said no.

With Eskridge and two policemen, Young helped lift King to a stretcher, rode to the hospital in the front with the ambulance driver while Abernathy sat in back with Doc.

Young stood outside the door of the receiving room, certain of the news they would receive, told reporters that King seemed to have had premonitions.

He called Jean. She was in the backyard of their home in Altanta, planting a peach tree (which would not bear fruit until the summer he helped Jimmy Carter secure the presidential nomination).

Coretta arrived and they flew the body back to Atlanta. Robert Kennedy supplied the plane.

Young carried Bunny, Doc's youngest child, off the plane on his shoulders, took part in the services wearing pulpit robes, marched behind the mule-drawn cart in denims—still a young man with already a lifetime of experiences crammed into his being in the wake of this man who had now crossed over.

"Let us stand with greater determination. Let us move on in these days of challenge to make America what it ought to be," said the Reverend Andrew J. Young, while in over a hundred American cities blacks looted and burned whole neighborhoods in another kind of testimony to the event.

The response by Young and SCLC was to carry on with the Poor People's Campaign. King got the idea for the campaign in late 1967 from a lady named Marian Wright Edelman. She knew about poverty programs from the viewpoint of Capitol Hill in Washington, D.C., and the shacks of rural Mississippi. Lots of help for the poor, she argued, was available from the government for the asking—if one knew how the programs worked.

That gave King the kind of idea for which he had been searching. In a matter of hours he had a vast new effort almost completely worked out. It would involve a second March on Washington, of Appalachian whites, Puerto Ricans, Mexicans, Indians—all the poor of the country—not just the blacks. They would converge on the capital from every geographical area by every means of transport, including mule-drawn wagons. They would set up a huge camp of plywood shacks, possibly on the Mall, where official Washington couldn't miss it. From there they would fan out to the various offices of government, presenting the case of the poor directly to the agents of power. It would be by far SCLC's largest undertaking.

"Before, we mobilized one city at a time," King said. "Now we are mobilizing a nation." And when he announced it, on December 4, 1967, he made sure he drew attention by projecting it as a campaign of "massive civil disobedience." That, he said, was the nation's only alternative to the riots.

At first King had no trouble getting the support of the rest of SCLC, and was even able to reach an understanding with Stokely Carmichael. But as problems with logistics and other matters became apparent, strong opposition began to develop within the Conference itself. King had mapped out even bigger things, involving organizing all the poor on a regional basis, unionizing them, and petitioning the government till their demands were met. Some people felt he had gone too far.

Andrew Young, who wanted to continue taking a good hard look at the difficulties, found himself swept along by King's enthusiasm. In January 1968 Young was calling the forthcoming campaign "a nonviolent crisis . . . that almost acts like a shock on a very sick person." In this instance the patient was the United States. Speaking of earlier large riots, he pointed out that conditions in Harlem and Cleveland had improved only slightly and that, after over two years, Watts was still no better off. The domestic situation was "very desperate," he said, and SCLC was prepared to go to any extent nonviolently, assume any amount of suffering and hardship to point that out.

"With an asinine Congress like this, things are bad, but they are doomed to get worse," Young declared. "We have waited around for almost a year looking for a sign of hope, and none came. So finally Dr. King reached the conclusion that something needs to be done to really shock this country into its senses." Young likened the campaign to a war without violence, compared to which the 1963 March on Washington would be a Sunday School picnic. "Something is going to change or we'll be in jail," he vowed. "This is do or die—not just for nonviolence but for the nation—and we'll do whatever is necessary to open the economic doors of this nation for the poor."

In Memphis, on May 2, less than a month after Dr. King's assassination, Young found himself sitting on that same balcony, part of a ceremony in which SCLC made the symbolic beginnings of the Poor People's March on Washington. The campaign proper had already started a few days earlier in Washington on April 29, with Abernathy leading a delegation of 150 to present to the relevant Cabinet officers a long list of their demands. These included jobs for every person able to work and a guaranteed annual income for those unable to work.

Young, now executive vice-president of SCLC, was second only to the new president, Ralph David Abernathy. Young had transferred his loyalty without hesitation. Before King's funeral, when Abernathy made clear to the Memphis marchers his intention to carry on, Young had rushed forward with tears in his eyes to congratulate him, and as they were leaving Mississippi, he could even opine that at that moment Abernathy was the better man to identify with blacks. Paul Good, a writer, heard Young say, "He can get on easily with the militants; his attitude is right. The brothers in the street, or out here, remember things he says even when they don't know his name or who he is. With Dr. King it was often the other way around. His language and concepts sometimes sailed over their heads. Ralph can talk the language."

Yet there was always some question of their compatibility. They were much more different from each other than King had been from either one. Whenever a demonstration started to get rough, King arranged for Young to leave the area. Abernathy would accompany him to jail; Young would carry on the demonstrations. As a result, Young went to jail only three times, and then, as he said, "only when I wanted to."

Young was judged to be closer to King philosophically, whereas Hosea Williams, who called himself King's "Castro" or his tough guy, was thought to be closer to Abernathy. There was talk of occasional personality clashes between Williams and Young, and even of shouting matches. Drew Pearson and Jack Anderson, the two muckraking columnists, said they had it on the best authority that after King's death the fiery Williams tried to persuade the other

SCLC leaders to get in step with the times by dropping their rejection of violence. Abernathy and Young refused, saying it would be a denial of Dr. King. And now they stood just as firmly together launching the Poor People's Campaign.

To the local and federal officials of the Washington area, the approaching Poor People's Campaign was a threatening apparition. Even Edward Brooke, the black Republican Senator from Massachusetts, questioned the wisdom of assembling so many people under conditions where the merest spark, "some irresponsible kid," could set off a riot. And Young made a quick flight to D.C. to assure the officials that there would be no vandalism or looting during the campaign.

The disorders that followed King's death, even more than his absence, intensified matters. Washington, after having thus far avoided the great urban riots despite its huge—and poor—black population, was the hardest-hit of all the cities in the "Martin Luther King" riots. Three separate sections of the city had been devastated, and all the bodies still had not been dug from the rubble. Young and the other SCLC officials knew that they would have to step carefully lest they reignite the turmoil. Yet, practically, the recent violence surely gave substance to their demands.

The site they chose for Resurrection City had that same sort of duality. Located in a beautiful, sprawling area of monuments and greensward, it was far from any populated neighborhood, black or white. This served to insulate it from those with a taste for riots. But it also meant that the demonstrators were more on their own, easy to surround and seal off. Abernathy, Young, and other SCLC officials were criticized because they set up headquarters in the black-owned Pitts Hotel uptown, in one of the riot areas far from Resurrection City.

From the beginning Resurrection City was not an outwardly friendly place. Resentful of the tourists who normally frequented the Mall and fearful of spies, youths guarded and patrolled the city closely; suspected curiosity seekers were firmly ejected. Much of the responsibility for security was left in the hands of gang members, recruited as an important part of the mix. Lance "Sweet Willie" Watson of the Invaders was there, as were the Vice Lords and the Blackstone Rangers of Chicago. To them good public relations were irrelevant: they were in town only to extract satisfaction for public wrongs. They were the poor, and proud of it.

New contingents of poor people kept arriving, and the problems of food, housing, sanitation, medical care, and security grew. The new arrivals were often already uptight because of prior difficulties. In Detroit one group of marchers was charged by police on horseback. The mayor apologized to SCLC, but Andrew Young still had to fly there to straighten out matters.

Then the rains came. May and June brought frequent and heavy downpours. The people of Resurrection City had scarcely recovered from one soaking when another and yet another followed. The hundreds of poor people stalking about looking for food, aspirins, and spiritual succor soon reduced the city, under a canopy of stately trees, to something resembling hogsheds awash in a lake of mud. People left, others entered, tempers flared. There were reports of rape and widespread theft. Youths took to stoning passing cars from the trees and bushes between the city and nearby scenic drives. A once sympathetic black cop now categorized the inhabitants as "some nasty people."

On May 18, with only one third of the planned two hundred plywood dwellings completed and the overnight population already estimated at 1,800, Bernard Lafayette, SCLC program administrator, produced, in Young's view, a "snafu" by indicating that the campaign was already in serious financial trouble, to the tune of $3 million. Actually, according to Young, the deficit was closer to $84,000.

A more serious development was the removal of Jesse Jackson from his job as Resurrection City manager. One rainy day he had led a crowd of about a hundred to the Agriculture Department. There they ate lunch in the cafeteria, running up a bill of $292.61, and left without paying, saying it was a tiny part of what the government owed to the poor. Attorney-General Ramsey Clark had protested to Abernathy.

Jesse Jackson actually lived in Resurrection City, and he was extremely popular with its inhabitants. Some were saying that if Jackson were the leader, they might already have gotten somewhere. Jackson's presence was simply too divisive. He had to go.

So on May 31, Young announced that Jackson was being sent back to Chicago on a field assignment that was "in no sense a demotion." Hosea Williams came up from Georgia to take Jackson's place as the "direct action leader." (Jackson eventually resigned from SCLC.)

No sooner had the Jackson brouhaha been settled than Bayard Rustin erupted. The centerpiece of the direct action in the campaign was to have been a giant demonstration by hundreds of thousands on Solidarity Day. Bayard Rustin was appointed specifically to coordinate this march, set for June 19. But on June 6 Rustin suspended his activities and gave SCLC one day to clarify confusion over the march. Rustin also issued a statement that was a modification of the campaign's original goals to a form that he thought was more easily attainable—that is, palatable to Congress.

By this time, through all the campaign's idealism, the basic obstacle was becoming clear: Congress's lack of response. The poor people, especially black poor people who dominated the campaign, did not as yet represent much in the way of votes or of campaign funds. As lobbyists, they were far different from the smooth, well-heeled men to whom the lawmakers were accustomed. As scattered acts of violence and threats of violence increased, the letters that the congressmen received, calling for "law and order" or asking whether the mules were being treated right, took precedence over feeding the nation's poor.

Rustin's revised goals not only upset some SCLC officials, but also enraged the more militant participants in the campaign. They called him "a sellout to the white liberal establishment." Hosea Williams called the modifications "a bunch of foolishness," and Abernathy said Rustin had issued them without consulting him. Rustin replied that he had tried to reach Abernathy and, failing that, had cleared them with Andrew Young. Abernathy replied that Young was "only the executive vice-president of the SCLC." ("Abernathy," one Administration official said, "has lost control of the thing and is bobbing along like a cork in the current.")

Sterling Tucker, a D.C. Urban League official, replaced Rustin, and Solidarity Day took place as scheduled, with 50,000 demonstrators, but it made no deeper impression on Congress than any of the other actions. The mule train arrived at last and was waiting just outside the city, but Young announced that it was not brought in to march on Solidarity Day because it would have caused too much confusion. By this time many were grumbling that SCLC had already expended entirely too much effort and money on the damned mules.

Meanwhile, the other marches were getting out of hand, forming and unfolding spontaneously out of impatience with the leadership and having predictably undesired results. Back on May 30, a group of Indians and others stormed the Supreme Court building, broke windows, and forced entry into a basement room filled with file cases before the security guards pushed them back out. The afternoon after Solidarity Day, eighty were arrested for sitting in at the Agriculture Department. Those not arrested were returning to the city when they tangled with the police, who unleashed a barrage of tear gas.

Resurrection City's days were numbered. In Congress, of the seventy-five bills that were submitted to accomplish the city's demise, one cleared committee. It would have closed down the city on June 16. Young spoke out: "If they close down the city they might have to close down America." But now, after having extended the camping permit, the government left no doubt that it would enforce its deadlines, and the "City of Hope," already sodden with rain, frustration, and fury, ended in a welter of curses, broken glass, brandished cudgels, wrecking bars, and proud mottoes tramped out of sight in the mud by police boots.

On the twenty-third, the day the permit expired, a white visitor was robbed inside the city and shot in the knee. Earlier, four white youths had been invited inside and were similarly beaten and robbed. Their assailants, the victims said, did not appear angry, but seemed to be acting "more like they were carrying out an obligation."

On June 24, Reverend Abernathy led a column of marchers to the Capitol where he was arrested with 300 others. Escaping arrest at the Capitol were 150 of his youthful followers, who fled uptown to 14th Street. There, in that most militant of riot corridors, they provided the long-feared spark. Looting and smashing broke out, and National Guard troops had to be called in. For now the dream was shattered.

Andrew Young was left behind to preside over the razing of Resurrection City. "We got too bogged down in Resurrection City and wasted a lot of energy here," he said, in a mood quite different from that of a few weeks earlier. "In one sense," he continued, "whoever it was who ran us out of here maybe did us a real favor."

The Poor People's Campaign did not end with the dismantling of Resurrection City. While Abernathy was in jail, Young kept taking up the slack with his reduced forces. In his ears rang the desperate cries of the youths fleeing from the doomed city: "We're going to see Stokely. If you're interested in Black Power, come with us. We're sick of this nonviolent stuff."

The philosophy of nonviolence, already challenged before the campaign, seemed to be collapsing. If SCLC left Washington in defeat, "we'd immediately be written off that we can't make it without Martin Luther King," Young said. The problem was that without King "people will accept what we say but they will not accept us. . . . They have not demonstrated a willingness to take us seriously." Yet Young, as always, was optimistic. "Look who we're fighting," he said. "Even Russia doesn't have the confidence and power to take on the United States government and that is exactly what we're trying to do. . . . We don't have to win this one. We just have to show we can do battle. . . . By February or March we'll be back with something else."

Two days after the riots and the closing, Young bitterly attacked Agriculture Secretary Orville Freeman for returning to the Treasury $227 million of unspent customs receipts that were supposed to be spent on surplus food distribution programs. Young was shocked that Freeman could not find the authority to spend the money to feed the millions of Americans who were starving. The government also seized the twenty-four-mule train, on the grounds that the mules were not being cared for properly. Young contended that they did so because the mules "were attracting too much attention."

Young had announced a demonstration of 300 clergymen from the Philadelphia area, to be held the day after Resurrection City closed, but it failed to materialize. Now, from his jail cell, Abernathy cried out anew for help from his fellow ministers. Finally, on June 30, Young was able to lead 500 clergymen, nuns, and ex-residents of Resurrection City on a silent march around the Capitol, one of seven such planned circlings to match the number of times that Joshua led the Israelites around the walls of Jericho. Meanwhile, his denomination, the United Church of Christ, asked its 7,000 loçal churches to contribute up to 5 percent of their parish budgets to help fight poverty.

Abernathy vowed to carry on the Poor People's Campaign at the two presidential political conventions that were coming up, and he tried. At the Republican convention in Miami Beach, he made a number of appearances but with little effect. And though the mules made a showing in Chicago at the Democratic gathering, that convention was so harried by other urgencies, inside and outside, particularly the struggle between the anti-war demonstrators and the Chicago police, that the poor people never had a chance to be heard.

In May 1969, SCLC staged a second "Poor People's Campaign" lasting only a week. In an intensive lobbying effort SCLC tried to wrest from the Nixon Administration commitments to guarantee incomes for the unemployed, make food stamps free, and make available $2.5 billion "to wipe out hunger." The effort failed. Daniel P. Moynihan, Nixon's assistant for urban affiars, thought the talks had gone well, and was astounded at Abernathy's disappointment.

Abernathy had no time to explain his disappointment to Moynihan. Between arrests, he was too busy in a struggle that he and Andrew Young were waging in Charleston, South Carolina.

The Charleston campaign is important because it was the first that SCLC undertook that hadn't been originally planned by King. SCLC pursued it vigorously and before long secured a triumph that was as clear as any that King had achieved. It was also important because the unions, especially the Teamsters and the United Auto Workers, poured hundreds of thousands of dollars into SCLC's coffers just when the money was needed most. This was the first time that a major national union threw its full weight behind a SCLC campaign.

Charleston was also to be Young's swan song with the organization.

In Charleston, 500 black workers, mostly women, employed in such nonprofessional slots as cooks, nurses aides, and orderlies, were conducting a strike at two hospitals, one run by the county and the other by the state. The issues were much the same as with the sanitation workers in Memphis. The main thing the workers wanted was recognition of their union, though as part of their long-range plan they were also interested in improvement of their base pay of $1.30 an hour. By the time that Abernathy addressed his first church rally, on March 31, 1969, Charleston had already experienced several unexplained hospital fires, charges of police brutality, and over a hundred arrests.

SCLC had seldom been in a contest involving so many groups. Aligned with the striking workers were the fledgling union chapter, Local 1199B of the Drug and Hospital Workers Union, at least two other, larger unions, Charleston's black population, and SCLC, and they were encouraged at the outset by the first joint statement of all the major civil rights groups (except SNCC) since King's death.

On the opposing side were the hospital administrations and the governor's office, and they received some support from the Charleston City Council, in the person of its chairman, J. Mitchell Graham, the state legislative body, and South Carolina's national congressmen.

Caught somewhere in the middle were Charleston's mayor, J. Palmer Gaillard, its businessmen, clergy, and police, the National Guard, and the U.S. Department of Health, Education, and Welfare.

Still, it was basically a contest between Governor Robert E. McNair and the SCLC leadership.

For Abernathy and Young, although the physical stresses were great, their philosophy was simple, straightforward, and easily followed. After employing techniques tested and proved over fifteen years, they would agree to anything that satisfied the workers.

For McNair it was not so easy. The hospitals were resisting on the ground that the law prohibited state agencies from recognizing and negotiating with unions representing public employees. Governor McNair backed this stand unequivocally. He remained faithful to the State's anti-union tradition. One of eighteen states with right-to-work laws, South Carolina had been highly successful in attracting industries.

Abernathy and Young came to Charleston on the wings of inspiration. The debacle of Resurrection City was almost a year behind them, and in the interim the SCLC leadership had experienced a revitalization. In an attempt to "bury King" and thereby start moving on their own, Young had suggested that they submit to exorcism by close psychological self-examination.

So in the late fall of 1968 he invited a psychiatrist and a psychologist, both black and working in San Francisco, to come to Atlanta. The SCLC leaders removed the beds from a room in Paschal's Motor Hotel, put cushions on the floor, and locked themselves in for two twelve-hour days. In the ensuing encounter sessions they confessed their shortcomings and their fears and gave and suffered severe psychic chops. Among other things Abernathy revealed an envy of King. Young admitted that his workload was too heavy because, in part, he was too jealous of his prerogatives to share it with others. Nothing (it is claimed) was too private—sexually, racially, or otherwise—to escape scrutiny. It was a remarkably revealing session for all concerned. The exchanges between Young and Hosea Williams—still unrevealed—were probably the most interesting and important of all.

On April 22, when the strike was a month old, Abernathy set out at the head of 700 marchers, ready to go to jail at once. (Young, as usual, prepared to direct things on the outside.) Failing of arrest, Abernathy tried again on the twenty-fifth, this time leading a crowd of 3,000 to the Medical College Hospital in defiance of an injunction against the union's conducting large demonstrations. After a brief, courteous palaver with the police chief, he was duly packed into a patrol car.

"If the union is recognized, we will go home," Young promised. But the hospital relented only to the point of offering to rehire the first twelve workers who had walked out.

On April 30, Coretta King led a force of 2,000 to the Medical College, where, exuberant, they knelt, sang, and prayed. Meanwhile spirits rose elsewhere in Charleston: Governor McNair called in the

National Guard, posting a hundred men in the streets to guard against "the danger of fires, vandalism, break-ins, and other harm which may come to persons and property."

All along, while Abernathy was in jail and Governor McNair was trying to hold the anti-union line, Young and others were working for a settlement. On May 1, Young announced that SCLC was willing to drop its demands for union recognition in exchange for the rehiring of the workers, some form of job security, and recognition of some kind of employees' organization. He received no reply from the opposition. Several days later the city's growing tension erupted in incidents of rock-throwing, window-breaking, fire-bombing attempts, and other acts of vandalism. Abernathy left jail to lead another march of 2,000 supporters.

By mid-May the South Carolina General Assembly showed signs of wanting to see the affair ended because of increased pressure from their black constituents. The hospitals were believed ready to start serious talks, but Governor McNair was still adamant.

After a second frustrating meeting between the Governor and the workers, SCLC escalated agin. They conducted a gigantic "Mother's Day March" of 12,000 through Charleston. Included were five Democratic Congressmen, including Allard Lowenstein. On the day of this march, Walter Reuther of the United Auto Workers gave SCLC a check for $10,000 and promised $500 more a week.

A few days later it came out that in Charleston there was, indeed, a state agency, the South Carolina Port Authority, that for years had been dealing with a union, an organization of railway workers at the docks. Thus there was precedent for bargaining with the black hospital workers. And the state budget men were getting uneasy. It was costing $10,000 a day to keep the guardsmen in Charleston.

SCLC never let up. On May 30, Coretta King and Abernathy addressed a nighttime crowd of 4,500 in a football stadium. Young disclosed plans for the type of "hydraulics" that had worked in Birmingham. After daily "shop-ins," in which long columns of demonstrators would wind through the aisles disrupting sales but not buying anything, the message would be transmitted through the businessmen to the Establishment.

As Young later disclosed, on June 5 a committee representing the workers and the hospitals' boards of trustees met secretly and made commitments for a settlement. Governor McNair approved them on June 10, but when asked about this, McNair would only say, "No comment."

This agreement probably fell apart because Representative L.

Mendel Rivers and Senator Strom Thurmond intervened. The U.S. Department of Health, Education and Welfare had added to the pressure on the hospitals by ordering the Medical College not only to rehire the workers but also to improve its racial attitudes. This was the result of a study that had been started long before the strike. The Congressmen visited HEW Secretary Robert Finch and persuaded him to delay a cutoff of federal funds till complete verification could be made of HEW's findings.

As the strike ended its third month, the International Longshoreman's Union disclosed that it was entering the struggle. In sympathy for the hospital workers, it threatened to close down the port of Charleston, the Atlantic seaboard's fifth largest port. The pressure on the South Carolinians thus became unbearable.

The evidence is that on June 20 at least half a settlement was reached. Much of this agreement was achieved through Andrew Young's search for common ground with the opposition. He found it in the son of Dr. William McCord, the president of the Medical College. The son had been a missionary, and having once wanted to be a missionary himself, Young was able to gain considerable rapport with Dr. McCord.

Unfortunately, something unexpected happened. That night Abernathy and Hosea Williams started out on a march with about 400 supporters and were arrested. Youthful black supporters did not like the way the SCLC leaders were hauled away, and they assaulted the guardsmen and police with bricks, rocks, and boards. Abernathy and Williams, picked up for the familiar parading without a permit, found themselves later charged with a felony—inciting to riot—the most serious charge that Abernathy had ever faced.

The settlement hung fire. A curfew, which had been imposed and then lifted, was reimposed. The acts of violence continued. One morning around this time Young woke up to find that someone had vandalized his car.

Abernathy went on a fast. This landed him in the hospital for treatment of the ulcers that he shared with Stokely Carmichael, James Forman, and so many other civil rights workers. (Though not with Andrew Young. Young's exercise habits, carried forward from his school athletics, stood him in good stead through the strains of the civil rights movement. In addition, he had begun to follow the well-known dietary recommendations of Adele Davis, with yeast supplements, etc.)

On June 27, the strike at the Medical College ended. The terms included a grievance procedure in which one employee could bring along another employee, and that, essentially, constituted de facto recognition of the union. In addition, all striking employees were to be rehired, and there would be a credit union, which would permit a payroll dues checkoff. Young and the other leaders of SCLC and the workers gathered in Abernathy's cell, where it was decided that, though his bond had been decreased from $50,000 to a more manageable $5,000, Abernathy would stay in jail till an agreement had also been reached with the Charleston County Hospital. Young suggested that they all kneel and sing "We Shall Overcome" in the cell. The next day he was in a pulpit explaining the situation.

"You remember when you all walked out of the Medical College Hospital, those people at the County Hospital said, 'We'll help you,' and they walked out too?"

"That's right."

"Well then, it wouldn't be right for us to go back to work and forget about them."

"That's right!"

The Charleston County Hospital said that of its seventy-one striking workers, it would rehire only thirty-nine, while the others would be taken on in two other hospitals. It turned out that they had already hired sixty replacements and had promised them permanent status. To keep both sets of workers would cost $250,000. The strikers said take all or none.

Abernathy finally left jail, in time for Independence Day, saying that he was leaving matters to the good offices of Charleston and returning to Atlanta. When he came back, it would be to "demonstrate or celebrate."

At last, with SCLC having suspended its demonstrations for some time, but with new tensions building in Charleston as the summer wore on, the other half of the strike ended. Forty-two of the workers were invited back, and the City Council promised to make "every effort" to rehire the others within three months.

After Charleston, Abernathy and Young repeated their success with much more ease in Baltimore and, after a twelve-week strike, in Memphis. But as the first day of the new decade approached, Andrew Young found himself an extremely tired assistant to an even more fatigued leader of an exhausted organization. Charleston was in some ways more remarkable than several of SCLC's previous campaigns; yet it was destined, along with the other hospital campaigns of 1969, to be obscured behind the picture of SCLC's fadeaway.

"We're not really strong enough to take on any national issues like Birmingham or Selma," Young said now. "We're not healthy."

One problem was money. Young pointed out that although SCLC had taken in $1.6 million in 1969, as much as in any year when they weren't conducting a major campaign, they had so many smaller projects going that they had spent $2 million. Also, the recent elections had channeled to peace candidates funds that SCLC might normally have received.

Another factor was the physical toll. Abernathy had been in the hospital suffering from pneumonia as well as ulcers; Jesse Jackson had sickle cell anemia; Hosea Williams had spent months fighting bronchial pneumonia. In addition, some of the staff members were getting tired of constant movement and agitation and were ready to settle down. "There are a lot of personal adjustments going on inside the organization," Young said. "But we know that we are going to go on for another ten or fifteen years, and there's no need to plunge ahead blindly because we see the job as really just beginning."

Perhaps. But with the new decade the times were clearly changing.

In Atlanta the black population formed a large part, as much as 40 percent, of an important congressional district, the Fifth. White liberals made up another large part of the electorate. Andrew Young was interested.

For two years Young had served Abernathy, and striking out on his own was not easy. Later Abernathy made this poignant statement: "Dr. King . . . was never alone because I was always there. And I thought that I would never be alone. And the person that I looked forward to really standing with me all the way was Andrew Jackson Young. But it did not work out that way."

In early 1970 Young sounded out Julian Bond, a native Atlantan who had been a Georgia state legislator for several years, as to whether he intended to run for the seat. Bond answered, in effect, "Be my guest."

On March 3, 1970, Andrew Young formally announced his entry into the Democratic primaries. Among those at his side were Coretta King, Bond, and several members of the Alliance for Labor Action, including representatives from the Teamsters and the United Auto Workers. To give full time to campaigning, after nine years Andrew Young resigned from the Southern Christian Leadership Conference.

The Lions in the Arena

THE NOMINATION

Julian Bond was one of those slick nigger bucks,
  Like Stokely and—somewhere between these two—Andrew Young, except that Bond
  Never stole no hubcaps or tried to sneak bluffs past envious whites.
  Julian Bond was born to be an academic, an individualist, bred to place no one higher than himself, and gently of course, taught to consider
  No one lower.
  In the 1890s a grandfather
  Went to the Supreme Court to try to eliminate segregation in the Kentucky schools. In 1954 Bond's father, Horace Mann Bond,
  Helped write the brief in the celebrated case of *Brown v. Board of Education.*
  Julia Washington Bond, his mother, held two masters degrees.
  The Bonds
  Were black studies in themselves.
  Julian. Bond, the oldest son, wrote poetry, was anthologized several times, seemed to be following in the footsteps of distinguished forebears,
  Until he met two Kings—
  M.L. King, Jr., hero of Montgomery, teacher of philosophy at Morehouse,
  Reading the first sentence of the day's passage, reciting the rest from memory, and spending the remainder of the session rapping on civil rights;
  And Lonnie King, no relation to M.L., seeing black students like

themselves conducting sit-ins in North Carolina and deciding it would be a good thing for Atlanta: "You take one side and I'll take the other," said football hero to poet. "We'll run up and down the tables."

"Why me?" asked Horace Mann Bond's son, who feared violence more than was good for the nonviolent.

He was arrested the very first time, and deciding that ten hours were enough,

He never went to jail again, Julian Bond,

Six-feet-one, retaining far into adulthood the face of the cute, good-natured infant who never needed to be spanked, sonorous straight-talker,

The peachfuzz prince.

COHAR, the Atlanta Committee on Student Rights, founded by himself and Lonnie King, 4,000 students trained in sit-ins, kneel-ins, and picketing

Was soon absorbed into a bunch of fire-eaters called SNCC, a group that instructor M.L. King, Jr., helped breathe into being,

Bringing together the students at Shaw University in 1960 and for a time warming himself against their fire.

But Julian Bond seldom went into the bushes

Like Stokely. He was appalled by threats, guns, and the still supple lynch ropes. Instead he worked out of Atlanta as SNCC's PR man and eventually became its highest paid official

At seventy-five dollars a week,

Sired four children in the accepted manner of the big-timers (King, Carter, Young, Abernathy),

And in 1965 entered politics

In a black Atlanta district Bond won easily

And was about to take his seat in the Georgia House when John Lewis first had this statement to read:

We are in sympathy with and support the men in this country who are unwilling to respond to a military draft which would compel them to contribute their lives to United States aggression in Vietnam in the name of the "freedom" we find so false in this country.

When Julian Bond would not disavow this sentiment and his comrades of five fearful years,

He was refused his seat. In a year he won two more elections for the same seat but considered giving up the incredibly bitter fight, quit SNCC when Stokely started taking things somewhere else, and finally,

Like his daddy
And his granddaddy,
Took his case to the United States Supreme Court.
The crackers who had barred him from the state house and then refused to be sworn in with him
Made Julian Bond the best known state legislator of all.
In 1968 he carried a toothbrush to the Democratic National Convention in Chicago, intending
Only to protest Lester Maddox's control of the Georgia delegates, and won again, helped crush the unit rule, and Lester, another ol' baby-face, had to divvy up the delegates with this uppity young buck,
And
While Dick Gregory was outside yelling through a bullhorn to the Yippies and the other anti-war demonstrators, *Tell them we're going to our fathers' house, tell them . . .*
And while the Chicago police left blood in the streets and SCLC's mules, almost unnoticed, completed a weary circuit around the convention hall,
And while Hubert Humphrey was losing the presidency before leaving the building with the nomination,
Julian Bond became the first black man to have his name offered up for the vice-presidency.
Throughout America hearts fluttered as the bright-eyed, curly-haired, ineluctably urbane Georgian stepped to the mikes and said, *I deeply appreciate the honor of having my name placed in nomination. Unfortunately, I have not yet reached the age and must therefore ask that my name be removed.*
He became the darling of the liberals, timber for a presidential dreamboat, and in the next few months made two hundred speeches, developed a paunch,
Went home to Atlanta as the South's foremost black politician,
The dangerous cherub always ready to lend his weight to the solid, lesser-known causes—the Black Coalition, the Southern Election Fund, the Southern Poverty Law Center—
Yet remaining ever one of those wary, suspicious SNCC dudes
Who lacked the thing that the hero of Montgomery had aroused in others, especially in Andrew Young,
Not the ambition to be elected Congressman from Georgia, appointed ambassador to the United Nations, or considered America's most powerful black man,

So much as the willingness to seek out and grab the biggest picture in sight
Having never ceased being the sensitive, blood-abhorring poet,
the individualist,
And never one to sit for long at anyone's feet.

Chapter Ten

BRIGHT DAY IN THE MORNING

IN HIS EFFORTS from March through November of 1970 to get the eligible voters of Atlanta to register and then to vote for him, Andrew Young did not have much time to look at the other Georgia races. If he had, he might have thought it Old Home Week.

Young's own opponent in the Democratic primaries was Lonnie King, who had been a civil rights compliance officer for HEW, head of the Atlanta NAACP, and before that had teamed up with Julian Bond to organize the early Atlanta student sit-ins. Hosea Williams was running in the Republican primaries for secretary of state, and his wife, Juanita Terry Williams, was in the race for comptroller-general. C. B. King of the original Albany movement was running for governor, as was J. B. Stoner, an old nemesis from the St. Augustine days. (His platform was "I am a racist.") Also in that contest was an erstwhile moderate state senator from southwest Georgia, Jimmy Carter, who was swinging to the right in order to break past the front runner, ex-Governor Carl Sanders.

Hosea Williams and Julian Bond had set up a group called the Black Coalition, with visions of a massive, state-wide black slate. Such a ticket had failed to materialize, but the Coalition was raising funds to support Juanita Williams, C. B. King, and D. F. Glover, who aspired to be lieutenant-governor. The Coalition hoped to benefit from Young's proven expertise in organization and fund drives. Politicians all over the state considered it a particularly damaging blow to C. B. King that now those resources were all to be channeled into Young's own campaign.

It all seemed to fall on Hosea Williams, who also had one further problem. With Young gone, SCLC would not accept Williams's resignation. For that reason he withdrew from the primaries just before election day.

The incumbent in Georgia's Fifth Congressional District was Fletcher Thompson, a conservative Republican, and Young broke from the gate charging that Thompson had provided no leadership to either the blacks or the whites of Atlanta. From the first Andrew Young ran his campaign as if he knew what he was doing, though later he felt that it had suffered from a lack of direction. With six months to go before the primaries, he devoted much of his time, up until about August, to recruiting workers, including many white students, and conducting voter registration drives. He held many street rallies and get-out-the-vote parades through black neighborhoods.

His role as a spokesman for SCLC had left him unusually well equipped for campaign rhetoric. He predicted early that he would be "the most powerful freshman who ever walked into Congress." He had helped draft his share of civil rights bills and had always either accompanied King, or been one of his chief delegates in the high councils, so that there was "not a senator or congressman with any power that I don't already know or have a rapport with."

A black man, Maynard Jackson, had recently been elected vice-mayor of Atlanta, getting votes of whites as well as blacks, and Young called this a "new force" in Atlanta that would help elect him, too. Included in this new force were poor whites and blue-collar white workers. Though these people were working harder, they were earning less; they would vote for someone like himself who would give them "some new leadership and talk about the issues."

The Vietnam War was still a major issue in congressional elections. In May a group of college educators formed a national antiwar coalition called the Universities Antiwar Fund, selected eighteen candidates for the House and the Senate whose views they favored, and contributed, for starters, $50,000 to their primary campaigns. One of the recipients was Andrew Young, who had publicly opposed the war from the first.

Young's prestige gave him access to other funds from far beyond the boundaries of Atlanta. This led to attacks from his primary opponents. The rest of the field consisted of Lonnie King, and two whites: Ray Gurley, a realtor and ex-evangelist, and Wyman C. Lowe, an attorney and ex-Army officer. Young and King differed from Lowe and Gurley not only in skin color, but also in age. Both the black candidates were in their thirties; the whites were in their late sixties. Gurley however, had one thing in common with Young: both had been preachers.

Lowe, a perennial bachelor, was a pugnacious little man who had been running for political office for the last twenty-four years, trying to win that same congressional seat. Nine times he had entered; three times he had withdrawn; six times he had been beaten. But now, glimpsing only the two black candidates, he smelled the sweet scent of victory. "The black vote," he raged, "is a set vote, a fixed vote, and a manipulated vote." And he, Wyman Lowe, was the only man who could beat Republican Fletcher Thompson. Lowe really felt put upon when Ray Gurley announced. Gurley and incumbent Fletcher Thompson lived around the corner from each other. Their wives were good friends. Gurley's candidacy was a trick, Lowe argued, to split the white Democratic vote and enable Thompson to win by beating the eventual black winner of the primary.

Gurley denied the charge. He shared Young's vigorous opposition to the Vietnam war, but he was remarkable chiefly in that he would accept no campaign contributions. It was from that point of view that Gurley joined in the most concerted attack against Young.

Lowe, as usual, was the angriest. "Enormous blocks of money," he said, were financing Young's campaign from "New York, Los Angeles, and Detroit." By contrast he estimated that in all his years of running (and losing) he had spent a total of only $50,000. Lonnie King charged that Young had given his out-of-town contributors the impression that he was the only black man in the race.

Young remained calm. He said he wished he had the kind of money that his opponents were mentioning; in fact, his Georgia contributions "probably by far exceeded" his funds from out of state. When Lonnie King mentioned that Sammy Davis, Jr., was going to hold a benefit for Young in Washington, Young brought up the fact that King already had had a "little benefit" of his own in Washington. Was King criticizing him for having a better benefit?

Young had entered the race several weeks after Lonnie King, because he felt his chances of winning were better, but once he was in the race Young showed uneasiness. He was far more comfortable dealing with his white opponents than with King. King pointed out that he was a near life-long resident of Atlanta, whereas Young had lived in the city for about ten years. Lonnie King had been baptized by Martin Luther King, had gone to jail with him, had been married by him. He asked the black voters to remember that while Young was still figuratively wet behind the ears, he, the younger man, had organized 3,000 people to picket and sit in at stores throughout Atlanta. (He didn't mention the relatively quiescent years he had spent since then, mostly in Washington, while Young had been running one difficult campaign after another.)

Lonnie King directed most of these appeals to the black community. Young, working from the base of his SCLC and labor support, and his endorsements by most of the top black leaders, including Abernathy and Martin Luther King's entire family, carried his campaign into the white and black districts impartially. "This is not going to be a vote for a black man or a white man, but a good man," was his motto. A key issue, he said, was Thompson and how long Atlanta could survive and grow "without a representative in Congress." (Among other things, Thmpson had seldom been seen in black neighborhoods.) Young opened four headquarters, as many as all his opponents put together, with five paid staff members and 200 enthusiastic volunteers.

The media tended to look on it as a Young-King race, with Lowe hungrily looking on from the sidelines. Having gained in the past as much as 46 percent of the vote, he was thought to have a chance to beat Young. But neither Gurley nor the idea that he was a Thompson tactic to cancel out Lowe was taken seriously. Why would incumbent Thompson worry about a six-time loser?

With the approach of fall, the race heated up for Andrew Young. Back on April 15, ABC-TV had telecast—not in Atlanta—a thirty-minute documentary about the Black Panthers. In it Young gave an interview that was so interesting to Thompson that he was trying to get a copy. Thompson quoted Young as saying, "Western technology and Western militarism has interfered with the right or the possibility of, say, democracy in Latin America, or real freedom in Africa or Asia. . . . If the white West is incapable of brotherhood with the colored peoples, then that small body of colored peoples, black people within the white West, may be the revolutionary vanguard that God has ordained to destroy the whole thing." When asked if he would support the destruction of Western civilization "if you were convinced that the rest of the world would thereby be liberated?" he answered, "I probably would."

Lowe pounced on this answer as proof that Young was unfit for the office. Young replied that the remarks were taken out of context, for he had immediately added, "I really believe that Western civilization and especially Western technology and business and management skills are the key to feeding the hungry of the world and providing medical care and economic development."

However, although the conservative black newspaper *The Atlanta World* thought an explanation was needed, these remarks do not appear to have kicked up much of a fuss. Atlantans were beginning to have other concerns. For instance, there were quite a few people who, while looking at their beloved Chattahoochee, the "River of Flowered Stones," were becoming concerned with ecology. To them the problem went far beyond the power of groups like the Panthers or the Weathermen to overthrow anything. Andrew Young got their message. And perhaps they got his. If, as seemed likely, the longest-lasting legacy of Western civilization was to be untold tons of radio-active garbage that would remain deadly to most forms of life for many times longer than all of recorded history, then maybe a little less Western civilization was just the ticket. However, the four Democratic primary candidates ended the campaign concerned not with Western civilization but with issues like inflation and the war. They all viewed inflation as a principal threat, and they all wanted to end the war.

Lonnie King assured the electorate that he was the only one who could beat Thompson "because he can't pull out all the stuff that will polarize the community on me like he could on Andy."

Young said he was confident of victory. "The question is whether I can win it big enough without a runoff."

Lowe repeated his conviction that he was the only one who could beat Thompson, and he predicted that if he won the primary, he would receive as many black votes as Young or King.

Gurley called himself the candidate of the "silent majority" and, referring to Young, said that "a candidate who is not able to pay his own way would make a weak Congressman."

Over in the Republican primaries, Fletcher Thompson was running unopposed.

In the 1970 Democratic primary for the Fifth Congressional District the outcome was 34,330 votes for Young, 21,586 for Lowe, 8,102 for Gurley, and 7,997 for King. Young now faced a runoff against Wyman Lowe. (In this second try for the governor's seat, Jimmy Carter was in the same situation. In an upset that lifted a lot of brows, he collected 48 percent of the votes to only 38 percent for Sanders, and they were in a runoff too. C. B. King came in a distant third.)

Instead of girding himself for Thompson, Young now had to take a close look at Wyman Lowe and at what had happened at the polls. Nothing had gone according to plan. He had gained more white votes than expected, actually beating Lowe by over a hundred votes in conservative Sandy Springs. This led him to discount damage by the Thompson charges that he was "un-American" or a Black Panther.

On the other hand, he had not received the black support on which he was depending. Lonnie King had not taken away those votes. Instead, Young reasoned, black people, not wanting to agonize over choosing between him and King, had stayed at home.

Gurley immediately threw his support to Lowe. He combined two charges by saying that Young had spent $170,000, with most of it coming from "white panthers" in New York, Chicago, and Washington. "That boy," he said, "is just not what I would call a true American." Gurley claimed that some of Young's people had threatened him, until, at age sixty-eight, he "offered to meet them anywhere and let them choose their weapons," whereupon, he said, "they took off like rabbits leaving a cut wheatfield."

Lowe similarly tried to equate Young with violence, charging that the Black Panthers were behind Young's candidacy and that his workers had bought guns at a local motel.

Meanwhile Young was adding to his support people like Ben Brown; Leroy Johnson; the famous Atlanta educator, Dr. Benjamin Mays; and the Atlanta vice-mayor, Maynard Jackson; as well as Lonnie King, who said that the main thing was to beat Thompson. Young didn't take Lowe seriously, he said, because "he is incoherent most of the time." The only problem he saw was getting out a heavy vote because he expected the segregationists to come to the polls in large numbers.

Lowe certainly sounded incoherent at times. He said he was going to station "burly guards" at every black precinct, with orders to beat up any wrongdoers.

"Mr. Lowe passes himself off as being interested in law and order, and now he's trying to bring mob rule to the polling places," Young commented. Lowe said he would send in "defenseless black women" to observe the voting and then install his "burly guards" after 7:00 P.M. "The shortage of black votes in Mr. Lowe's column was probably more an assessment of his ability than a judgment of his color," Young replied.

Lowe charged that Young had spent between $150,000 and $200,-000 while he, in contrast, had spent only $10,000. And calling SCLC a communist-front group with Black Panther members, he tried to associate Young with the communists.

Meanwhile Young tried to make the voters see that their real problems were not Lowe's alleged perceptions of him but the war in Vietnam, the need to revitalize Atlanta's public schools, the economic losses that Atlanta had sustained by not having adequate rail and airport systems, the drug traffic.

This second phase of this election ended with 52,790 votes for Young and 35,471 for Lowe. (Jimmy Carter simultaneously smashed Carl Sanders with 60 percent of the vote, and only Hal Suit, the Republican candidate, stood between him and the Georgia governorship.) The third and most difficult round was about to begin.

Fletcher Thompson had the usual advantages of an incumbent, plus that Black Panther TV documentary with its damaging statements by Young. He had obtained a copy of the film, and he opened his campaign against Young by showing it—minus Young's praise of various aspects of Western civilization, which had been edited out by ABC—to groups of twenty voters each in his campaign offices.

Young was not dismayed. He considered his victory against Lowe a triumph over smears. "Anybody," he said with some understatement, "that knows me at all knows how ridiculous it is to try to say I'm a Black Panther."

"Let's just say this," Thompson answered. "I'm not making these statements. . . . If there's any smearing, he's smearing himself."

Young thought they should be talking about the issues that affected Atlanta—rapid transit, better schools, housing, and health care. "He is doing in fact the very thing he's accusing me of doing," Young elaborated, a little weary of the constant personal attention that he received from his opponents. "It's this kind of politics that has alienated students, that has made blacks lose faith in the political system, and I think has. . . created a lot of the tensions in our society."

The general election was held on Tuesday, November 3, 1970. While Jimmy Carter was overwhelming Hal Suit with 62 percent of the vote, Young's supporters were noting a disappointingly light black turnout. In the end Fletcher Thompson beat Andrew Young handily, with 78,540 votes, or 57 percent, compared to Young's 58,394, or 43 percent. The blacks had failed to go to the polls in the required numbers. Only 56 percent showed up. Most ominous to all those interested in increased black political power was the theory that blacks were too turned off by the system to vote for anybody.

If that was so, Andrew Young was going to be given the opportunity to fight the apathy. In mid-November Atlanta Mayor Howard Massell appointed Young chairman of the Atlanta Community Relations Commission (CRC). It was a job suited to Young's experience and abilities. The CRC was of considerable importance to the black community. As far back as August 1967, an article in *Harper's* by David Halberstam recounted a conversation in which Young spoke of a low-income white community in Atlanta that was turning middle-class black.

And so, of course, as soon as they've moved they all get together and have a big meeting about how to keep the neighborhood clean. . . and they want that garbage picked up, you know all that, and in the middle of the meeting, a man stands up at the back of the room and he tells them they're kidding themselves. "Forget it," he says, "just forget it, because you're not going to get those services. I work for the sanitation department and I want you to know that they've just transferred twenty men out of this area, so you can just forget it all."

Young put his gaughters into a racially balanced school in Atlanta, only to feel that, after three years, their white teachers had been treating them as if they were socially retarded. So, although reluctantly because they wanted their children to learn about both worlds, he and Jean pulled them out and put them in a predominantly black school where they did much better. Every house on Young's block had been burglarized at least once. These were the kinds of problems that Young would now be confronting in more direct ways.

The CRC was an advisory group without any powers of enforcement, one of a number of such city-financed organizations in urban areas with large black populations. The emphasis was on bringing to the attention of the city government any municipal problems, especially those of a racial nature. The CRC members were thus essentially ombudsmen for the people with the authority to do little except, as Young said, "to put Band-Aids on cancers."

When Young was sworn in, he said he would try to place emphasis on the problems of the young, the landlord-tenant relationship, and the consumer. He anticipated his style in later posts by saying he wouldn't fix the agenda; he would consult Nat Welch, the commission's vigorous executive director, and the other CRC members and the advisory council. Under him the CRC would be more than a riot-stopper; its members would push as hard as they could, and it would be up to the mayor and aldermen to rein them in.

He started by taking up the complaints of some citizens who wanted a swimming pool. Since the time was November and the outside temperature below freezing, some though that was an odd thing to worry about. Young quoted Martin Luther King's words: "Our summers of discontent always result from winters of neglect."

Under him, in 1971, the CRC intensified its drive for the hiring of more black and Spanish-speaking police and appointing of more black judges. It asked that real estate signs be banned to discourage "block-busting." The CRC had members who specialized in matters such as garbage collection, but Young got into it by mediating in a sanitation strike and inspecting the facilities. He found matters had become so critical that some of the supervisors were accused of carrying guns. The CRC's recommendation that more blacks be made supervisors was subsequently followed.

Young continued to support MARTA, the rapid rail system. His foresight was borne out a few years later when the system was completed with far fewer delays and initial bugs than those in San Francisco or Washington. He expanded neighborhood representation on the CRC by naming thirty new members in 1971 and thirty-nine more in 1972. Under him the commission compiled an extensive report on bias in the city water department. It looked into the services that were being denied handicapped blacks. It started an extensive program in 1972 aimed at making Atlanta an "open city," meaning that housing would be available to all.

In 1972 Young kept his pledge to help the consumer with the hiring of a full-time consumer affairs specialist. He continued to show his interest in the problems of the young by demonstrating to adults the need to change their attitudes in education. Often, he told them, they were trying to raise children according to the ways in which their parents had raised them. They weren't taking into account the dynamic ways in which society had changed, nor how such changes affected youth. He asked adults to relax their control and let the children advise them. Among its activities the CRC established a young citizens night.

His term on the commission had begun with a proposal by the mayor that the Atlanta Youth Council and other youth groups be merged into the CRC. It ended with Young's repeated admonitions to the young and to Atlantans in general about the problem of drugs in the city. Atlanta, he said, was becoming the hub of drug traffic in the southeast, and he recommended setting up full employment programs. "We have a gigantic hustlers' army of young people creating their own employment because they can't get into ours," he pointed out. He also proposed international police action and the establishment of a National Service Corps in which young people would serve for two years, for example, in hospital, police, or educational work. He avoided a moralistic approach, feeling that to become too righteous about drugs would cloud one's practical thinking, and instead he urged businessmen to focus on the dollars and cents costs of the problem.

The chairmanship of the CRC, which was a nonpaying post, called for Young to work in just the kind of areas in which he had already been involved for years. During his previous campaigning when his experience was questioned, he had been quick to point out that he was called into practically every dispute that arose in the city by both sides. In the late 60s, for instance, he mediated in several labor disputes. Now, his activities merged naturally into his next political campaign. When the spring of 1972 arrived, he merely had to intensify what he had been doing all along.

This time the candidate waiting over on the Republican side and running unopposed in the primaries was Alderman Rodney Cook. (Fletcher Thompson was running for the senate.) In the Democratic field with Young were another black candidate, commercial photographer and Alderman Henry Dodson, and two white candidates, one an Alderman and attorney named Wyche Fowler (only thirty-one years old and Young's most serious threat) and the other a tax consultant named Howell Smith.

From the beginning Young was clearly the man to beat. As usual, everyone else campaigned against him. With the backing of the civic, business, and labor communities, Young always felt that he could win the primary. But he needed to win big if he were to avoid another expensive, strenuous runoff, during which the Republican Cook could leisurely raise a large campaign fund.

Young saw faults in his 1970 campaign that he now meant to correct. He would especially work much harder at getting out the black vote. He couldn't afford to have them stay at home again.

For a long time, till about the final two weeks before the primaries, the candidates campaigned in a low-key manner, pacing themselves. Both Dodson and Fowler took shots at Young's spending. Young called his greater expenses necessary if he was to avoid the divisiveness of a runoff. Fowler, a vigorous man, took exception to Young's assumption of the win. He also criticized the endorsements that Young kept getting, such as from the *Atlanta Constitution,* and called Young the "anointed candidate." Both Fowler and Dodson portrayed Young as the Establishment candidate.

The problem was that Young was the kind of candidate whose back Fowler was far more likely to see than his face. That is, they were likely to find themselves on the same side of any given issue. Fowler was against the guaranteed annual income that McGovern had proposed, but he supported things like an income tax credit of up to $100 a year for property tax payers, a close examination of all tax shelters, a freeze on the price of agricultural products until the prices stopped soaring, government provision of jobs to any able-bodied persons who needed them, and continued public assistance to anyone who needed that. Young said he couldn't seriously argue with any of those stands, but in addition he backed establishing Civilian Conservation Corps-type program and giving business tax incentives to create jobs.

Fowler painted Young as having no experience qualifying him to be a Congressman. The Congress, Fowler said, pointing to his own three years as an alderman, was no place for "on-the-job training." Young in turn questioned Fowler's accomplishments, even with his powers and those of the other eighteen aldermen; Young suggested that, as the chairman of the CRC and having no legislative power at all, he had contributed much more toward solving the city's problems.

As election day drew closer, things heated up, particularly between Young and Dodson, who became abrasive. Dodson viewed Young and Fowler as middle-class candidates who were out of touch with the ghetto's problems. Young saw no serious problems with the city's welfare system; Dodson proposed scrapping it entirely and puting in a new one with fewer bureaucrats. Dodson bitterly opposed MARTA; Young saw it as bringing in $1.4 billion in development and jobs.

One day in mid-July, at Dr. King's Ebenezer Baptist Church, Young suggested that Dodson might be guilty of "corruption." Later he said that corruption might be too strong a word, but there were still some things that had happened "before and during the campaign" that he would be happy to discuss "in a friendly, non-public environment." After a radio program two weeks later on which all the Democratic candidates appeared, when Young wouldn't back off far enough, saying that Dodson had been "picking" at him all through the campaign, Dodson called him a "lying preacher." He also said that maybe Young himself had something to hide; after all, his pretty blue campaign buttons cost sixty-nine cents apiece.

A few days later Dodson charged that Young had demonstrated that he was unfit to be a Congressman by bowing to the pressures of the campaign. The issue was a speech Young had made before an audience at Morris Brown College. During his civil rights days, Young said, "I used to pray that I'd catch one of those crackers one time alone. And I guarantee you that I would not have been nonviolent." Young said he was serious about that. But later, after a debate between Dodson and himself, after the press and most of the audience had left, he made a sort of joke while explaining the remark.

"You know, for ten years I was nonviolent . . . because I was convinced that the destiny of the black community depended on my remaining nonviolent. . . .I am a well-controlled and well-disciplined individual, and when the interests and needs of my community demand that I be nonviolent, I am nonviolent. But when one brother gets me in front of a bunch of white folks and starts loud-talking me and threatening me, I have to just tell him that if he doesn't shut up, I may have to kick his ass."

Dodson promptly seized upon this. "He's running scared," Dodson said, "and a man who is scared makes mistakes. And if I can press him during a political campaign, God only knows what will happen when he gets to Washington."

"If I had it to do over again, I don't know if I would say it," Young answered. "It's a very rare occasion when I use that kind of language. But . . . he's impossible to deal with. I guess I thought that was the kind of language that he would understand."

Wyche Fowler leaped to take advantage of the battle between blacks. "Although we all have such urges," he conceded, "a leader not only learns to control them but also refuses—in a political campaign where emotions run high—to appeal to violent emotions." All along, while Dodson had been emphasizing that he was the one best qualified to represent the black community, Fowler and Young were agreeing that what Atlanta's Congressional seat required was a liberal and that his race should not be a factor. Now Fowler exhibited a letter signed by many of the black leaders who supported Young which said, "Andrew Young is the only black candidate that can be elected to Congress this year." Fowler, claiming that he had never asked anyone to vote for him because he was white, condemned this letter as a direct appeal to race.

The actual arrival of the primaries, held on August 8 that year, was marked by the bizarre. Dodson reported an anonymous phone call from Chicago to the effect that Young might have worked as an undercover agent for the CIA while he was with SCLC. Young responded that Dodson had printed and circulated an endorsement of Young and other candidates by some prominent blacks in which the sample ballot number shown next to Young's name was actually Dodson's number on the official ballot.

All in all, Young had picked up too much strength. In spite of the fact that Young's workers provided up to fifty cars for transportation, only 30 percent of the black voters went to the polls. But the white turnout wasn't much better, and Young still won a smashing victory and avoided the runoff. He received 35,226 votes, or 60.7 percent of the total, while Fowler had only 18,854, or 32.4 percent. Dodson and Smith lagged far behind with totals of 2,995 and 996 respectively.

The Republican candidate, Rodney Cook, was forty-eight, a former alderman and the operator of a one-man insurance agency. He was married and, like Young ("Bo" was not yet around), the father of three children. He was considered a liberal or at least a moderate. Observers considered the race between him and Young to be particularly dramatic because both had recently lost big races, and another loss was likely to be crippling. (Young covered that by saying that he had never been "hellbent on politics" anyhow.) In 1969 Massell had defeated Cook in the mayoral race by 10,000 votes, with Cook attracting little black support.

Despite the nagging problem of low black voter turnout, the fact that Young had taken from Fowler 35 percent of the count in the northern, predominantly white precincts was encouraging. He started door-to-door canvassing in those areas and enlisted the aid of many college students, while in the black neighborhoods, voter registration drives soon added another 5,000 to the rolls. The worsening situation in SCLC, though damaging to the officials there, also served to help him. With SCLC lacking funds to pay its workers, Stoney Cooks, the executive director, and Tom Offenburger, a communications expert, both resigned and started—or picked up again—their long careers in Young's camp.

Young and Cook opposed each other against the backdrop of the 1972 presidential campaign. As the Democratic prospects against the Republican incumbent steadily grew worse, Cook repeatedly tried to link Young to George McGovern and his proposals for generous government assistance to the disadvantaged. Young concentrated on issues like saving the Chattahoochee River, along the city's northwest border, from development and pollution and opposing the disruption of neighborhoods by the construction of more freeways.

Cook kept trying to draw Young out on other issues that he thought would trip up a man courting polarized constituencies. One such issue was busing to achieve racial balance in the schools. Cook said that he opposed forced busing but favored quality education.

Young likewise straddled the question but in more detail. He was against busing, but said he would not vote for an anti-busing bill because it would probably be unconstitutional. He also thought attracting more federal funds, for which he felt well qualified, would be a big help. Cook opposed Senator Edward Kennedy's plan for a program to put health insurance under the federal government. Young said he would probably vote for a national health care system. Young supported the sharing of revenue by the United States Treasury with state and local governments. Cook said he didn't believe the federal government had any revenue to share. Yet he supported increased defense spending; Young said that the days of the arms race were over, and he prophesied that for the next twenty years the battle would be over economics. Cook supported "right-to-work" laws; Young did not.

Their struggle, which remained on a consistently high level throughout, was most clearly seen in their statements on welfare. In the debates that they conducted nightly, Cook kept saying that Young could not "escape responsibility" for McGovern's "giveaway" proposals. Young responded that he didn't think the plans of either McGovern or Nixon would help the situation in Atlanta. He denied that Atlantans had a welfare crisis, and he said quite strongly, "This whole issue of welfare makes people emotional about something that should not be played with. The survival of our blind, elderly, sick, and homeless young children should not be made a political football."

Young emphasized his past achievements as a mediator. Cook said that implied a talent for not alienating people that would hurt a Congressman. "At some point you've got to vote."

"The main role of a Congressman," Young replied, "is to bring together a variety of opinions that a lot of people can support."

Responding to the anxiety about American prisoners, which was becoming almost the only reason why Americans felt the need to stay in Vietnam, Young said that if North Vietnam reneged on any agreements to release the prisoners after a ceasefire, the United States should wage "all-out war with no holds barred." Cook immediately suggested that the man who had stood steadfast with Martin Luther King, Jr., throughout the antiwar protests might be advocating nuclear war, and he said rather pityingly that expecting the return of all the POWs and the MIAs was to ignore "the lessons of history." Instead, Cook favored Nixon's plan for a gradual troop withdrawal. In addition to his regular plan—stop the bombing, arrange a ceasefire, collect the prisoners, and get out—Young recommended that first a C5A cargo plane be used to fly out everybody in South and North Vietnam who wanted the United States to stay. "You probably wouldn't get more than a planeload," he suggested.

Meanwhile, Fletcher Thompson, running for the Senate, was labeled by a Ralph Nader report as the least effective of all Georgia's Congressmen. For a long time he seemed to be running against anti-war activist and actress Jane Fonda instead of against opponent Sam Nunn. He accused Senator Herman Talmadge of ganging up against him with Julian Bond, Mayor Massell, and Governor Carter. Then he stumbled into deep trouble over the use of his congressional mailing privileges. Finally he and Carter were at each other's throats after Carter suggested that he quit his congressional post ahead of time so that a special election could be held to fill his seat.

Thompson didn't resign, and Young and Cook continued campaigning in gentlemanly fashion—until Maynard Jackson, the black vice-mayor, accused Cook of having called Young a "boy." (Jackson later called the story "apocryphal," said he heard that Cook had made the remark in a private conversation, and didn't know for a fact that Cook had said it.) Cook accented his strong denial by claiming Young, himself, had expressed a desire to be "an errand boy" for his constituents. Cook also attacked a letter on Young's campaign stationery calling for his election as Georgia's first black Congressman in modern times. Cook used Wyche Fowler's argument: Young was asking to be elected because he was black. Young commented that the issue could never be avoided. "My race," he said drily, "is an issue every time I walk into a room."

Around the end of October, Young and Stuart Eizenstadt, who was Young's issues coordinator and later became President Carter's top domestic advisor, took strong exception to what they called "fear and hate" ads. In these ads, adjoining columns featured the faces of Cook and Young over contrasting statements on issues like welfare and busing. The picture of Young was particularly unflattering. Cook tried to argue that his own picture was no winner either and that, anyway, everyone in Atlanta already knew that Young was black.

They came down to the wire with everyone agreeing that the race was too close to call. Young's people said that to win, he needed the usual formula: a large black turnout, of which he was expected to get 95 percent, together with about 23 percent of the white votes.

The election was held on Tuesday, November 7, 1972. To the early despair of Young's workers, it was a day of cold rains. Nevertheless, history was about to be made. The South was sending a black man to Congress. The final returns showed Young with 72,289 votes, or 52.8 percent, compared to Cook's 64,495 votes, or 42.7 percent. Despite the rain, the black turnout was about the same as the white, 58 to 60 percent. But besides sweeping the black vote, Young had gained between 30 and 40 percent of the votes in many white precincts. This compared to the average of 20 percent that white Atlantans had given to George McGovern. Young had spent only $10,000 more than Cook, or about $160,000.

Young quickly established the tenor of his next career. He was less impressed with being the first black Congressman from the South since Reconstruction than with being perhaps the first black Congressman who had been elected in a predominantly white district. "This proves what I have said before, that the South is going to have to show the nation how we can live together and work together as brothers."

The Lions in the Arena

DEVOTION

Ralph David Abernathy was always there. When Martin Luther King, Jr., arrived in Montgomery to take up his ministry, he was given his first meal by Abernathy. Fourteen years later, when the rifle cracked, Abernathy, a container of shaving lotion in his hand, was among the first to know that something was amiss.

Abernathy was always there.

In the name of civil rights, the Reverend Ralph David Abernathy saw the insides of various jails thirty-six times, and on seventeen of those occasions he shared his incarceration with Dr. King.

"Violence is the weapon of the weak," Abernathy preached, "and nonviolence is the weapon of the strong. It's the job of the police to use mace on us. It's our job to keep marching. It's their job to put us in jail. It's our job to be in jail."

Ralph David Abernathy was a country boy whose father had somehow amassed five hundred acres in west-central Alabama. The midwife declared that among Willie L. Abernathy's twelve children this would be "the strange one," and his career would be "national and informed." (Abernathy, who lived within legend, can be suspected of creating myth.) Ralph David, the tenth child, eschewed the soil. He studied, ran errands for his mother, taught Sunday school when he was ten, got a degree in mathematics, heeded the Call, and met Martin Luther King, Jr.

"I was told by my daddy not to fight—but if I ever saw a good fight, get in it."

Rosa Parks was one of his flock. The Montgomery Improvement Association that engineered the desegregation of the Montgomery bus system in 1955 was Abernathy's idea.

But they elected King president.

Abernathy didn't mind. He and King became a team. They worked out routines. Abernathy would warm up the crowd with good old home-style preaching, the plain, simple, down-to-earth homilies, the tears. Then King would come sailing along, dangerously close to the tops of heads with concepts from Tillich and Hegel, Carlyle and Gandhi.

When they were arrested, for the first twenty-four hours they would fast, to gain strength. Then King would read and write and Abernathy would provide spiritual support.

It was hard to take a picture of King without including the broader, darker visage of Ralph David Abernathy. In the press conference, King always fielded the questions, while Abernathy amened. Abernathy had been everywhere King had been, had observed and endured to the same degree, and he also had things to report. He was saltier than King, humorous, likely to joke. During his pursuit of civil rights, he was sued for $3 million, had his car taken away and auctioned off, suffered the loss through an unfair judgment of property that he had inherited.

Abernathy was always there—in Oslo for the Nobel Prize, in Berlin to inspect the Wall, at the Vatican for an audience with the Pope, at universities to pick up King's numerous honorary degrees. (Finally Abernathy got one himself and thereafter was pleased to be called "Doctor.")

Dr. Abernathy stoked SCLC's engines while King steered the ship. They reached all the decisions together, and Abernathy had a say over all that were hired and the few that were fired. *Now there's a nice, respectful, sharp young man,* one imagines him musing upon the arrival of the calm, cool, deferential dentist's son, Andrew Jackson Young. But he couldn't see that smoothie in jail, and jail was where it was at—arrests, discomfort, heart trouble, peptic ulcers, phlebitis, fatigue, bail, strategies.

In all the accounts, one never glimpses an outward show of fear in the actions of Ralph David Abernathy.

Often King had presentiments of death. Abernathy thought that when the time came, there would be tickets for two. Hadn't they observed the angel of death winking at them from the faces of Bull Connor, Hoss Manucy, and innumerable rural sheriffs? Wouldn't they head up the celestial path together, arm in arm, at the appointed hour?

Abernathy was always there, ate the same hurried meals, waited in the same airports, bus terminals, courthouses, town squares, watched the same faces florid with hate and the myriad trunks of pitch pines flashing past, swelled to the same applause and ignored the same curses, suffered the same assaults, made himself comfortable in the same cell, expected the same bomb, the same bullet . . .

"He looked at me but he couldn't talk. Still, I'm certain he tried to talk to me with his eyes. He gave me a good, long, solid look as if to say, 'See, Ralph, didn't I tell you it would happen this way?' "

As was his due, after the mule-drawn cart had carried King's body to its rest, Abernathy took up the reins of SCLC. He had his doubts. For seven nights and seven days he fasted, gathering his strength. Hadn't Doc already chosen him for the job years before? If Doc said he could, then he would.

"Dr. King had a dream, but I do not have a dream, I have a vision," Abernathy announced. "I don't have to tell you that I am the leader. Baby, I am going to show you. We will get to the Promised Land. It will happen in my time and under my leadership."

Yet as the new president of SCLC, he impressed hardly anyone. There was too much grit in his craw, his leadership appeared too jerky, his ambition too forced. He couldn't strike fire; it was as if he were using matches still damp with grief. With Andrew Young's help, he won a big one that King hadn't planned, at Charleston. But later Coretta was more interested in raising funds for her own King memorial, Jesse Jackson remained in Chicago with his People United to Save Humanity, and Andrew Young chose politics.

When he tried to step down from SCLC's helm in 1973, Abernathy was applauded back into the post. But times kept changing. Things were tough; they would have been so even for King. The money still wouldn't come in, the antiwar protests had soured the strategy of pouring people into the streets, Watergate swept through, then the energy crisis, and more and more blacks were being voted into office . . .

Andy's handy. He can ride the white horse and the black. I can only ride the black. But I accept that. Even Martin was nimbler—he could ride the white horse while the black was bucking. My black horse is bucking too, but I'll stay up. . . . I must.

In 1977 Abernathy again resigned. He attempted to follow Young into the seat of Georgia's Fifth Congressional District. In the primary he collected just 4.8 percent of the vote.

At last this devoted husband and father of four, security blanket to an immortal, thirty-six times a prisoner in the war against injustice, this "President of the Poor," Ralph David Abernathy, attained his nirvana, after having been denied passage through the turnstile that passed Martin through. He was what he had been in the beginning, what King kept trying to return to but never could, a black Baptist minister attending to the needs of his flock in a southern town.

Greater love hath no man.

Chapter Eleven

THE INSIDE GAME

ANDREW YOUNG'S EXPERIENCE with King's political expectations differed somewhat from Ralph David Abernathy's. Young didn't recall that they often discussed political matters, and he thought King would be surprised at his election. He remembered King's feeling that the first black congressman would most likely come from somewhere in the Black Belt.

The distinction has to be made that while Young was the first black congressman since Reconstruction from Georgia, on the same day some Texans were one-upping Georgia somewhat by electing the South's first black congresswoman of any era, Barbara. C. Jordan. She had been elected in a district that was only one or two percentage points more black than Young's, but with the importance difference that another 15 percent was Mexican-American. Still, her share of the vote, 80 percent, was so high that it meant she, too, had received a large number of white ballots. And thus the two of them arrived in the 93rd Congress together, the cool, hip royalty of black politics.

Shirley Chisholm of New York had already been the first black congresswoman ever, and there were several black congressmen. The difference among them was that Young favored a "New South Coalition." He exhibited a powerful pride in the South, and he and Jordan (as well as Carter) were about to demonstrate that there was, indeed, something special about what the South, in its awakening, could produce politically.

Young and Barbara Jordan lived in the same apartment building, but they seldom visited each other. They were too busy beginning their separate ascents. They had to endure an intense round of welcoming parties. At one, held in the Cannon Office Building, Young

deal, Young did not confine himself to finance, but regularly re-
was not ashamed to tell Rep. Carl Stokes of Ohio, "I haven't learned
yet what the bells mean."

Stokes, then the chairman of the Black Caucus, put an arm
around his shoulders, and they pushed through the crowd to the basement reception room. There a panel of lights blinked above the door.
"Three lights are for a quorum," Stokes said. "Two are for a roll call,
and one is for teller votes."

"I guess I can ignore them for a while since I'm new," Young
said.

"But you gotta be careful you move on that second buzzer!"

Several years later Young revealed that when he and his staff
moved into their congressional offices, they discovered some memos
that Fletcher Thompson had "obligingly" left behind. The memos
were from the FBI to Thompson and covered in detail Young's 1972
campaign appearances. As a footnote, a retired FBI agent told the
House Intelligence Committee that even earlier, during the 1970 race,
he had been assigned to obtain copies of SCLC stationery and the sig-
natures of several of King's associates, including Young. The idea,
apparently, was to use phony letters to cause disruptions within
Young's organization. However, when this was revealed, in 1975,
Young couldn't recall any spurious letters having gone around during
that period.

Young was not too busy being feted and learning the ropes to
neglect his commitments. He made it a point to speak at a church on
the edge of the 14th Street riot corridor where war protestors were
preparing for the second Nixon Inauguration Day. Urging them to
remain nonviolent, he referred to some recent killings in New Orleans by a militant black sniper. "Brother [Mark James] Essex gave
up," he said. Undeterred by some boos that answered the remark, he
went on to stress the virtures of hard work, which was strongly on his
mind following his strenuous campaigns.

It wasn't long before Young was placed on the House Banking
and Currency Committee, a plum assignment for a freshman. The
concerns of the committee, however, were not areas to which he had
devoted much earlier study, and visitors to his office later noticed
shelves of books indicating that he and his staff were taking self-
taught, crash courses in such matters as economics, finance, world
trade, and currencies. This added to the impression of him as a model
freshman congressman, seen but not often heard. Yet, reflecting the
mind-boggling array of subjects with which all congressmen have to

vealed his positions on a wide range of subjects, both local and national.

He had hardly been sworn in when he was joining the equally new Georgia Senator, Sam Nunn, in sponsoring legislation in the extended struggle to make the Chattahoochee River a national park. (One of the best examples of Young's writing is his article, "Chattahoochee: River of Flowered Stones," published in the December 1975 issue of *National Parks & Conservation Magazine.*)

At the end of January he was joining his fourteen black colleagues, the Black Caucus, on the floor of the house, in criticizing Nixon's upcoming State of the Union message and its budgetary proposals. His share of the attack focused on the cutbacks on rural spending, which was not as incongruous for him as it seemed. The large urban centers such as he represented soon felt the impact, in the form of migrations, of rural poverty. "I hope," he said, "Congress will put aside the old rural-versus-urban politics and give united leadership."

He carried on this attack in the spring, saying that the Nixon policies were about to bring on a recession if not a depression. And he tried to point out that he wasn't screaming only on behalf of blacks. Prices for meats and the "fancy packaged materials middle-class white families buy" had jumped, while those for pigtails, neckbones, and hamhocks were still fairly reasonable.

Young's principal interest in these days was rapid transit systems. As a member of the Banking and Currency Committee, he also served on its subcommittees on mass transit, consumer affairs, and international trade and finance. In the works was the Urban Mass Transit Act, which was intended to help systems such as MARTA. Young devised and got early committee approval of an amendment that would allow blacks and other minorities to have a say in the development of the systems. He conceded that the Act was essentially a "big business boondoggle," but he could justify it to the black community, since, if passed, it would pour over $1 billion of federal funds into the Atlanta system. "We're fighting in Atlanta to see to it that we [the black minority] have 30 percent of the jobs, 30 percent of the contracts. Well," he said, "30 percent of a billion and a half dollars is a lot of money."

The Nixon Administration had declared a federal moratorium on financing new housing. Young was disapproving. He pointed out that the moratorium hurt more white people than black through its effect on the building trades and the savings and loan associations.

Meanwhile, in SCLC, conditions were continuing to deteriorate. The question, as Young's aide, Stoney Cooks, aptly put it, was, "In light of these times, what should an organization like this be doing?" Young, who had become a board member, did not feel that SCLC needed to remain a large national organization. Hosea Williams disagreed. He predicted that people like Young would turn SCLC into an Urban League and it would die. "Those guys left Abernathy holding the bag. Any black man could be congressman, but the years Andy Young and Walter Fauntroy [the D.C. delegate] had in the movement could have been used much more for black people in the civil rights movement," Williams said.

Young replied that serving in Congress was a logical extension of his service in SCLC. "My own feeling about my move to politics was that I felt the local feeling in Atlanta was ripe for a change in direction. . . . You also have to say that there was a whole generation of guys on the front lines for years who need a break." And later he added, in celebrating the political advances of black people, "Everybody has been wondering what's happened to the civil rights movement. . . . You don't have to march on the sheriff when you can pick up the phone and call someone." He paraphrased Kwame Nkhruma, the late president of Ghana. "See first the political kingdom and then all things beneath it."

This summer he presaged his later efforts in Africa by making his first bit of impact on legislation affecting affairs outside Atlanta. With the help of some southern Republicans he attached to the foreign aid bill an amendment authorizing the President to cancel any aid to Portugal that that country in turn was using to combat the liberation movements in its African colonies. The House passed the amendment.

In the fall, Young became involved in a perennial civil rights controversy. Efforts were underway in the House to pass a tough anti-busing bill. Four liberal congressmen tried to attach an amendment that would soften the legislation, a plan involving gradual school integration with a small federal role and no busing. They sought out Young and Barbara Jordan, "two freshman black congressmen considered less dogmatic than their colleagues," to join them in supporting the amendment. The amendment ran into immediate heavy fire from civil rights groups. Clarence Mitchell, the influential NAACP lobbyist, was especially angry. Young got the civil rights leaders together one weekend to talk about it, but the result was that in deference to people like Mitchell and Kenneth Clark, the famous New

York psychologist, Young and Jordan eased out of the coalition.

And then the Watergate scandal broke open.

Young was one of twenty-five congressmen who supported starting preliminary proceedings for the impeachment of Nixon. In November—second thoughts?—he said he didn't think Nixon would be impeached. The bitter fight that it would involve wouldn't, in his view, do the country or the Democratic party any good. What the party should do, he advised, was to "let the President stew in his own crises."

In the meantime Vice-President Spiro Agnew had been forced to resign. Andrew Young would have to vote on his successor. Gerald Ford was nominated.

In 1965, while the most important of the civil rights measures, the Voting Rights Bill, was being debated, Gerald Ford, a Republican from Michigan, had been one of the sponsors of a weaker substitute. His civil rights record was uniformly bad, while as House Majority Leader, he was widely known as a somewhat ordinary, maybe even mediocre, but mainly decent man. Everyone stressed that he was decent—though he had tried to water down the voting rights of blacks.

Andrew Young surprised everyone by becoming the sole black congressman to vote for Gerald Ford's confirmation! Young not only joined 386 of his colleagues in voting "Aye" to Ford's confirmation, but he also gave a speech explaining why, since he had just finished saying, "I've studied his record and I find it impossible to look the American people in the eye and say this man is the most qualified person for the vice-presidency."

Standing in the well of the House, Andrew Young said he expected Ford "to rise to the occasion of assuming his high office, to grow in that position as many have in the past. . . . Out of my own southern experience, I have confidence that people can overcome past parochial views and develop a broader perspective which takes into account the interest of all the people. Decent men, placed in positions of trust, will serve decently." Young added that he believed he was aiding the orderly process of succession, in case Nixon resigned or was impeached, when no one should expect a successor chosen by him to have a different political philosophy.

The congratulations to Young for this action were practically unanimous, though fellow black congressman Ron Dellums of California, while generally praising him, thought he should have stood up on principle a little better, and members of his own staff were bitterly opposed. Young calmed the angry members of the Black Caucus by bringing in additional arguments (which were academic in any case, since the vote for Ford was 387 to 36): if Ford had been rejected, they might have ended up with someone worse. In addition, it wouldn't hurt to have a member of the "club," that is, Congress, as Vice-President.

Dellums repeated the most general comment; he admired Young's courage. Shirley Chisholm said that Young's action showed leadership, and she hoped he would one day become chairman of the Black Caucus. The *Atlanta Constitution* proudly called him a "man of stature."

As his first year in office neared an end, Young's approach to his congressional colleagues was becoming clear. It was an outgrowth of what was called the "Atlanta style." Black and white Atlantans met in private conferences to resolve their differences instead of resorting to public set-tos. In Congress the same kind of thing was called the "inside game."

An early admirer of Young was Morris Udall. Young, according to Udall, had enough star quality to play the *outside* game if he wanted to. "He could make public statements and play to public opinion and get attention. But he doesn't. He plays the inside game, works within the Congress, and does it very effectively."

A large part of his success was attributed to his readiness to negotiate and mediate. Shirley Chisholm said that Young reminded her of Martin Luther King in his personal attributes. "You know, this business of really loving your neighbor. Andy operates on the basis of what his conscience tells him to do. . . . In the Black Caucus Andy will sit and listen, then in a very cool way will kind of get all of us together."

It's worth noting, however, that in the vote for Ford there was something shrewder than conscience at work. Three years later Young was looking at a presidential election in which both candidates, to varying degrees, owed him something. And he gave an interview in which one can almost see the guarded twinkle as he said that he did it "to get Nixon out of there," and also because he thought, mistakenly, that Ford was a "harmless conservative. Just incidentally," he added, "Atlanta has received close to a billion dollars this term [of the 94th Congress]. I don't know if that had anything to do with it. Whenever I can I cooperate with an administration. . . . Got to sell out something to get something. . . . But I don't want my fellow members to think I did it for that reason. . . . Well, some things are better left unsaid."

In 1973, Young's son "Bo" was born. Not long after, his family moved up from Atlanta to a house in Washington. At the Christmas recess, he took a trip to Tokyo to attend a seminar on trade and commercial development. Unlike the trips of some of his Georgia colleagues, his expenses were privately paid, by Columbia University, which was sponsoring the seminar.

The winter of the beginning of his second year was marked by the energy crisis or the "gasoline crunch." Young, who earlier predicted that the energy problem was "going to keep us on the fringe of trouble for many months to come," was one of six legislators who petitioned the Federal Trade Commission to act on ads by the oil companies that seemed to absolve them of any responsibility for the shortage.

Another issue on which Young made himself heard during this period (while Congress was steeling itself for the ordeal of impeaching a President) was the Equal Rights Amendment. Still requiring ratification by thirty-seven states in order to become a constitutional amendment, it had been rejected by the Georgia General Assembly. Young blamed the defeat on "Neanderthal" legislators. The occasion for this remark was a dinner in observance of the twenty-fifth anniversary of the civil rights coalition in the United States, and Young criticized Nixon for slowing down on civil rights. It was here that he first invoked Jimmy Carter's name in connection with the 1976 congressional elections, citing his leadership in trying to unseat Republicans from Congress. If the Democrats could get "forty good guys in the House and four or five in the Senate, it would be a whole new ball game," Young said.

He had good reason to desire Nixon's impeachment. The President had submitted a transportation bill that threatened harm to the most important of Young's local issues, mass transit. The trouble was that funds would not be specifically earmarked for urban rapid transit and instead could be diverted to other transportation needs if the governor decided they had priority—or if politics so dictated. Young believed, instead, in furnishing large operating subsidies.

In this period Young attempted to block the appointment of a former ambassador, Nathaniel Davis, to a high State Department post. It had become known that the CIA, on the instructions of the White House, had financed political forces opposing Chilean Marxist President Allende at the time he was overthrown and killed by the military. Mr. Davis, then American ambassador to Chile, was believed to have been involved.

Young, who seems to have been playing more of the "outside game" than was commonly thought (but quietly), next came up with a charge that multinational corporations using foreign funds to inject their influence into campaigns were a threat to the American political process. He called for strictly limited private contributions supplemented by public financing.

He returned to his concern with housing for low income families by introducing a bill called the National Homestead Act of 1974. It was based on the original Homestead Act of 1862, whereby a family could move onto up to 160 acres of land for a fee of $10, build a house and live on it, and become the owner within five years. The Department of Housing and Urban Development had on hand thousands of abandoned inner city homes whose original owners had lost their mortgages. Young proposed that after paying a fee of $100 or less and rehabilitating and living in the house for five years, the home would become the tenant's without further payment. Modified versions of this plan soon became standard practice of HUD and local governments in several large cities.

By late spring of 1974 it was clear that Nixon was likely to be impeached. Once Young suggested that even rising prices might be grounds for indicting the President. Nixon had been accused of approving increases in milk price supports in exchange for campaign money, which Young regarded as an impeachable offense.

Just before Nixon's resignation, Young began his drive for re-election. He had compiled a solid record. To his usual labor support, he added large segments of the Atlanta business community. He ran unopposed in the Democratic primaries. Late 1974 was the best of times to run against a Republican. To face Young in the November general election, the Republicans selected a singularly willing sacrificial lamb—none other than the indomitable Wyman C. Lowe. Finally losing patience with "black-dominated primaries," Lowe had switched parties. Young and everybody else recognized that it was not going to be much of a battle. While it was in progress, however, in September 1974, after Nixon had been out of office for hardly a month, Gerald Ford pardoned him, and was immediately attacked from all quarters. Even many of those who favored pardoning Nixon thought that the new President had acted too soon. Young took a different tack and, while well on his way to achieving a consistent 95 percent rating by the ADA, he again leaned away from his fellow liberals. He stepped up and said he supported the pardon.

Why? Young simply didn't relish the spectre of Nixon under indictment, a Nixon whose taste for vengeance was well established and who would come out swinging hard. He had visions of Nixon "going around the country holding one hundred dollar-a-plate defense dinners" and stirring the emotions of extreme conservatives and the remaining hard core of Nixon loyalists. The pardon had effectively taken him out of public life. In addition, Young felt that the case would have dragged on for as long as three years, and then the tapes that had brought on Nixon's downfall might not be admitted as evidence on the grounds that they violated the Fifth Amendment guarantees against self-incrimination.

During the campaign, however, Young strongly advocated firing what he called the Nixon holdovers. He was especially critical of Secretary of Agriculture Earl Butz, whom Ford would in fact fire, but two years later, for making a remark that slurred black people, and of Arthur Burns, the chairman of the Federal Reserve Board. Actions such as Burns's maintenance of high interest rates were, in Young's opinion, leading the country to "the brink of economic disaster."

In September 1974, Young made an appearance before a House education subcommittee. He said that because of past discrimination (from which he himself had suffered as a college applicant twenty-three years earlier), he approved of affirmative action programs in which, for instance, an economist would be picked for a job solely because he was black. He could live with this until being black no longer meant being poor.

Congressman Jack Kemp, a former quarterback for the pro football Buffalo Bills, disagreed. He believed that persons should rise solely on the basis of their talent, their skill. Unlike Young, he didn't believe that there was a black economics and a white economics, or a female economics and a male economics. Kemp suggested that Young himself had gotten where he was not because he was black but because he was an able, articulate spokesman.

"I was successful, frankly," Young said, "because my daddy was a dentist."

"A dentist?" Kemp asked.

"A dentist. He had enough money to send me to school. That was not true of the other kids in school with me. There were a lot of kids

... that were a lot smarter than me that went to jail, went to the Army and were killed, went everyplace but to school. It was never on the basis of merit. It was on the basis of economic opportunity."

He pointedly added that his father had become a dentist because, after the Civil War, the churches "maybe practiced a little reverse discrimination. . . . They set up hundreds of schools and colleges in the South for ex-slaves."

Young was re-elected in November with 72 percent of the vote, compared to Lowe's 28 percent. House Speaker Carl Albert appointed him as the first black to serve on the Rules Committee, a powerful post, since that committee controlled the flow of legislation from the other committees to the House floor. That same month, December 1974, he took his first trip to South Africa, where he stayed for one week. A long-standing tennis fan, he accompanied Arthur Ashe (at whose wedding he officiated) on a tour of that country. This time his expenses were paid by the United Church of Christ's Commission on Racial Justice.

He was appalled by the conditions in South Africa. They were far worse than anything he had experienced in the Deep South. He thought he detected "tremendous reservoirs" of good will among whites in the antiapartheid Progressive party and the middle ground United party. But in his conversations with Nationalist leaders, he was struck by their lack of guilt. He was surprised when they expected him to agree with statements like: "If all of them [the South African blacks] were like you, it would be okay [to end apartheid], but they're not, so we've got to continue it."

While in South Africa he met the widow of Chief Albert J. Luthuli, the winner of the 1960 Nobel Peace Prize. One of her daughters was then a teacher at Atlanta University. It was also on this trip that he met Robert M. Sobukwe, the exiled leader of the Pan-African Congress, which years earlier had split off from Luthuli's more moderate African National Congress. Young was quoted as saying that he wished he could become South African long enough to lead a nonviolent movement there.

But he was a black American, and in the next year, 1975, the Voting Rights Act was due for extension. Young prepared for the fight early. He pointed out that a third of the eligible black voters in the South were still not registered. His efforts were successful. The act was extended for seven years this time, until 1982. The media hardly noticed. It was already gearing up for the 1976 presidential primaries. Could Ford be elected president in his own right? Or would some hopeful from the scrambling ranks of the Democrats get the nod from the electorate?

One of these hopefuls, a former governor of Georgia, was still scarcely known nationally, and one of the jokes from this period came to be, "Jimmy who?" But for some time Andrew Young had known very well who Jimmy Carter was. America, unaware, was nearing the point where it would begin to hear a great deal of both men, separately and together.

The Lions in the Arena

THE TEXAS CLUB

People were always fascinated, wondering what Barbara Jordan was going to do.

It never mattered that she was heavyset and ungainly and had the bearing of the principal of the toughest high school in town,

Or never had a husband, reveled in the collected works of Gladys Knight and the Pips, lived in a pink house, and played her cards close to the chest,

Kept her own counsel, so that nobody was ever, ever

Going to get next to her—all right!

People always watched, wondering what she would do.

Barbara Jordan's father was a Baptist minister who, when he

wasn't preaching, worked in a warehouse, and liked to see his three
girls bring home straight A's.

Barbara Charline, the youngest, did her best to please him, but
soon she was wondering what she would do

To please herself, having realized that God had set atop her
shoulders

An object of rare quality, more durable, more useful to herself
and to the world, and in the end infinitely more beautiful

Than the figure of a pom-pom girl.

But, being black, being a woman, and living deep in the heart of
Texas,

She wondered what she would do with it.

She wanted to do great things and to be famous. For a while she
thought of being a pharmacist. But who ever heard of a famous
pharmacist?

One day Edith Sampson, of Massachusetts, visited her class.

Edith Sampson was black, female, and famous. She was also a
lawyer.

Barbara Jordan took all her A's to Texas Southern University
and then straight up to the Boston University Law School, the only
woman in a class of 128,

Passed the bar in Massachusetts and Texas, returned home,

And wondered what she would do.

She wanted to be powerful and famous and to help people. But
those things took time. So for several years she mainly practiced
law, using her parents' dining room table as her desk, and later
worked in the office of a county judge as an administrative assistant.

Once Barbara Jordan started doing something, those who had
wondered what she would do

Were always confident about her timing, about the certainty
that she knew what she was doing. In 1962

When almost all the big struggles still lay ahead for King and
Young,

Barbara Jordan ran for the Texas State House of Representatives and lost. But 46,000 voters had liked her style, and in 1964 she
ran again, and lost, and she

Decided she had set her sights too low. So in 1966 she ran for
the Texas Senate and won easily.

I have a tremendous amount of faith in my own capacity, she
said. *I know how to read and write and think, so I have no fear.* In
the Texas Senate

She was not only the only black person, but also the only woman. She quickly learned the language, the rules, and the personalities, was voted the outstanding freshman member,

Chaired committees, was elected president pro tem, saw half the bills she submitted enacted into law,

Establishing the Texas Fair Employment Practices Commission, a minimum wage law, an improved workmen's compensation act, blocked a law that would have impaired voter registration,

And caught LBJ's eye,

Especially when at the 1968 convention in Chicago she helped keep the Texas delegation on record as supporting his Vietnam policies,

Though she was no hawk or goddess, but just a politician whose chief art, she claimed, was that of persuasion.

In 1971, as vice-chairwoman of a congressional redistricting committee, she helped carve out a new district in her native Houston, the Eighteenth, and promptly ran for the seat, swamping her opponents,

And when she arrived in Washington, LBJ put through a few calls before he died and she found herself first among the new members

Of the House Judiciary Committee.

As she had done in Texas, she looked around to see whose hands grasped the reins, and found that quite a few belonged to white, male Texans

Whose language, rules, and interests she knew almost better than they did.

Of the twenty-one standing committees in the House, seven were chaired by Texans. They called such power

The Texas Club. And if the 1974 impeachment proceedings are remembered for anyone except Nixon himself or House Judiciary Committee chairman, Peter Rodino, that individual will be Barbara Jordan,

The personal representative on that committee of LBJ and the blacks, the Mexican-Americans, the poor, and yes, liberal and conservative whites, the Texas Club.

On television she nailed the nation to the wall when she stated her case, in the voice that Andrew Young described as making one think that "the Heavens themselves are about to open up." The Constitution was the crux. When it was framed, she had not fallen under its guarantees. But through its processes things had changed, and

Today I am an inquisitor. I believe that hyperbole would not overstate the solemnness that I feel right now. My faith in the Constitution is whole, it is complete, it is total. I am not going to sit here and be an idle spectator to the diminution, the subversion, the destruction of the Constitution.

And all eyes stayed on Barbara Jordan throughout the rest of the deliberations, watched her casual-appearing votes

As if she were a chocolate mountain about to erupt, as if whatever she decided would be subtle, sensible, and correct.

And two years later people were only slightly less surprised when at the Democratic National Convention in New York she again stole the show

From Andrew Young and Jimmy Carter, as keynote speaker:

If we promise, we must deliver. If we propose, we must produce. If we ask for sacrifice, we must be the first to give.

In the thunderous acclaim many thought she looked

Just like a Vice-President, and Carter put her on his list of fifteen possibles.

But, never one to fool herself or others, Barbara Jordan knew her chances. She liked

The attorney-general job. She had the background, the keen, legalistic mind, the presence, and a talent for persuasion second to none. She had everything except membership

In the newest club.

Barbara Jordan returned to her offices, struggled with physical ailments, announced that she would not run for another term.

And while Andrew Young had already left Congress with its tedious and often frustrating routines and was working on matters as weighty as how to free the black South Africans,

Everyone wondered what Barbara Jordan would do.

Chapter Twelve

THE ENDLESS WAR

They did not face racism in their lives and tended to rule it out. Nixon and Ford did not face it because they were, in fact, racists. . . . They were racists not in the aggressive sense but in that they had no understanding of the problems of colored peoples anywhere.

Andrew Young, Interview in *Playboy*, July 1977

THE MEDIA FOCUSED ON THE accusations of racism that Andrew Young made on the plane to London and in his *Playboy* interview, which was published at about the same time. Certain politicians reacted with predictable criticism. William E. Brock, chairman of the Republican National Committee, called Young "a diplomatic incompetent who should be fired." Barry Goldwater said that Young "can get both feet, his hands, and his hat in his mouth at the same time." When asked what he would have done if he were president, Ronald Reagan answered, "I wouldn't have an Ambassador Young." Harris pollsters reported that the public was critical of the way Young was handling his job by a margin of thirty-five to thirty-one, although almost 50 percent thought he would be instrumental in working out a solution in Africa.

Young spent the early part of June 1977 reporting on his trip. He appeared before a Senate Foreign Relations subcommittee and then the House International Relations Committee, and he met with President Carter. He told the Senators that he was concerned that his critics had extended their attacks to include the President. Having al-

193

ways stressed the importance of assuming full responsibility for one's actions, he said that he would ask Carter to treat him henceforth as an ambassador rather than as a friend. Continuing that theme, he told the House committee members that he would "much rather be fired for trying to do what is right, to help the country, than to be a retired, successful ambassador who never did anything."

The Congressmen pressed. Representative William Goodling of Pennsylvania told Young that "a congressman has to count to ten before putting his mouth and brain into gear. An ambassador ought to count to a hundred."

"I am what I am," Young said. "I can't change that."

The committee chairman, Clement J. Zablocki, of Wisconsin, asked whether Young couldn't try to be "more of an ambassador and less of a politician."

"I can't promise, Mr. Chairman," he answered.

After talking with Carter for half an hour in the White House, Young emerged saying that he had not been asked to resign, that Carter, who had given a "hot" interview of his own to *Playboy*, had read his remarks, understood what he was trying to say, and had not muzzled him. "I don't think the President has to encourage it, but he didn't tell me to shut up either." As for the shots from the right, "The Republicans have really had so little to criticize in this Administration that if I didn't do what I'm doing I think they'd have to invent me. In a way I think that's what you guys are doing," he told the reporters, "trying to invent me."

There was some justice to his charge. How else explain such questions as that directed to Young by a reporter in Pennsylvania: "Do you plan to say anything outrageous while you're here?"

But he was continuing to do it to himself as well. The reason had to do with the need to define a racist. Till then it seemed a racist had to be at least a Bull Connor. Members of the House International Relations Committee had asked if Young wouldn't regard Kennedy and Johnson as racists too. He said he would. So then did it also extend to Lincoln? asked a reporter. "Expecially Abraham Lincoln. . . . There I go again," he added, "giving you another headline."

As for Nixon and Ford, he said that he hadn't intended the remarks to be critical of their personal lives. What he had in mind was the insensitivity to cultural differences which was causing the United States great difficulties. Colonial oppression based on color had "created a dynamic in the world today that can be terribly destructive if ignored. . . . Unfortunately I haven't been able to find a word other than racism. I wish I could, because people react emotionally to that word and don't pay attention to what I'm trying to say."

Though in *Playboy* he had already said that he personally tried to "demoralize racism and call it 'ethnocentrism,' " he began to feel gratified by the debate that he had started. Always trying to relate things to the issues rather than to himself, he felt that it was causing people to think about the effect of racism on the struggle to bring majority rule to southern Africa. Like Ian Smith, he avoided saying "black majority rule" because it implied the exclusion of whites. Awareness of racism by the nationalist movements lay behind their distrust of Western negotiators, while the negotiators' failure to recognize its virulence made them vulnerable. Rhodesia's weakened government could collapse at any time, resulting in chaos, and the front-line countries, having a better grasp of old scars than Britain or the United States, were better equipped to deal with that. And Young said he had deliberately picked on the British because he was "nervous" about them and about what they might not perceive from their own past.

Once what he said—and the criticism—were properly digested, Young started picking up support. President Carter said that the Third World nations "now look on the United States as having at least one representative—I hope more, but at least one—who understands their problems, who speaks their language, who will listen to them when they put forward their woes and their hopes for the future." Jesse Jackson had already come strongly to Young's defense, and three of the highest officials in the NAACP, including Roy Wilkins, said that "Black Americans are proud . . . that we have a spokesman at such a high level willing to speak the truth." The Council of Bishops of the powerful African Methodist Episcopal Church similarly commended Young and denounced the press for distorting his views.

Indeed, Young had solid black support. The black public was aware of what he was doing in Africa, and he said nothing that the overwhelming majority could not support. For generations they had seen legions of black people ousted from all kinds of elevations at the merest hint of speaking their minds and not "knowing their place." The longer Andrew Young remained unaware of "his place," the more beautiful it was.

Britain's Ivor Richards kept saying that Young's comments had hurt their relationship "not a scrap." And a Swedish delegate said that his countrymen were less concerned by Young's "Swedish" remarks than were many of their friends. In fact, at about this time many Swedes were beginning to realize how little room they had allowed in their psyche for the many immigrants now in their country. Even the 180,000 Finns—blond, blue-eyed, and next-door neighbors—had not been well accepted. It was another example of a continuing circumstance: people could scream about Andrew Young's remarks but had great difficulty refuting them.

The controversy over his remarks died down in July, a slow, quiet month around the United Nations, when Young spent considerable time in Europe familiarizing himself with its outposts in Paris and Geneva. On his return, the State Department announced that in August Young would visit ten countries in and around the Caribbean.

This was in fulfillment of a pledge made by Carter after Young returned from South Africa. The ambassador would now "shift his emphasis toward other developing nations outside Africa." Heretofore Carter's chief representatives in that area had been his wife, Rosalynn, who had already visited Latin America twice and was supposed to go back a third time, and Cyrus Vance. "Andy Young is part of this effort because if somebody like him goes there it highlights our interest in the area," said a high State Department official. The area was of great importance not just because of its nearness or historical ties or the presence of difficulties such as Cuba and the Panama Canal, but also because it was the source of some interesting imports. Among these were—and are—25 percent of our incoming oil, two-thirds of the bauxite needed for making aluminum—and nearly all the illegal immigrants.

Young had already visited Jamaica, his first stop, eleven times, the first exactly twenty years earlier. Then he had been so struck by the sight of blacks in important positions that he later took his family, including his parents, to see the contrast to a place like Louisiana. Jamaica also was where he had shared King's last vacation. Now his arrival as ambassador symbolized how far the United States had progressed. "I consider myself Jamaican!" he told the welcoming party.

At the moment Prime Minister Michael Manley was, at Young's

urging, in Colombia to attend talks on the Panama Canal. The Panamanians themselves had asked Young to talk Manley into coming.

Young's twelve-day swing through the Caribbean, beginning August 5, was accurately described as a whirlwind tour. The goals were mainly to show himself, to exhibit the interest that the United States had in the problems of each individual country, and to stress that, far from indulging in "creeping isolationism," the United States was interested in the development of the Third World and in its liberation movements.

In Jamaica he encountered some opposition at the outset. Students from Tanzania demanded that the United States supply liberation movements with arms. "I find people are committed to violence almost in inverse proportion to the distance they are from it," Young answered.

On this trip he was also able to announce more United States aid to the area. This added up to almost a five-fold increase in the case of Jamaica. Before Young left, Manley returned with the news that prospects were good for an agreement on a canal treaty between the United States and Panama within ten days.

In Mexico next, Young spoke of a White House plan that would give legal residence status to all illegal aliens who had been living in the United States for at least seven years, and then after five more years they would be eligible for citizenship. The plan also included putting 2,000 more guards on the border, which was not as favorably received by the Mexicans as the prospect of improving trade so that there wouldn't be as much incentive for Mexicans to leave their homeland. "Mexico will never be really satisfied until it is able to export commodities and goods and not people to the United States," President Lopez Portillo informed him. The whole thing was another sticky wicket for Young since the Mexicans felt that the emigres were only repopulating land that the United States had taken from Mexico in the days of the young Abe Lincoln.

Whereas Young's arrival in the first two countries had been accompanied by formal welcomes, Costa Rica was different. Foreign Minister Gonzalo Facio ran out to the plane in the rain and reminisced about hearing Dr. King's "I Have a Dream" speech in Washington in 1963. He said that Costa Rica joined the United States in its emphasis on human rights, that Costa Rica's own record was clean, and that the president himself, Daniel Oduber Quiros, had asked Rosalynn to ask Jimmy to send Andy.

In Guyana on the tenth, the theme was that despite early United States hostility because of Prime Minister Forbes Burnham's vow to create "the first orthodox Socialist state" in South America, the United States was going to increase its aid there too, from $1.1 million to $12.3 million in the next three years. This was in keeping with Young's proposition that not helping such countries destabilized America's perimeter.

Joshua Nkomo, head of one of the two forces comprising the Patriotic Front, the guerrillas fighting in Rhodesia, happened to be touring the Caribbean also, and in Guyana, by prearrangement, their paths crossed. Nkomo told Young that he was not optimistic about reaching a settlement with Ian Smith, whom he called "an impossible character," nor did he think the United States had a role to play in the negotiations, except to support Britain. Nkomo stressed that though he thought matters could be resolved only through force, he wanted the white minority to stay, and Young said he was surprised at Nkomo's moderation.

In Surinam on the eleventh Young praised Cuba's role in urging the Panamanians to reach an early settlement. But in Trinidad and Tobago on the same day, Young attacked Cuba for human rights violations, though he admitted that he was not an expert on the country. Venezuela, for all its oil-exporting importance, was an equally brief stop. There he said that the Panama Canal treaty would be the first test of the Carter Administration's "new approach to Latin America." Anticipating the difficult struggle to secure ratification, he added that the United States Congress was perhaps "not up to date with this approach."

In the Dominican Republic he had lunch with President Joaquin Balaguer. Then it was on to neighboring Haiti, smaller and poorer than most of the Caribbean countries, and also looked on by some as a testing place of Carter's commitment to human rights. President Jean-Claude Duvalier was an improvement on his father, "Papa Doc." He had abolished his father's force of hatchetmen, the Ton-Ton Macoute, and he had just released seven hundred political prisoners. But he was thought to be still strongly under the influence of his mother and other hard-liners. Nobody could deny that there was still much repression in Haiti.

Before Young left New York, thirty Haitian demonstrators had picketed him, recommending that he bypass the country. He said that he couldn't do that, but he invited them all in for a talk. Even as he was traveling to his rendezvous with Duvalier, three large boatloads of Haitians were seeking refuge in the United States. With Haiti still a dictatorship, what Young would do there was awaited with great interest. In the past the United States had landed Marines in Haiti for reasons not often having to do with human rights.

Young told the Haitian officials that their actions with regard to human rights would directly affect the amount of aid and other cooperation that the country received from the United States. (Among other things Haiti enjoyed a monopoly on the manufacture of baseballs.) He made a strong appeal on a moral basis, and he handed Duvalier a list of twenty political prisoners. The President promised quick action: either to prosecute them if there was evidence that they had committed crimes, or to release them. He also pledged that the government would soon pass new laws protecting the rights of detained persons.

After a last swift stop in Barbados, Young returned home, feeling that he had created many new ties in the 'Caribbean. He recommended an integrated partnership between the United States and these countries, a relationship that would emphasize cooperation in place of the large doses of American aid that had characterized the last era of strong interest in the area, the Kennedy years.

Five days after he left Barbados, Young was in Lagos, Nigeria. The occasion ostensibly was a week-long United Nations conference for action against apartheid, with five hundred delegates from over one hundred countries. (The same day, August 22, Kenneth Kaunda's Zambians lofted up to thirty rockets across the lake onto the Rhodesian resort town of Kariba, forcing the tourists to take cover. It was the second such attack in three months.) Kaunda and General Obasanjo of Nigeria were among the distinguished figures who gave speeches urging economic sanctions and a total arms and oil embargo against South Africa. But, in general, the West had already rejected such measures as counter-productive, especially while South Africa still had the potential to bring about peaceful change in Namibia and Rhodesia.

Accordingly, the United States and Britain came up with a new plan to bring majority rule to Rhodesia, and as it happened, Lagos was important because in the process of pushing the plan, Young would be leading from his African strong suit, Nigeria. Young and British Foreign Minister David Owen intended first to meet in Lusaka, Zambia, with the presidents of the five front-line countries. If they approved the plan, the guerrilla leaders, Nkomo, operating out of Zambia, and Mugabe, operating out of Mozambique, were expected to join in. Thereupon Young and Owen would push on to Rhodesia or South Africa or both.

At first the details were secret, but on the twenty-third Young presented the plan to General Obasanjo, and on the twenty-fourth, before the Anglo-Americans could even get to Lusaka with it, it was leaked in full.

The main feature was the establishment of a three-part peace-keeping force consisting of segments of the guerrillas, the Rhodesian Army, and, mainly, the Nigerian Army, with Tanzanian units added. It would involve the gradual demobilizing of both the guerrillas and the Rhodesian Army. In addition, Ian Smith would voluntarily step down, and a British administration would take over and hold elections on the basis of "one man, one vote," designed to give the black majority responsible roles in the government. The white settlers would be encouraged to stay by making available large sums of money to shore up the badly sagging Rhodesian economy.

After hearing considerable condemnation of the United States at the conference, Young reminded the delegates that the United States probably had been even more bitterly condemned by South Africa for the policy that Botha and Vorster called "strangulation with finesse." Then he flew as Owen's guest in a British jet to Lusaka. By this time their strategy was set. If successful with the Front Liners in Lusaka, they would move on to Pretoria, South Africa, for two days of talks, then would wait in Nairobi, Kenya, for two more days to sit out the parliamentary elections in Rhodesia before flying on to Salisbury.

Already the Rhodesians were wondering why Owen and Young were taking the trouble. They had said they were going to turn thumbs down as soon as the proposals were leaked. Disbanding their army was even more absurd than the thought of Ian Smith's stepping down voluntarily. Every day someone in Rhodesia was shouting that they wouldn't accept it, and in Pretoria Smith and Vorster again got together for a huddle.

Owen and Young left Lusaka without having gained complete approval of their plan from the black leaders. The front-line leaders left it to the guerrillas, and the sticking point was the insistence of Nkomo and Mugabe that while the Rhodesian Army should be fully dismantled, their troops should stay armed. Having done the fighting for liberation, it was only fitting, they thought, that they should police the transition.

It was not completely clear what the Anglo-Americans expected to get from Vorster. Andrew Young's previous trip to South Africa had upset the white government no end. This would be his first meeting with John Vorster. The plan was thought to be mainly a British production, and since black leaders like Nkomo and Nyerere had always insisted on the British taking the lead, Young's role was expected to remain chiefly one of United States support.

In contrast to his earlier visit, Young, not wanting to distract from the talks, said nothing about the South African government's oppressive policies or nonviolence. The most he permitted himself was a wave to some black gardeners waiting to greet him after one of the sessions and the filming of a television segment as he sat in a limousine reading *The World*, a black newspaper then on the verge of being outlawed. In the talks Vorster directed almost all his questions to Owen; however, he was courteous and correct with Young at all times and did not rule out future efforts to "get along."

But the South Africans, after many grueling hours of talks, gave Owen and Young no encouragement, saying only that they would leave the matter to Rhodesia's best judgment. Owen and Young had hoped to talk South Africa into seeing that its best interests involved pushing Rhodesia toward the plan. But the South Africans, in the meantime, had been pressured so heavily toward majority rule in their own country that they were retaliating by saying "hands off."

On the way to Nairobi, Young and Owen stopped off in Dar-es-Salaam to discuss the plan again with President Julius Nyerere, the leader of the front-line countries. Then, after the elections, won by Ian Smith's Rhodesian Front Party, they arrived in Rhodesia.

Andrew Young got a better reception in Salisbury than did the plan. Ian Smith, like Vorster, was meeting the American United Nations ambassador for the first time. He found Young and his team "more pragmatic" than the British and not nearly so "vindictive" toward the minority government. But the Rhodesians, as they insisted they would all along, rejected the plan.

Smith, as was his habit, did not leave closed the possibility of further considering the scheme, but the fact was that he had decided something about the blacks in Rhodesia. He felt that as a whole they were far more conciliatory toward the whites than were the several thousand guerrillas of Mugabe and Nkomo. There were at least two leaders without troops, Muzorewa and Sithole, who might be trusted, with white help, to bring about the inevitable transition without the devastation of white interests. If this large majority could be won over, the guerrillas could be shut out.

Now Smith and Young set out on differing courses that would continue for many months to come. In his attempt to work out an internal settlement, Smith would indeed meet in Salisbury with Bishop Abel Muzorewa, the Reverend Ndabaningi Sithole, and Chief Jeremiah Chirau, of whom only Muzorewa had a national following. At the same time Young and Owen would conduct a conference on the island of Malta with Robert Mugabe and Joshua Nkomo, trying to persuade them to accept the Anglo-American plan.

In February 1978 Smith reached agreement with "his" three black leaders. Under its terms, he would remain in power until new elections were held at the end of the year when, on the basis of "one man, one vote," rule would pass into the hands of the black majority. Yet it would be done in such a way that whites would retain effective veto power over key matters, the most crucial of which was land reform. The Rhodesia Army would remain intact while the guerrillas would be required to disband.

Nkomo and Mugabe angrily denounced this as a bogus agreement, saying there would be no peaceful settlement because they would not allow one. And to Andrew Young, Smith's plan, with its exclusion of the guerrillas, raised the immediate spectre of an Angola-style civil war, a prospect that confirmed the depths of the risk that Smith was taking.

While others worried that not accepting the internal settlement invited Soviet-Cuban involvement on the side of the guerrillas, Young's views prevailed among the British and Americans, and they sought a formula that would include a vital role in Zimbabwe's government for the guerrillas.

The same month of Smith's agreement, Robert M. Sobukwe, Young's friend and best hope for nonviolent leadership in South Africa, died of cancer at the age of 58.

The endless war raged on.

The Lions in the Arena

THE
TWO-THOUSAND-
YEAR
TREK

We pray very hard for our children. . . . Young Africans know from infancy upwards . . . that their strivings after civilized values will not, in the present order, earn for them recognition as sane and responsible human beings. . . . The argument [of white South Africans] goes like this: "It has taken us two thousand years to reach our present civilised state. A hundred years ago the natives were barbarians. It will take them two thousand years to catch up with where we are now."

—Albert John Luthuli, *Let My People Go* (An Autobiography)

Albert John Luthuli, though he was a South African, was born in present-day Rhodesia, sometime around 1898, five years after Mohandas K. Gandhi was thrown off his first segregated train while journeying to Pretoria. At the hands of his mother the young Luthuli received a disciplined upbringing, mastered the Christian ethic, justice and dignity for all. Love.

In 1913 the first Natives Land Act was passed, confining the blacks, who outnumbered the whites 5 to 1, to tribal reserves amounting to 13 percent of the land.

Fluent in English, rock-steady, and instantly receiving respect even as a young man, for fifteen years, from 1921 to 1936, Albert John Luthuli lived the calm, contented life of an academic, teaching Zulu history and literature at a mission college.

In 1923 the Native Urban Areas Act gave government ministers the power to restrict the free movement of Africans into towns and cities.

The Industrial Conciliation Act of 1926 and amended in 1937 and 1956 bound Africans into labor agreements in which they had no say. Once the demands of white members of unions were met, employers could write into the contracts anything they liked concerning Africans.

The Immorality Act of 1927 forbade sex relations between Africans and whites.

"In the days when Professor Matthews and I were young teachers at Adams the world seemed to be opening out for Africans. It seemed mainly a matter of proving our ability and worth as citizens, and that did not seem impossible."

The Natives Representation Act of 1936 provided that no African could qualify as a voter.

The Natives Land and Trust Act of the same year followed up the earlier Natives Land Act in assuring that whites would have an average of 375 acres each from which to wrest a living, compared to the 6 acres available to each African.

In 1936 Albert John Luthuli followed in his uncle's footsteps and was elected chief of their tribe of 5,000, the Abasemakholweni. For the next seventeen years he served as a combination president-judge, settling disputes in the sugarcane fields and beer halls, assessing fines, working to increase agricultural yields, representing the tribe in contacts with the white authorities.

The Apprenticeship Act of 1944, with the Industrial Conciliation Act, excluded blacks from skilled labor jobs in industry.

The Natives (Urban Areas) Consolidation Act of 1945 pushed "redundant" blacks out of cities and onto white farms or overcrowded reserves. It set up the townships such as Soweto, imposed curfews, and set strict controls on the lives of every urban African.

The Asiatic Land Tenure Act of 1946 confined Asiatics to certain areas in the same manner as had been done with the Africans.

By his wife Nokukhanya, to whom he was married for forty years, Luthuli sired four daughters and three sons.

The Mixed Marriages Act of 1949 barred marriage between *whites and blacks or coloreds, and, as amended the next year, forbade sex between white and colored.*

The Population Registration Act of 1950 fixed every inhabitant of South Africa into categories: white, colored, Bantu, etc.

The Group Areas Act of 1950 imposed rigid residential segregation. Africans could be resettled with expropriation of their property.

"We pray very hard for our children," wrote Luthuli.

The Suppression of Communism Amendment Act of 1950 gave government ministers the power to bypass courts in dealing with agitators and to declare not merely the Communist Party but any organization as unlawful.

The Separate Representation of Voters Act of 1951 provided that no colored could qualify as a voter.

The Bantu Authorities Act of the same year set up tribal, regional, and territorial authorities, starting with the African chiefs, in effect clamping control on Africans by the white power structure through the chiefs.

As early as 1938 Luthuli traveled to India, while serving as a delegate to the International Missionary Council. Yet he made no mention of meeting Gandhi and would almost seem to have arrived at his principles of nonviolent protest independently. In the mid-forties he became involved with South Africa's counterpart of SCLC, the African National Congress (ANC), and soon became president of the ANC's Natal division.

The Natives Abolition of Passes and Coordination of Documents Act of 1952 continued the requirement that all Africans, including for the first time women, carry identification, in the form now of "reference books," wherever they went.

In 1952 the ANC launched a Defiance Campaign. Thousands of Africans staged sit-ins protesting racial segregation in public places. The government ordered Luthuli to leave the ANC or be deposed as a chief. Luthuli replied that as a Zulu chief he was first a leader of his people and only later a government official. In the first of a long series of such moves, the government stripped Luthuli of his chieftainship and barred him from visiting any of South African's large cities and towns for a year.

The ANC promptly elected him its president-general, and for

the rest of his life he was always called "The Chief."

The Criminal Law Amendment and Public Safety Acts of 1953 imposed harsh penalties on anyone participating in acts of civil defiance and passive resistance.

By the Riotous Assemblies Act of 1953 the Minister of Justice could bar public gatherings for any duration.

The Native Labor (Settlement of Disputes) Act of 1953 made strikes by Africans illegal and barred them from any role in settling labor disputes. Henceforth they would be represented by state officials in negotiations with employers.

"What have been the fruits of moderation?" Luthuli asked then. "The past thirty years have seen the greatest number of laws restricting our rights and progress, until today . . . we have almost no rights at all."

The Reservation of Separate Amenities Act of 1953 imposed racial segregation on vehicles and in art galleries, museums, libraries, and other public places.

The Bantu Education Act of 1954 was designed, in the words of Premier Hendrik Verwoerd, to educate Africans to be equipped "to earn their living in the service of Europeans." Classes would consist of a minimum of 65 students per teacher, the lessons would last for only twenty minutes each, and the teachers would work double sessions.

In 1956, following the end of another ban that had confined him to his home in Groutville for two years, Albert John Luthuli was arrested on a charge of high treason and with 64 others was imprisoned for a year. In 1957, immediately following the bus boycott in Montgomery, Alabama, and in the wake of the ANC's efforts, Africans in townships outside several large cities stunned white South Africans by launching a bus boycott that lasted for months and was total, despite the necessity for thousands to walk so many miles every day that they arrived at their jobs too tired to work. Luthuli's ANC negotiated an end to the boycott in which the Africans gained all their demands.

Through the Promotion of Bantu Self-Government Act of 1959, the several white representatives of the Africans lost their seats in government, and the Minister of Bantu Administration assumed control of Africans living in the reserves or bantustans.

The Extension of University Education Act of 1959 excluded Africans from universities, except for a chosen few who were per-

mitted to attend "ethnic colleges," thus helping to keep the different tribal groups separated in their reserves.

In 1959 Albert Jon Luthuli undertook a series of speaking engagements that were attended by so many whites as well as blacks that he was again arrested and subjected to a ban lasting five years. Luthuli, who had had to retire to the sugarcane fields to read a smuggled copy of his "greatest inspiration," King's *Stride toward Freedom*, received a letter from the author. "I admire your great witness and your dedication to the cause of freedom and dignity," wrote Dr. King. "You've stood amid persecution, abuse and oppression with a dignity and calmness of spirit seldom paralleled in human history."

In March 1960 Robert Sobukwe's more radical Pan-African Congress staged its National Anti-Pass Campaign, which climaxed with the killing of sixty-nine Africans by police at Sharpeville and the beginning of the detention that would last for the rest of Sobukwe's remaining seventeen years.

Albert John Luthuli, in Johannesburg for the continuing Treason Trial, publicly burned his own passbook, called for a national day of mourning, was seized and beaten by police, and received a nomination for the 1960 Nobel Peace Prize.

The South African government dragged its feet before letting Luthuli out of the country on a ten-day passport. The Chief delivered his acceptance speech in Oslo dressed in a tribal robe of blue and black, with a necklace of leopard teeth and a leopardskin cap fringed with monkey tails. "A free and independent Africa is in the making, in answer to the injunction and challenge of history: 'Arise and shine, for thy light is come.' "

Then he returned to the little cinder-block house that he had built himself, in the cane fields, and died, with his people living under far worse conditions than when he was born.

The Terrorism Act, enacted in the year of Luthuli's death, 1967, authorized mass arrests, arrests without warrants, confinement for indefinite periods, solitary confinement, mass trials, and mass convictions.

". . . I do not agree," he mourned, not only for himself and his people, "that white South Africa, at the end of its two-thousand-year trek, is displaying at present the high virtues of civilization."

Chapter Thirteen

THE CANDY STORE

IT IS GENERALLY ACCEPTED that Andrew Young was the earliest and most steadfast of Jimmy Carter's black supporters. But confusion exists: Was (and is) Young a good personal friend of Carter's? And did they become allies long before the 1976 campaign, or was it just before the Florida primaries in March 1976 that Carter sought Young's assistance?

They first brushed against each other while both were establishing themselves in Georgia politics in 1970. Prior to that they had moved in separate circles, Young with SCLC in its last, often painful years, Carter in the Georgia Senate after losing his first bid for governor in 1966. At the beginning of 1970 Young may have been better known nationally, but by the end of the year both had received considerable notice, Young by making a credible run at Atlanta's congressional seat, Carter by coming from nowhere to become governor.

Three and a half years later, as Young was starting his second term in Congress and Carter finishing his term as governor, the two of them could be found slogging together through a subdivision in north Atlanta where rains and overflowing creeks had repeatedly damaged constituents' homes. As one reporter, Ron Taylor, neatly put it, "The footprints both men left in the mud looked a little like a campaign trail." At another point, when Young was trying to get to a meeting called by Carter, the governor had a state trooper bring Young to the meeting. Dazed, Young said it was the first time he had ever sat in front with a Georgia state trooper and that it was "quite a trip." And in December of 1974, almost a year and a half before the 1976 presidential primaries, Young announced that while he didn't want to be locked into Carter's candidacy, he planned to help Carter in Florida, in the North, and wherever Carter wanted him to go. He thought Carter was a good man and had done a good job and he was interested in seeing that the Georgian got "a fair hearing by the American people."

Young believed in keeping his options open. After all, he was a bona-fide liberal, in spite of the vote for Ford, the approval of Nixon's pardon, and the juggling acts he had to perform to satisfy all segments of his multi-hued district. And the leadership of his party was dominated by other liberals who, in the beginning, were even more attractive than Carter. Thus, Young had expected to support Teddy Kennedy, but in September 1974 Kennedy had removed his name from consideration. So now Humphrey still looked good, and so did Morris Udall, the Congressman from Arizona who had been one of the leaders of the ill-fated busing compromise.

That year of 1974 marked a turning point in American politics for reasons other than Nixon's resignation. By law, Jimmy Carter could not succeed himself as Georgia's governor. The constitutional limitation to one term explains why other politicians as ambitious as Carter resorted to various contortions to stay in the public eye. Lester Maddox, who had preceded Carter as governor, had got himself elected lieutenant-governor, and now he, too, regardless of what Young called his "ax handle politics," was interested in the presidency, as, for a while, was his antithesis, Julian Bond.

So, nearing the end of his term, Carter volunteered to run around the country helping to elect Democratic congressmen—which was also one of Young's favorite hobbies. Robert Strauss, the head of the Democratic National Committee, happily gave Georgia's lame-duck governor the assignment, not realizing, as the *Washington Post* put it, that "it was like giving a kid the key to a candy store." With his young assistants Jody Powell and Hamilton Jordan at his side, Carter helped Democrats to get elected all right, though in 1974 that wasn't difficult. Meanwhile, he was making important contacts, collecting the names of potential workers and quantities of political IOU's, and making himself better known in all sections of the country.

As soon as the 1974 elections were over, Carter announced his candidacy for the presidency, though it burst on the Democratic scene with less than explosive impact since well over a year remained before the primaries. After Kennedy's withdrawal Carter found himself joined by a pack of other runners, many of them veterans of past presidential races having strong allies among the traditional power brokers. Jimmy Carter, an unknown on the national scene, would have to think of something.

Carter and his people had already proven themselves adept at thinking of something.

The first "glancing contact" between Carter and Young seems to have come at a party in an Atlanta suburb early in 1970 when Vernon Jordan announced an interest in running for a congressional seat (which Young later won). After Carter became governor and while Young was chairman of the Atlanta CRC, a BBC reporter named Jonathan Powell relayed to Carter word that Young had described him as "ideologically ignorant" but a man who occasionally did the right thing. Far from being dismayed, Carter received Young, when he came to explain what he had meant, and quickly invited him to a dinner at the governor's mansion.

Yet Young remained skeptical of Carter. He had watched the gubernatorial race Carter had run, though he could not have been very dismayed at a Carter promise to meet Wallace. Young had always met the enemy. Later he would say that he always welcomed white South Africans into his office in Congress, and "the meaner and whiter they are the more I like 'em to come by." But he doubted, as the BBC man had suggested, that the new millenium had arrived or that Carter represented a big change in white men's hearts. The increase in black voters was the big factor—and he was putting together a bit that he would often use on white audiences. "The politicians were frank. They used to call us niggers. But when blacks in a community got 30 percent of the vote, we became nigras. Later on, at about 40 percent, we were Nee-grows or colored people. And when we got the majority, we became their black brothers."

Still, he had met Carter's mother while she was fraternizing with a group of black welfare mothers, and he had been impressed at how she had fit in, showing not the slightest sign of discomfort or condescension. To him she appeared completely free of racism.

And then there was Carter the man, never to be detached completely from Carter the politician, but still . . .

Carter the man, safely ensconced in the governor's chair, promptly announced an end to discrimination in the state government. In his inaugural address the man who had gotten 75 percent of the white votes and somewhat less of the black told his fellow Georgians, "No poor, rural, weak, or black person should ever have to bear the additional burden of being deprived of the opportunity of an education, a job, or simple justice." He appointed twenty or more black people to important boards. He made no attempt to interfere in the state-wide integration of Georgia's public schools. He helped push through the state's first open housing law.

He also hung a portrait of Martin Luther King, Jr., in the State Capitol.

"Especially that," Young told an interviewer much later, as he described how he had remained adamant in his refusal to be impressed. But it was an act of such high symbolism that he had to give it a closer look. A little later Carter announced for the presidency, by which time Young was beginning to wonder whether, on matters of race, one of the new crop of southern governors might not be a better choice than a northern liberal.

He had already been through some difficulties with such men, capped by a debate in Congress over whether the United States should send money and supplies to the South African-backed National Front for Liberation in Angola. He thought several of the liberal candidates had been wishy-washy on the issue, whereas Carter, in Young's view, "understood very well" why the United States should not support the South African side. When Young sought to impress the point on the liberal candidates through their black assistants, he discovered that they had few if any black staff members; Carter had twenty-six blacks on his campaign staff.

Young recalled the Kennedys. In the civil rights days they usually had had to be pushed into doing the required thing; Carter, the white man's candidate, had often done the right thing on his own. Carter, the Southerner, had grown up with race problems. His father had been a hardcore conservative. Carter knew the evils of racism at first hand; John Kennedy had been acquainted with it only through textbooks and therefore had had a hard time taking it seriously. From the allegedly freer North Young had repeatedly fled back to the South, with the feeling that it was the region of the greater hope. And now that seemed to be borne out. The old-guard hard-liners were being deposed in various ways, and that redemption of which he, Abernathy, King, and the others had dreamed seemed finally to be at hand.

The "New South"—which Young, to differentiate it from other efforts of the same name that had failed to flower, sometimes called the "New, New South"—had not only risen, but also was on the move. And in a nation that had been fragmented by political issues, whoever was at the head of this movement would have the potential to put together more of the pieces than anyone else. And if that person were successful while serving in the job, after having been elected, he might just be able to cement the fragments together as good as new. No other notion could have been so attractive to Young, who was always interested in bringing people together.

Setting aside for a moment the unplumbable depths of personal ambition, such thoughts were as much in Carter's mind as they were in Young's. The two men were essentially braiding opposite ends of the same rope, and whether or not Carter sought out Young first, as has been claiimed, Young needed Carter just as much as Carter needed him. So it is probably more accurate to say that their interests simply grew more mutual until finally, following the Florida primaries in March 1976, they couldn't do without each other.

All this helps to explain why Young stood for so long as the lone national black figure in Carter's camp, with the exception of Martin Luther King, Sr. (and even "Daddy" King's presence was believed to have been considerably encouraged by Young). All along Young had been working out a far-reaching national plan, while the other black leaders were merely reacting to whatever came along. To them Jimmy Carter did not represent the spearhead of a total philosophical commitment but simply the candidate who had happened to keep his head above the waters longest. So most didn't come aboard until the Democratic national convention, after they started perceiving that, as yet, thanks to Andrew Young, Carter didn't owe them much, and that, if he became much more successful without their help, he might become "vindictive."

But first, to Young's mind, there was one big barrier that would prevent that "New New South Coalition" even from forming sufficiently, much less leap past the Mason-Dixon line. That was George Wallace. Though crippled by a would-be assassin's bullet, Wallace still had a long-standing coalition of his own, with strong bases in the North as well as in the South. But it was a coalition based on negative aspects, the worst of what certain Americans saw in themselves, yet regarded as necessary if they were to preserve "their" way of life. George Wallace and his people had not shared in that redemption that the movement had brought to the South.

To dislodge Wallace, then, Young was prepared to back Carter or one of two other southern ex-governors of the new breed. One was Rubin Askew, of Florida, and the other was Dale Bumpers, of Arkansas. But Bumpers was elected to the U.S. Senate, and Askew delivered a speech that inadvertently turned off Young. That left Carter, the home candidate, the man whom Young referred to as his friend.

Knocking Wallace out of the race was one of Carter's chief interests. He would not be a credible candidate to the rest of the nation if he did not appear to be preeminent in his own region. Reaching an accommodation with Wallace would be far from enough. The man would have to be beaten, and it would have to be in some key place in the South—Florida, which in 1972 had cut down a number of progressives.

Carter prepared for Florida as he prepared for the rest of the nation. He worked early and he worked hard. He campaigned through Iowa harder than anyone else, just to get recognition in the first state to choose delegates to the convention. Only 12,000 people in a population of 3 million trudged through 10°F weather to vote for him, but they were all Carter needed. Then, with the help of the New Hampshire conservatives, he won that primary. He rode into Florida a proven vote-getter outside the South.

Meanwhile, for months, for years, Andrew Young had been getting out his index cards, making calls, touring Florida, giving speeches. He had kept the names of more than six hundred persons who had passed through the training program at Dorchester Center. Now they were leaders in communities throughout the South. Young also had the names of almost as many ministers in the South and elsewhere with whom he had made contact during the civil rights days.

Carter had pulled Young into his camp by asking for help and advice rather than for a commitment. Similarly, Young asked his friends merely to hear Jimmy Carter out. He didn't know how successful that would be, though he had seen Carter campaign in some impressive ways.

At Paschal's Motor Inn in Atlanta, after giving a speech to middle-class blacks, Carter had been just as enthusiastic and at ease shaking hands with the cooks and dishwashers back in the kitchen. Young saw how comfortably Carter could stand in black pulpits and stir the spirits of the congregations. By the time he introduced Carter to the Black Caucus Young was so confident that he asked Barbara Jordan to fire the hardest questions she could think of. She said she would be delighted. Carter hadn't flinched. In contrast, the conventionally liberal candidates generally seemed ill at ease in the midst of these black inquisitors, though all had walked the halls of Congress.

Carter defeated Wallace in Florida, with 34 percent of the vote. The margin was narrow (Wallace got 31 percent), but it was enough. Now the Carter bandwagon looked like it was rolling, and the time had come for his black Georgian supporters to decide whether, for their own purposes, they should stay on or jump off. Julian Bond, who supported Carter in Florida, switched his support to Morris Udall and became one of Carter's persistent critics, calling him, among other things, "punitive and preachy." Bond was unworried about whether or not Carter would be vindictive toward him or other blacks who did not give their support. "So what?" he asked. "What can he do to us?"

Along with "Daddy" King and Ben Brown, a state legislator, Andrew Young stayed on.

Earlier, Young had made it clear that he was going to help Carter in Florida and North Carolina "out of friendship," after which he would switch to Hubert Humphrey, who had not been an active candidate but was expected to make a late break into the lead. But Humphrey's candidacy never got off the ground, and Young did not have to make that choice.

Actually, since he had committed himself even prior to Florida, it is hard to see how he could have jumped off if he wanted to. He *had* made all those phone calls and speeches, he had kept philosophizing about the "New South." A month before the Florida primary Young had said, "I'm beginning to get scared he's going to win. . . .It's one thing to get out and try to help a friend and after it's over you can pat each other on the back and say, 'Well, we did our best.' But when it dawns on you that this man stands a good chance of being president of the United States, the responsibility of what you are doing shakes you up."

A key decision of the Carter people was to contest every primary to some degree. That strategy produced an enormous drain of money and other resources. If the men to whom Carter lost here and there had been one and the same (or even two and the same), things might not have gone so well. But the candidates who beat him earlier could not keep it up, and the ones who beat him later were chiefly nuisances. Jerry Brown, the governor of California, beat Carter in no less than five primaries including Maryland and California, but in this campaign of sharp strategies, Brown seemed to be only testing the course for a later run.

In North Carolina Carter and Young beat Wallace again, this

time with a clear majority. Immediately they wheeled north, into Wisconsin, New York, and Pennsylvania. Shirley Chisholm, the keen observer, the player *par excellence of the outside game,* called what happened next a case of Young making an end run—which was totally compatible with Carter's policy of bypassing the regular power brokers in favor of taking his case as close as he could, *with his own people,* to the actual voters. She claimed that the moment they turned north after Florida and North Carolina, intent on contesting everything, they "messed up the game plan" of the northern black, liberal, and labor leaders.

"He [Carter] caught a lot of black politicians sleeping," she said. "This was a result of the movement and machinations of Andy Young and some of the most clever political practices I've ever seen. . . . Some members of the Black Caucus were annoyed at Jimmy Carter for running in their districts without first clearing it with them. But Andy had already touched base with the preachers and, to a certain extent, they delivered."

Besides influencing the black vote, Young, in campaigning through seventeen states, was almost as important to Carter with respect to the labor and the liberal vote. The coalition had now truly flowed over its old borders and now included not only Southern whites and blacks but also labor, liberals, and northern blacks.

It was not easy. Even before Florida a "Stop Carter" movement was in the air. Besides being prejudiced against the idea of a Southerner serving as President, they didn't like the idea of having a man with whom they possessed practically no leverage.

This angered Carter's southern liberal supporters and made it even more difficult for them to switch. Patricia Derian, a Democratic National Committeewoman from Mississippi, was enraged, and like Young, she made trips into the North to point out to the liberals the kind of bias that they were not supposed to be harboring.

For Young the biggest crisis in his efforts for Carter was the "ethnic purity" controversy.

Speaking in Indiana on April 6, 1976, Carter said that he didn't think the federal government should take the initiative to change the "ethnic purity" of some urban neighborhoods or the economic homogeneity of affluent suburbs. In the same context he also used the terms "alien groups" and "black intrusion."

Carter's principal opponents immediately jumped on the phrases. Senator Henry Jackson of Washington called the remarks "amazing." Morris Udall said, "Much worse than his ambiguity, which has become as much a trademark of Jimmy Carter as his grin, are some of the words and phrases he used to express himself on this issue."

But the worst effects were produced within Carter's own camp. His supporters cringed at these remarks. Primaries were still to be held in Wisconsin, New York, Pennsylvania, Maryland and Ohio, all of which had large cities with black cores, some adjoined by "ethnic" neighborhoods, and all surrounded by prosperous white suburbs. Carter's comments might draw votes from the supporters of Wallace, who was withdrawing from the race, but they could also undermine the support of the blacks and the liberals.

Young voiced that fear: people who had insisted, "You can't trust a Southerner," were now going to say, "See, I told you so." The whole manner which Young had outwitted and outmaneuvered other black politicians, as Shirley Chisholm put it, was now threatened. His credibility seemed to be in question.

Of course Carter tried to clean it up in the stock way: he apologized without actually backing too far from his original statements—he had never been one to miss extending a hand to voters of any kind, even the hardcore Wallace people. He crumpled up "ethnic purity" by saying he didn't think America had any ethnically pure neighborhoods, and in any case "purity" had been an unfortunate choice of words. "Character" or "heritage" would have been better.

But the onus remained on Andrew Young. What would he say when the press and the candidate called?

At first all Young could think of was George Romney's remark on "brainwashing" about the Vietnam war, to which the former governor of Michigan said he had succumbed. That had cost Romney a good shot at the 1968 Republican presidential nomination. So, fearing an instant knockout after months and years of effort, Young decided he had to come on strong. He told an interviewer that Carter's remarks were a "disaster for the campaign," and later he said he had told the candidate as much over the phone.

Soon he elaborated, in exactly the tones Carter would later use in defending him: "This doesn't mean to me he's a racist. It means he's made a terrible blunder that he's got to recover from." Young said he didn't think Carter realized how loaded with Hitlerian connotations "ethnic purity" was. "My theme all along," Young continued, "has been that white liberals would eventually follow blacks to support him. But this gives them some reason not to. . . .He's kind of put himself into this trap. . . .He's got to find a way to get out—and frankly I hope he does."

That was followed by some slapstick over what Young had actually said. Carter denied that Young told him he had said it was a disaster for the campaign. Young repeated that he had said it to the press. Then it all settled down into agreement that while Young had conveyed to Carter his impression of the dimensions of the "disaster," he had used somewhat gentler terms over the phone.

A little later, after lifting his head from the reflexive ducking to see what was happening, Young discovered yet another phenomenon that was to become common to himself and Carter following most of their slip-ups—the expected hailstones were at best only a few badly aimed spitballs. No blacks poured into the streets to protest Carter's statement, and soon the main thing Young had to worry about was whether the press might yet be able to promote it into a full-scale catastrophe.

Coleman Young and Maynard Jackson, the mayors of Detroit and Atlanta, who had been poised to support Carter, were black leaders who did not seem to be affected at all by the uproar. Just to be sure, Carter quickly returned to the heart of his black strength. On April 13, at a racially mixed rally at Central City Square in Atlanta he listened happily while the Reverend Martin Luther King, Sr., said, "I have a forgiving heart, I'm with you all the way." Dr. Benjamin Mays, a highly respected educator, and Jesse Hill, an insurance executive and one of Young's top supporters, gave Carter their endorsements. On the other hand, Ralph Abernathy, who had promised to come, was unaccountably absent, and on the fringes Hosea Williams led a small group of demonstrators who sang, "The black leaders are selling you out today / Oh, deep in my heart I do believe."

While Young was saying that he doubted that the "ethnic purity" remark had been such a disaster after all, Julian Bond predicted that the impact would show in the Pennsylvania primaries, held on April 27, though he was "surprised at the number of people that can take that bitter pill without throwing up."

Carter beat Jackson in Pennsylvania, and, after losing to Brown in Maryland, went on to another big victory in Ohio. In fact, history records that there wasn't a day in 1976 when Carter was losing a primary or two that he wasn't winning one somewhere else.

Bond was far from alone in the black community in distrusting Carter, for all the support that Young's network of ministers had drummed up. As the convention week drew closer and black leaders took readings to see where their best prospects lay, they kept finding things to criticize in Carter. Sometimes these were based on general impressions—they thought he was insincere and they were angry at Young for supporting him. Curiously, they were not *too* angry, for in the same breath they were capable of saying that Young was the one who should have been running for President. At other times their grievances were more specific, such as Carter's selective inclusion of Dr. King's name on his list of standard American heroes. Carter said his list was made up only of ex-Presidents but he included King whenever he saw black faces in the audience.

By the middle of June, with Wallace's endorsement in his pocket, Carter could no longer be stopped. He slid into the convention in New York in mid-July with the nomination locked up. This was a far cry from 1972 when he had unsuccessfully tendered his availability to be the Vice-President on George McGovern's ticket.

During the convention, just before Young's seconding speech, Carter met with a large group of black leaders and gained their support, after he pledged to name blacks to high-level jobs, especially in areas outside those in which they had customarily served, and after he promised not to push replacing Basil A. Paterson, a popular New Yorker, with his own man, Ben Brown, as vice chairman of the Democratic National Committee. Young attended this meeting but kept a low profile—just another face in the crowd.

Though he had the inside track on placing Carter's name in the nomination, Young at the last moment deferred to Peter Rodino, the veteran congressman from New Jersey who had chaired the House Judiciary Committee when it voted to impeach Richard Nixon. Nevertheless, against a Democratic tradition of boisterousness and discord in its convocations, Young is credited with preserving much of the harmony of the convention through his very presence and the acknowledgment of his contributions toward having brought them all there together. He clearly conveyed this tone and his optimism when in his seconding speech he said, "I'm ready to lay down the burden of race. And Jimmy Carter comes from a part of the country that, whether you know it or not, has done just that."

It was too bad for Jimmy Carter that, following "Daddy" King's stirring benediction to the convention, he could not carry his famous smile, which was fully justified that day, directly into the national election, for then he would have beaten Gerald Ford by a landslide, instead of by the whisker into which his huge lead, four months later, had degenerated. The country was thrilled by the spectacle of good will that the convention had offered. It was just the kind of tonic that Americans needed, in order to think well of themselves.

The loss of that lead can be blamed on many things. Carter made a few more mistakes, such as the *Playboy* interview (though Young believed that it helped Carter by changing his image in the minds of those who had considered him too pious and sanctimonious), and he was the first to slip up in the television debates with Ford. But the lead was unnaturally large to begin with, and the interval gave Ford time to continue disentangling himself from Richard Nixon. He, like Carter, was a decent man, so that those not given to looking too closely could see little to choose between the two.

Another factor was that people like Andrew Young were now of less use in helping Carter extend the coalition. Given Carter's huge initial lead it could be assumed that the traditionally Democratic black, labor, and liberal segments were not likely to desert him for Gerald Ford. The chief target would be all those millions whom the Republicans called "the silent majority," and they were best approached by Carter himself.

So while Carter was out trying to ease more of the pieces into the coalition, Young concentrated on one of his traditional activities during any election: registering voters. He was elected chairman of an organization that had been formed by the Democratic National Committee and given $2 million for the purpose. At the same time, along with Ben Brown, he had the delicate task of seeing that the black leaders who had supported Carter before the convention were not forgotten while he sought the support of others who had not been Carter people.

Also, especially in the closing weeks, Young had to engage in a contest of his own.

One of the benefits of working in the presidential campaign was that he had become a politician of national stature, sure to go on, if Carter won, to have influence in the executive branch. In the meantime he had picked up several other powerful assets, including the widespread admiration of his congressional colleagues and his positions on the Banking and the Rules Committees, especially the latter, which gave him, as he liked to say, "subtle influence on every piece of legislation." Having won easily in his previous bid for reelection, he had what could be called a safe seat, and for a time he could enjoy the luxury of being unable to remember the name of his Republican opponent, Ed Gadrix, a young attorney who was running in his first race.

In the election on Tuesday, November 2, 1976, Jimmy Carter became President-elect of the United States by barely one percentage point. And in the heavy voter turnout in Georgia, 68 percent, Andrew Young was reelected to a third term, with 95,955 votes, far more than the 80,000 that he had first dreamed of getting and which since had seemed almost unattainable and even unnecessary for a healthy winning margin. Ed Gadrix received 47,965 votes.

The voting map showed the spread—or the slimness—of the coalition that Carter, Young, and others had breathed into life in Georgia and in Florida. Carter's strength decreased in direct proportion to the distance from Georgia. The South remained solid till he got up to Virginia, where the open spaces started appearing. In the Northeast and Midwest he gained some important states here and there, just enough to put him over the top, while west of the Mississippi stretched an almost completely unbroken desert.

Later analysis revealed how important Carter's 94 percent of the black vote turned out to be. He was truly a son of the New South, for he could not have been elected without the passage of the 1965 Voting Rights Bill and the subsequent increased registration of black voters; he could not have been elected without the help of those black people who were in office through that Act and who perceived that, beyond being a white man, he was a good man. Slightly more white voters in the South had chosen Ford over Carter, and only the black voters had provided his margins of victory. They supplied the same kind of help in several northern states. If the black vote had been absent in Mississippi, Louisiana, and Maryland, plus Ohio and Pennsylvania, Carter would have been 52 electoral votes shy of the 270 he needed to win.

But those were matters for future study.

What counted was that all of Andrew Young's philosophies had been borne out, as usual. Yet, while he might have been wryly amused at being considered the country's "top nigger," no problems were really solved. He fondly remembered King, once more saying, "Influence is like money in the bank. It's good only as long as you don't spend it." His new status meant only that he had a chance to get closer to where he could really attack the problems.

The voters had made their choice, and he would have to make his. He would search his soul before settling on one of the attractive courses that lay open before him. But the weight of the past and of the future pressed so heavily that there can be little doubt that he had made his choice long ago.

Andrew Young knew exactly what he had to do.

A NOTE ON SOURCES

For this biography of Andrew Young I have relied extensively on contemporaneous descriptions of events as reported in newspapers and magazines. The newspapers that have been my chief sources are located in the cities where major events occurred: Atlanta *Constitution*, Atlanta *Journal*, Atlanta *World*, Chicago *Tribune*, Los Angeles *Times*, New Orleans *Times-Picayune*, New York *Times*, Pittsburgh *Courier*, and Washington *Post*. The chief magazine sources for interpretative periodical coverage were *Atlanta* magazine, *Christian Century*, *Ebony*, *Esquire*, *Harpers Magazine*, *The Nation*, *National Parks and Conservation Magazine*, *New Directions* (published by Howard University), *The New Republic*, *Newsweek*, *New York* magazine, *Playboy*, *The Reporter*, *Rolling Stone*, *Saturday Review*, and *Time*.

Books that provided valuable background information were these:

Bennett, Lerone, *What Manner of Man*. Chicago: Johnson Publishing Company, 1968.

Bishop, James Alonzo, *The Days of Martin Luther King, Jr.* New York: Putnam, 1971.

Fager, Charles E., *Selma, 1965*. New York: Scribners, 1974.

Forman, James, *The Making of Black Revolutionaries.* New York: Macmillan, 1972.

King, Coretta Scott, *My Life with Martin Luther King, Jr.* New York: Holt, 1969.

King, Martin Luther, Jr., *Why We Can't Wait*. New York: Harper, 1964.

Lewis, David L., *Martin Luther King: A Critical Biography*. London: Allen Lane, 1970.

Lokos, Lionel, *House Divided*. New Rochelle, N.Y.: Arlington House, 1968.

Luthuli, Albert John, *Let My People Go.* New York: McGraw-Hill, 1962.

Metcalf, George R., *Up from Within.* New York: McGraw-Hill, 1971.

Miller, William Robert, *Martin Luther King, Jr.* New York: Weybright and Talley, 1968.

Neary, John, *Julian Bond, Black Rebel.* New York: Morrow, 1971.

Parks, Gordon, *Born Black.* Philadelphia: Lippincott, 1971.

Reynolds, Barbara A., *Jesse Jackson: The Man, the Movement, and the Myth.* Chicago: Nelson-Hall, 1975.

Schulke, Flip, ed., *Martin Luther King, Jr.: A Documentary, Montgomery to Memphis.* New York: Norton, 1976.

Seller, Cleveland, *The River of No Return,* New York: Morrow, 1973.

Williams, John Alfred, *The King God Didn't Save.* New York: Coward McCann, 1970.

INDEX

Page references in italics refer to photographs.

224